A FUT
WORLD V

THE REFORM OF COMMON SENSE IN THE 21ST CENTURY

Richard Smith

With a foreword by Andy Thomas

Published in 2015 by Vital Signs Publishing
Broom Cottage, Ashdown Road, Forest Row, East Sussex, RH18 5BN

Website: *www.vitalsignspublishing.co.uk*
E-mail: *info@vitalsignspublishing.co.uk*

Edited by Andy Thomas

Cover images, title page and page 6 variation: *The Sunrise Over St Paul's*,
by James Burns. Details of James' work can be found on page 272 and at:
http://londonfromtherooftops.com
Email: *james.rawimages@gmail.com*

Photographs on pages 12 and 250 by Richard Smith

ISBN: 978-0-9550608-3-0

Printed by InPrint, Latvia - *www.inprint.lv*

CONTENTS

ACKNOWLEDGEMENTS

I am indebted to various authors of the italicised comments at the beginning of each chapter. Profound insights that have found their place in the commentary of history demonstrate that in order for wisdom to be wise, it must contain humour. I have collected interesting observations such as these for many years; to each author unknown, many thanks.

Thanks to Jim Lyons[1], whose physics lectures at various conferences in the last twenty years have inspired me to at least consider what I never hoped to understand; to the late Hamish Miller[2], all credit for demonstrating that advancing age is no barrier to fresh revelation; credit must also go to Andy Thomas[3], co-organiser of the Glastonbury Symposium each year, a consistent and indefatigable truthseeker bringing the quest for truth to a wider audience – he writes and speaks about truth and conspiracies in as honest a manner as you will find; meanwhile Iain McGilchrist's[4] book *The Master and His Emissary: The Divided Brain and the Making of the Western World* must rank as the classic explanation of where we stand today in terms of understanding human development, and where mankind may be headed. Here you will discover notes of cautious optimism; I also owe a debt of gratitude to Thomas Hobbes[5], author of *Leviathan*, published in 1651. We need to re-examine Leviathan and our relationship with the mighty ship of 'State'.

All thanks to those who pointed out in the first place that whilst these comments seemed to flow from and be inspired by the strong feeling of both personal and world change, they might be worth setting down in print. We all talk about 'change', but few seem to have much idea as to what it may be and how change might be effected – or what it is that needs changing. Thanks also to Sash Dhuri and the staff of *www.fernandeswoodencottages.com*, who deserve my gratitude for providing somewhere to 'stop the world and get off' in peace and sometimes quiet, and get this collection of words coordinated.

I have attempted to offer some suggestions for reform as a discussion framework, and I hope to have presented these in a straightforward manner. If I have failed anywhere to give credit where it is due, it is unintentional and I will be happy to correct this in any future editions.

Richard Smith

FOREWORD

by Andy Thomas

Here in the second decade of the 21st century, there is a growing feeling that we are being presented with an opportunity to move forwards into something new, something better, in terms of the ways in which we run our civilisation. New technologies offer hitherto undreamt-of solutions, while seemingly limitless communication methods mean that ideas can transmit faster and wider than ever before, presenting both dreams and nightmares. Yet still we seem dogged by some persistent anchors bumping along the sand, holding back crucial momentum.

Especially here in Britain, there is broad disaffection with the now obviously flawed social and political systems that in a better world might cradle us, but which instead are too rooted in methodologies that seem increasingly anachronistic in rapidly changing times. Public opinion voiced during recent elections has shown that although there is a resigned acceptance of the way things are, almost no-one has a good word to say about any of it. Trust in our leaders is at an all-time low, and the thirst for reform in all categories is steadily building from a general low grumble to a thundering oncoming storm that will surely have to find full expression and manifest a practical response sooner rather than later.

The rise of the Internet and social media means that we can now easily discover, should we care to look, who our elected leaders are really lobbying for in our parliaments, and it becomes obvious when self-serving behaviour or the desires of corporate masters and undemocratic but powerful 'thinktanks' are driving the agenda. The waste of public resources on inappropriate policies and the ineffectiveness of moribund electoral structures which hold back real change, meanwhile, add further layers of resentment for those of us wading through treacle as a result, while the people at the top of the glass towers enjoy an apparently eternal excess of privilege and wealth. Refusals of an academic elite, that seems to hold the establishment in its sway, to investigate new ideas and open up awareness of so-called fringe sciences in the face of sometimes impressive evidence is another blocked avenue that frustrates the more open-minded, while alternative solutions to the problems of overpopulation, global governance and the misuse of technology seem to be equally dismissed if the proposers are not from the traditional avenues of peer control.

This is not the blueprint for a healthy society; something has to change. But grumbling will not be enough to shift the stagnation. Only the willing proactive participation of everyone will tip enough dominos to start new patterns of improved governance and social revitalisation tumbling into action. The barrier that many people feel holds back their involvement in this process is the tangled procedure of trying to understand how things became the way they are in the first place, and the then torturous necessity of having to pull together the many complex threads that might help begin the healing. Where does one start? This book might help.

I have known Richard Smith for over 20 years, and during that time have observed his passionate belief in the need for multi-layered reform, and his campaigns against questionable transmission masts and the subsequent attempt to become a Member of Parliament, along with his journeys of investigation into some of the aforementioned 'fringe' areas mostly kept from us by mainstream media. I was always impressed by his resolute convictions and determination never to go quietly into passive submission. So when I heard from Richard, in a new phase of his life, that he was planning to spend six months on an Indian beach writing down some of his thoughts about the world around him, I was very curious to see the results.

When I was given the privilege of seeing the excitingly substantial file that I and a few fascinated friends of Richard received on his homecoming, I was immediately struck by the unusually practical tone that his writings exhibited. Here were some of the problems of modern society being identified and put under the microscope, yes, as is necessary to do when directly faced with its many dysfunctions, but here also were some well-thought-out solutions being offered. This excited me. I have long been an admirer of the writings of the eighteenth century libertarian Thomas Paine, who once lived in my birth town of Lewes, East Sussex, and whose words helped inflame both the American War of Independence and the

French Revolution. This is not because I necessarily agree with all of Paine's personal convictions, but more because I am impressed at how he never leaves the reader alone with feelings of despair at the ways of the world; he always emboldens them instead, using wit and wisdom, and actually gives sensible, practical solutions as to how essential changes could be made. Many of Paine's suggestions have indeed come to pass, even if it took centuries for them to percolate into modern law. But everything has to start somewhere. The seeds have to be planted.

Likewise, Richard's writings speak plainly with unabashed outrage at some wrongs, but also offer encouragement and insight for those seeking rights. They plant some seeds that I strongly felt should be made more widely available for those seeking answers to some of the dilemmas of our times. Richard and I discussed how this might best be done, and this book is the result. My own books, including *The Truth Agenda* and *Conspiracies*, attempt to do something similar by focusing on perhaps more overtly controversial matters, but Richard himself does not shy away from moving beyond what some might reductively call 'real world' issues, as the later part of the book shows. His willingness to widen out the implications of what reform might really mean for us if we apply it to all ways of thinking, even ones rejected by the mainstream, is admirable. His views on conspiracy theories, for instance, are fair and balanced in ways which certain media pundits might take a lesson from.

As with Paine's work, I may not personally agree with every argument put forward by Richard, but I support their dissemination because I feel robustly that these views should be given an airing. If the world is to move forward, all voices must be heard and everything should be up for discussion. The unfortunate moves currently taking place in restricting human rights and creating ever-more repressive censorship of information that doesn't suit the establishment, through subtle and not-so-subtle legislation concerning the ability to express views and the availability of online sources, goes against everything that has made this country, for all its undoubted flaws, a bastion of law and democracy. Britain has inspired many other nations and has been a role model. This book does have a global outreach, but uses the home front as its main springboard, for history shows that what happens here often winds up influencing the rest of the world. Reform must mean going forwards, not backwards into an Orwellian nightmare. We must forge a more sensible balance between security and freedom.

No book can provide the solutions to everything, and Richard makes no attempt to do so here, but he does dissect some selected key issues in a way that might help kickstart wider discussion of necessary reform in a number of important areas. His analysis does a fine job of explaining the historical developments that have led us to be where we are, and it is refreshingly accessible and incisive. More importantly, Richard does not point the finger at the governing classes as the sole source of where required change must come from, but also shines a light on how we all might look again at the ways in which we live our own lives within the systems that currently bind us. Change, if change is to occur, must come from both inside and out, above and below. This willingness to see that we all play a role in shaping society is one of the strengths in Richard's approach, and his openness to what some might call a spiritual dimension adds further welcome depth.

As we enter times in which we in the West seem to be re-evaluating our engagement with everything, and the world as a whole moves towards shifting borders and uncertain outcomes in many different ways, documents like this are important and timely – and more are needed, from every source possible. If this entry into the canon tips even just a few extra dominos into caring a little deeper about how we are governed and how we live our lives, then those months that Richard spent in India, looking at his home planet with a new perspective, arranging his thoughts on positive change into coherency and usefulness, will have been time very well spent.

Andy Thomas

Andy Thomas is one of the world's leading truth and mysteries researchers and is the author of the acclaimed The Truth Agenda: Making Sense of Unexplained Mysteries, Global Cover-Ups and Visions for a New Era *and also* Conspiracies: The Facts – The Theories – The Evidence *(see page 273 for information on both titles), amongst several other books. Andy widely lectures around the world and has made many TV and radio appearances.*

More on Andy Thomas and his work can be found at: **www.truthagenda.org**

INTRODUCTION

There is a strong and growing feeling that all is not well with the world. That is not a particularly unusual sentiment, but what appears to be different are both the symptoms and speed of the growth of the malaise. I set about putting down my observations on the current age initially because I had the strong impression that my personal freedoms were somehow being eroded by the back door, and I wasn't being told how or why. Was it just me? The resolution of that unsettling feeling gradually unfolded in the ensuing years. I felt an internal need to put down on paper what the concerns were that many folk seemed also to feel might be worth further articulation.

This process began whilst on holiday in November 2006, four months after the Glastonbury Symposium conference[1] of July that year. At this conference, my feeling that there was without question a unification of existence, and that everything is in fact connected, appeared to be confirmed by the presentation of, amongst others, the now late Hamish Miller, wordsmith, dowser, and a blacksmith of the highest order. The penny, in other words, began to drop. His dowsed patterns of subtle earth energies matched exactly the polishing pad patterns used in the ophthalmic optical manufacturing industry, where I had spent so many years. Hamish put the key into my door of perception, which I was then able to slowly open. Jim Lyons used the word 'toroid' in his presentation delivered at the same Symposium, a variation of which happens to be the astigmatic correction 'toric', i.e. a non-spherical lens form used by the lens-making fraternity. I am grateful to Jim for his expression 'the intelligent aether', which is that great unseen which appears to unify everything.

I have unashamedly appropriated and adapted the phrase 'Inferential Scrutability' from the work of David Chalmers[2], the Australian philosopher who wrote the outstanding work *Constructing The World*. My interpretation is a plain language understanding of this analytical thesis. The phrase appealed strongly since inferential scrutability involves knowledge by inference: 'Every truth is scrutable, or derivable from a limited class of basic truths'. In other words, one can come to know a great many things by knowing certain truths. Amen to that. This seemed to me to be an apposite description, particularly applicable to the possibilities of institutional cover ups and the offerings of conspiracy theorists. Anything may be possible, and this is something we are increasingly being asked to believe by various agencies. It helped me to coordinate the various strands of enquiry that form the basis of this book.

It is important here to emphasise that I am not especially interested in analytical or reductionist philosophy. This would be of no interest to the majority and would not further my objectives of clarity. I stress an ordinary-language philosophy; plain language is helpful and rather less prone to misinterpretation. 'Inferred scrutability' is as far as I feel able to go in an attempt to clarify the distinction between fact and fiction, truth and nonsense. Why use the word 'philosophy', though? Is such terminology of practical use to us? I believe it is, since we may consider science as being the factual truth. To observe processes and to construct means is science – to criticise and coordinate ends is philosophy. That which lies outside science is therefore philosophical, or non-scientific unestablished evidence. As I see them, the five philosophical disciplines of Logic, Ethics, Politics, Metaphysics and Aesthetics greatly concern us, particularly the first three. The last two are less important since they may stray into the realms of possibility and objective opinion.

I offer two kinds of established methods of examining 'The Truth'. Philosophers will also typically offer a choice of two, *a priori* and *a posteriori*. To ask the question 'do you believe 2 + 2 = 4?' and preface the question by observing that this is not intended to be a trick question, is to ask the apparently obvious; i.e. it is an *a priori* self-evident truth. (That said, there are many who dispute the equation as being this obvious.) The second truth, only obvious after examination of the facts, is *a posteriori*. This is an extremely simple analysis but it suffices for our purpose.

That a growing number of people are concerned about the 'status quo' is indisputable. I have tried to address some of these concerns in a digestible way and I hope I have succeeded. I do not pretend to offer anything other than observations to questions that might be asked by any other thinking individual who feels sometimes that something isn't quite right and wonders 'what on earth (and perhaps elsewhere) is going on'? This involves an examination of what has hitherto been considered inconceivable, even fantastic. We should be bold. When we reach the horizon, we can and we will see further.

There are many published works, printed and digital, available on many of the topics discussed here. If the reader wishes to pursue these in the interest of acquiring further detailed knowledge, I urge them to do so. I provide an appendix summary of both people, publications and websites that may yield additional useful information at the end of these chapters. It was necessary, for basic clarity, to decide what factors seemed to be the principal contributors to the global mess in which we find ourselves. That it is in a mess in many respects is generally agreed. What is less clear is who is responsible and why, and what the key concerns are. Those concerns form the basis of these chapters. I have sought to answer questions that Mr & Mrs H.A.D. Enough might pose, and I have sought to provide some answers in a non-academic and, I hope, in a non-patronising fashion. Indeed, I confess wholeheartedly to not even pretending to be an academic here; on the contrary, I have tried to be Devil's advocate for the majority. We can complain by all means, but it is also useful to propose some solutions to raise the debate up a level. Whoever is lost to simply complaining has left that debate.

The primary concerns in this book are:

1. FREEDOM – Everywhere.

2. EDUCATION – At every level.

3. REFORM – At local, national and international level.

4. TECHNOLOGY – Good and bad.

5. HUMANISM – Everywhere.

6. WORLD GOVERNMENT – *not* a New World Order.

These are the themes of the chapters which I have assembled according to these broad but pressing matters. The quest for truth is a constant theme. Without it we founder, and this quest applies to all six of these concerns.

I appear not to be alone in having a very strong impression of impending change, both in what it should be to be a human being, and what the human race could properly achieve. The sense that individuals are being failed by whatever political system that purports to represent them, grows stronger. This in turn exposes other crucial issues which, in my view, seem worthy of our further consideration and reflection. The subject of 'consciousness' has come far more to the fore than hitherto, and the elevation of consciousness is now being much-discussed and coming to scientific attention. At its most basic definition, consciousness means awareness. Are we becoming increasingly aware? If so, of what are we becoming increasingly aware? And, once aware, what are we going to do about the problems we face?

To consider the implications of an aroused awareness in some people, though certainly not all, it is necessary to examine a number of subjects that are considered by many mainstream folk to be 'whacky', 'off the wall', 'ridiculous', or – the ultimate killer put-down – 'New Age'. There is a growing interest in all things spiritual, which seems to confirm that folk are undernourished and unimpressed by the current political climate. I argue that if this is indeed the case, then folk are good judges. An increasing awareness of, and interest in, 'spirituality' does not mean a corresponding increase in matters of religion. Many people will readily admit to being called spiritual but not 'religious'. This is an important distinction, and calls into question the future of religion as we know it.

As many people begin to lose heart in humanity itself, and also lose personal belief and confidence in both themselves and 'the system', they cast about for the truth, for it has become obvious to a significant number of people that they are being deceived by that system, which is simply failing to represent them and their needs. Manipulation of statistics seems to be continual. In short, we are being lied to by the authorities; by whom I mean government and the media, with whom the government unashamedly seems to cooperate. Mismanagement and unaccountability seem to be rife.

A free press is a mirage. What do we even mean by the expression a 'free press?' We need to ask whether the people who own the press are themselves free. The printed and digital media is owned by people of means; this is not to imply that money necessarily buys freedom, but it certainly does offer choice. Authentic freedom places demands on us. Commercially, the media owners' need to protect and enhance these substantial investments is an ongoing requirement. Inevitably, powerful interests become involved in order to obtain published influence, including governments. This is by no definition a 'free' press. There is no clear water between the political party interest and media voices; it is a muddy brown at best. Therefore we feel that there is very little difference in what we get as a result of who we vote for.

To politicians everywhere: the democratic deficit concerns us all. Your honesty and truthful intent is paramount, and if you have lost your connection with the truth, find it. Freedom must not be surrendered in the name of 'security'.

Richard Smith

1

AT FREEDOM CROSSROADS

"When you make a choice, you change the future".

The end of history?

At what point of development in our democratic history do we find ourselves? Is our democracy the finished article, and are we satisfied with its functionality?

The End of History and The Last Man, written by Frances Fukuyama[1], proposed that the end of the Soviet Union effectively meant that democracy had won the battle and communism had failed. We now know that this seductive proposition was very wide of the mark, and the book *The Return of History and The End of Dreams* by Robert Kagan[2] illustrates clearly why history didn't end after all. It should be noted here that Fukuyama was a signatory to the controversial thinktank The Project for the New American Century (PNAC), of which more later. Does democracy best serve today's society as intended? The answer must be no, and we need to look at what might be done to properly reform the democratic framework, not simply react to inadequacies and repair the existing structures. We are gifted complainants. We must complain by all means, but we must contribute to the solutions by every means. Today is important. How did our democratic freedoms arrive at where they are today, and what must we do to improve, maintain and enhance them?

I am from the European continent, specifically the United Kingdom (UK), so, as you might expect, my historical perspective comes from this geopolitical position. The UK has occupied a prominent, although now declining, position in world affairs since 1789, so I feel somewhat more justified in commentating from this standpoint than assuming any other. True, this prominent position of the oft-called 'mother of democracy' has been in decline since the end of the Great War in 1918, but we have our place. Internationally, is democracy even necessarily the best form of government? As we know, democracy has been variously described as the best system in a menu of poor options, but some variation of democracy must be preferable to dictatorship and the command economy. We also know that the export of democracy as understood in the United States of America (USA) is no automatic solution either. Who defines what democracy means to any nation?

There is little point in retreating to far distant times for solutions; there would be no obvious starting date. How we define 'modern times' is, of course, a matter of opinion. I personally feel it necessary to consider modern history as being from the French Revolution onwards, since this event spelled the beginning of some measure of European democratic agitation. Divine Monarchy was served notice to quit and the individual began to assert himself. Herself came later as we shall see.

A pattern emerges from thereon, and knitting together the events from 1789 France to the first Reform Act in 1832 Britain produces a 43-year pattern, a time period that 'events' show to be significant to the present day. This reminds me of the old truism that in order to know where we are going, we need to know where we have been, and we ought to be conscious that this statement remains valid today.

We live in an extraordinary age of rapid and life-altering change. How can we cope with the many philosophical questions that arise from these changes?

Neglected forums?

The poor consequences of failing to properly maintain our democracy is becoming more apparent. Any freedoms we possess came to us through national parliaments. These institutions must be healthy and properly functional to deal with the current social complexities. It is essential therefore that democracy mirrors the society it purports to represent, and in the second decade of the 21st century, in the UK especially, it is plainly failing. It is bloated both in numbers and cost, and is largely concerned with matters I argue are best left to a properly-structured local government assembly. I offer some alternative organisational ideas in Chapter 5. Do we expect our Members of Parliament to be legislators, or simply social workers, to whom we complain as the last resort? Until we resolve this question, we are doomed to mediocrity and indecision. Have we surrendered the long-term care of our future in favour of the instant message and the 'here and now?'

Wise or enchanted?

We are not doing wisdom well at the moment, and we should do better. I am fascinated by what the current age seems to expect of us as individuals, and our collective response to the challenges that we face today. I have tried to examine in a logical manner those questions which, in my view, we must ask ourselves. One salutary lesson to relearn is what we can learn to do without. I suggest that:

'Those who are poor are those who need a lot to live'.

81 days in India during the 2007–2008 winter taught my late wife and I just that lesson – that life can be lived without the mass of paraphernalia with which we surround ourselves. With the exception of small screens, this experience was repeated over 141 days during the winter of 2013–2014, and a further 42 days during the winter of 2015. This led me to question growth for growth's sake, and to consider 'steady state' alternatives. Humanity seems to be set on a course driven more by intellect than by wisdom. We become enchanted by technologies that excite us. Ought we to be more cautious? It has been forecasted that 2047 is the date when we may expect to see 'Singularity' to occur. Singularity in this context is the moment when the rules governing human existence alter so significantly that taking anything for granted is rendered impossible. This event is deeply important as we shall see, since this is when it is forecasted that available artificial intelligence will be greater than the sum of human intelligence. If we fail to grasp the full implications of this, we may get what we did not wish for.

I am reminded of a wonderful observation by Jalaluddin Rumi[3]:

"Yesterday, I was clever, so I wanted to change the world. Today, I am wise, so I am changing myself".

More of us

The tricky question of population numbers will not go away either. The 'great change drivers' of sheer numbers tell anyone with open-minded intelligence that we are in uncharted territory. World population at the time of the French Revolution stood at around one billion, and by the end of the Great War in 1918 at two billion; a doubling in 129 years. By the time that the Berlin Wall was constructed in 1961, there were three billion; another billion in just 43 years. In 2004, the number had reached six billion. In Chapter 8, *A Consideration of World Population* examines concerns about these numbers. It is difficult to imagine the consequences of our failure to cooperate and redistribute natural resources when faced with this rapid increase in world population numbers. It's tough, and we are not used to cooperation on this scale. We will have to learn.

Democratic devaluation

George W Bush[4] was the 43rd President of the United States of America. Do try to obtain and read a copy of *What Happened*, by Scott McClellan[5], for an interesting account of the White House administration under President number 43, George Walker Bush. As an example of how the democratic process and world peace can be derailed in the wrong hands, it serves as a clear warning. It also demonstrates the clear division of attitudes between a nation of experience and history, the United Kingdom, and a new 'deductivist' state dependent upon a short history, the United States of America, of necessity short on experience. Unchecked and unchanged, our uncoordinated collaborative behaviour bequeaths to our successors a grim international legacy of which none of us has a right to be proud.

The 'fluffy bunny' era is over

The 'fluffy bunny' era is firmly over, and just wishing the world to be something we feel it should be is no longer enough. Sadly, love and light alone do not pay the bills. The evidence of decades of poor management is there for us all to see. Some action must be taken to elect representatives with the ability to listen to those they represent, and to absorb what it is that concerns those communities they purport to speak for at all levels of government, and implement meaningful solutions to problems. We must consider our future potential with greater imagination than that with which we have ransacked the past. Once we have grasped the importance of our individual and collective dependency upon one another, the practical remedial direction we must accept will be obvious to us all. If this seems a step towards some form of enlightenment, it is.

Violence pays

Sadly, there are many instances in our recent history that demonstrate the success of outright war, theft, deception, plunder and financial deceit in order to gain advantage, either personal or national. This, as we shall see, is pretty much how the British Empire came about. The tentative, almost random, spread of personal freedoms, the all-too slow increase in wealth share amongst the world's population and the growing resentment of ordinary folk against waging pointless wars must be positive indicators of hope. If the young find fighting silly, all credit to them. There is therefore cause for cautious optimism. As always, the ability to manage ourselves properly is paramount. Later, I offer some practical suggestions as to how war might be made to be a truly lousy proposition; in effect, to make it both illegal and pointless. To those who scoff and declare such an objective to be ridiculous, do please share your own ideas. After all, this is a discussion document.

A return of the city state?

As the world goes 'global' through increasing centralisation, management of world affairs is in fewer hands, along with the money. The continual and unstoppable growth in urban conurbations and 'super cities' concentrates populations in groups of millions; are we seeing the effective re-emergence of the city state? For example, New Delhi in India is home to 22 million people, almost the entire population of Scandinavia and Finland combined. So in terms of inhabitant numbers, we probably are seeing the re-emergence of the city state and we ought to be planning accordingly. India alone has 50 cities in excess of 1 million people.

Is central government a continuing relevance locally, or is it too far removed from the very people increasingly disinterested in electing it? This would seem to be the case. The further removed people become from the seat of government, the less they feel any connection to what is done in their name by that government. There is a buck-passing mechanism seemingly built into local town halls – effectively the central government directive. It's always the fault of the centre stage. To regain any credibility, that mentality has to change. There is a strong and timely case to be made for far-reaching and deep structural reform – reform that returns the answers to local social questions to local people who elect quality representatives, who in turn have the power to get things done. Chapter 5 details how this might be done. There is an enormous need for structural alteration, as opposed to a process of 'incremental creep', which often results in little meaningful change at all.

This return to local accountability has national ramifications. As we shall see, national government would be concerned with supra-national issues, leaving the detail of local management to local people. National government therefore would become less of a daily 'target' for getting things wrong – city representation would become infinitely more important than it is now. Buck-passing would become impossible, and local accountability total. It really does appear that a re-evaluation of where the power to elect ought to lie is necessary, along with financial accountability. A system empowering local people to elect their representatives must be accompanied by the ability to raise and administer local taxes. Subsequent failure of management is swiftly identifiable and therefore there may be less inclination and incentive for the untalented to stand for office, and less inclination to occupy space and time and soak up attendance allowances.

SUMMARY

We are obligated to recognise the problems caused by increasing and shifting populations. It is apparent that our management institutions are unable, or

unwilling, to see that the growth of the middle classes in developing countries carries with it colossal challenges of expectation. We see a steady devaluation in democratic functionality, and an equally steady increase in materialism reflected in our swift adoption of fresh technologies. Further, a determined and resolute refusal to properly deal with urgently needed international and domestic national reforms threatens to undermine individual liberty through state intervention in our name. We must reassert our right to freedom. Where we go from here is of the highest importance; we should take the keenest interest in our future. Large numbers of people in the newer 'democracies', particularly Russia, are seemingly content to leave government in a 'strong and safe' pair of hands, as long as those hands leave them alone to simply make money. This is no long-term solution to stability.

2

THE MODERN HISTORY OF FREEDOM

"To be free is not merely to cast off one's chains, but to live in a way that respects and enhances the freedom of others".

The speed of change

When we consider the speed of change, the last two hundred years in our history are without question the fastest in modern times. One of the biggest challenges we face is the management of rapid population growth and the pressure on natural resources distribution as a consequence. We must also pay more attention to non-scientific questions; we have failed throughout the last two hundred years to show enough interest in the consequences of our creativity. If we continue to advance technically whilst failing to keep pace ethically, we will outstrip our mental resources to keep pace – from where then will we be able to import our solutions? Beginning with the aftermath of the French Revolution in 1789, we will concern ourselves here with six distinct and formative periods, which are:

1. 1789 – 1832
2. 1832 – 1875
3. 1875 – 1918
4. 1918 – 1961
5. 1961 – 2004
6. 2004 – 2047

The first five periods are a part of significant modern history and each period is around 43 years duration, almost bi-generational. These periods mark significant changes in social organisation and the subsequent development of relationships within the international community.

Significant events include:

1. 1789 – The French Revolution

2. 1832 – The first Reform Act in the UK

3. 1875 – The zenith of the British Empire

4. 1918 – The conclusion of the Great War

5. 1961 – The construction of the Berlin Wall

6. 2004 – The organised Western 'War on Terror'

The sixth and current period differs since the immediate past is a reflection of a set of circumstances not dissimilar to those prevalent in the 1790s, unlikely as that might seem. Technically, the 'War on Terror' may be said to have got underway after the 9/11 attacks of 2001, and it has clouded opinion since in a cloak of mistrust, as we shall see. This so-called war has parallels with governmental concerns in Britain in the aftermath of the Napoleonic Wars of the late 18th and early 19th centuries. The government of that time found good reason to limit individual freedoms and liberty with much the same lack of spirit as that of the Labour government in the first decade of the 21st century in the United Kingdom (an approach since unfortunately reinforced in the wake of the Paris terrorist atrocities of 2015), along with the Republican administration of the United States of America, both of whom saw fit to impose limitations on their citizens in order to 'protect their freedom'.

What we mean by the word 'freedom'

What do people mean by the words 'freedom', 'liberty' and 'rights'? We all use these words frequently, but which do we use and in what context? We might be 'at liberty', and we may know our 'rights' but *are we free*? Free from what, or to do what? Free from authoritarian supervision? Why is it that we must 'lose certain liberties in order to retain our freedoms'?

The philosopher Isaiah Berlin[1] once memorably described freedom in two ways, positive, and negative. Positive freedom he defined as being free to benefit from certain rights and entitlements in society. Negative freedom he defined as protection from the arbitrary exercise of authority. It is the latter proposition that concerns us here, since positive freedom has been amply considered by eminent philosophers from the Enlightenment onwards. We should be concerned that the current age shows every sign of a return to unenlightened government, which some might feel is merely a return to the post-Napoleonic period, when civil liberty concerns certainly led to grave restrictions on personal freedoms.

Being or becoming?

We seem at this time to have a need for future-forecast dates... why is this? We appear to be pretty much incapable of living today for today and for what today brings us. We are obsessed with forecasts, meeting targets, planning endlessly for tomorrow – and today goes by us, rapidly and often without our conscious involvement. We are obsessed with *becoming*, rather than *being*. Time is, after all, the consideration that events happen in sequence. We seem often to occupy time and subsequently ask ourselves 'where has it gone'? What counts in life is not just that we have lived – what we have done in relation to others will determine the significance of the life we have lived. Freedom is an enshrined human right. We need to examine more clearly what is happening today, to take a deeper interest, or indeed any interest at all, in legislation passed in our name. Failure to do this will continue to result in a growing set of laws we know little or nothing about, but to which we have agreed by default. There is no point in subsequently complaining that we live in a 'police state' if we do nothing to prevent it today.

I am not concerned to offer a detailed history lesson, nor would I pretend to a scholarly work of past events. However, I am concerned that a consideration of historical events takes place. If we fail to learn from past mistakes in the management of our communities, how will we make any genuine progress? We should all be very aware and sceptical when we are effectively ever told that a dubious legislation is 'for your own good'. Good governance is, after all, what our democratic procedures are designed for; for the people and by the people. Any interference that divides these two elements is dangerous - 'for' and 'by' the people is democracy. This is why I place the events of 1789 in France as the effective beginning of the modern era of democracy, European style. This date happened to be exactly 350 years after Gutenberg's[2] invention of the printing press. The United States of America were, in the 1780s, in their federal and national infancy, and did not come into stronger international reckoning until after their civil war ended in 1865. The United Kingdom, as it became in 1801, dominated the 19th century as we shall see. Democracy as it is currently understood was hard-fought for over a 100-year period. It remains necessary to consider contemporary events with what we might learn from past experiences that could affect our future more positively. I am concerned to illustrate those areas, particularly the political theatre, where negative 'progress' affects us all. This is oxymoronic; progress cannot be negative, but this is in effect what we are being sold by those in power. We have seen the results of democratic failure, and the awful consequences of despotic rule. We must remain perpetually vigilant. We must ensure that tyranny at the highest levels, wearing a cloak of legitimacy, is exposed for what it is; the grossest lie.

UK and US influence

How our world stands today and what intellectual results or otherwise stem from the behaviour of the UK and the US during the last two hundred years is of paramount consideration. World dominance of geopolitical events in that time have been shared by both countries, with no little encroachment by the now defunct Soviet Union. Collectively, how we have developed as people, how we think, how we apply our technology and how we deal with those nations no longer prepared to trail in our ideological and post-colonial wake, are what will affect not only the political theatre, but also the planet in the coming decades. The United States of America and the United Kingdom are very different types of democracies, as we shall see.

Printed freedom

We have made enormous progress since the invention of the first printing press in 1439. This allowed a small start to be made in the erosion of ecclesiastical and monarchical influence. The liberation of the individual had begun and the production of books was free to move away from the monastic scribes. More than 500 years have passed since Caxton[3] introduced the first printing press to England. The Dark Ages were almost over and a renaissance began that we may feel continues to this day. Individual freedoms would take another 450 years to achieve. Surely we cannot allow so many of those freedoms to be removed without the strongest informed debate? This debate must involve the truth on every aspect of the discussion.

Singularity in 2047?

Singularity – that moment when the normal rules of human existence change massively – may be heading our way sooner than we think. Where will we be at the turning of the next 43-year period in the year 2047? If, for instance, the growth of artificial intelligence threatens to overtake collective human intelligence, then who or what will run the world? Artificial intelligence is forecasted to exceed the sum of human intelligence by 2047. This is not a sci-fi question.

We need to accommodate our technological innovations at a similar speed at which we develop our understanding. Failure to do this will leave us woefully exposed to grave uncertainty as to who or what will be in charge. Furthermore, we need to be told the unvarnished truth of reportedly hidden so-called 'black' economies, projects and technologies that have been withheld from the public, and who might be involved in them. If such activity is pure fancy, then the rumours should be quelled by allowing an independent internationally-supervised audit to take place, free of vested interest concerns. Our collective sigh of relief at protracted periods of peace should continue, but we must constantly seek and rediscover the cumulative wisdom that ought to have accompanied those years, to not only prevent tyranny but to enhance our futures with reforming zeal and a continual questioning of the status quo.

Science cannot answer all questions

A naïve belief in 'scientism', that technology will make 'everything alright', we now know to be wide of the mark. A revised method of conducting our personal, local, community, national and international lives is becoming an obvious and urgent requirement – how to agree on what to do about it is less obvious. We must try. To leave the solutions of our problems to chance, technology, our neighbours, our children, is to walk away from a responsibility we can no longer shirk. We cannot allow the possibility of any return to a dark age through the removal of freedom in the name of 'security', especially not with the technologies now available to would-be oppressors.

The significance of the formative periods

Let us look at why the aforementioned periods appear to have real reforming significance.

1. 1789 – 1832

The French Revolution

The events in France in 1789 were as much to do with the overthrow of absolute monarchy as with the influence of the Romantic Philosophers' movement, of whom the best known character is Voltaire[4]. His admiration of England, the English and their system of governance is well known. The 'Encyclopaedia' movement of these French philosophers, particularly Diderot[5] and d'Alembert[6], had given enormous courage to those who dared to be outspoken. Criticism of the King and Catholic Church became a possibility, along with the keeping of one's head.

The French aristocracy cannot be compared to their English counterparts; their indolence and conspicuous consumption was not replicated as ostentatiously in England, and the demands of the revolutionaries were never likely to be matched by any mob in England. The absence of any organised class or organisation beneath the French monarchy left a vacuum which did not exist in England. Nonetheless, the government of William Pitt[7], a brilliant peacetime Prime Minister, sought to pursue the question of parliamentary reform. He was to be frustrated in this; the House of Commons was unconvinced and the proposals were quietly dropped. This did not prevent successive British governments from being extremely cautious about any revolutionary contamination from across the channel – the French uprising created shockwaves across the British Isles. George III[8], Britain's king, was not in any way an absolute monarch, and he knew full well that he depended upon Parliament to run the country. Until Napoleon[9] was finally defeated, the English monarchical and parliamentary system did not have a certain future.

Declaration of the Rights of Man

As approved by the National Assembly of France in August 1789, these today are the relevant articles of 'The Declaration of the Rights of Man':

Article 1 states: "Men are born and remain free and equal in rights. Social distinctions may be founded only upon the general good".

Article 4 states: "Liberty consists in the freedom to do everything which injures no one else; hence the exercise of the natural rights of each man has no limits except those which assure to the other members of the society the enjoyment of the same rights. These limits can only be determined by law".

Article 11 states: "The free communication of ideas and opinions is one of the most precious of the rights of man. Every citizen may, accordingly, speak, write, and print with freedom, but shall be responsible for such abuses of this freedom as shall be defined by law".

All seventeen articles in the declaration were set forth in response to the neglectful contempt of human rights, the ignoring of the citizenry and the excesses of the aristocracy. Small wonder then, that Edmund Burke's[10] remark "Whenever our neighbour's house is on fire, it cannot be amiss for the engines to play a little on our own" was, in retrospect, a significant lens through which to view the reaction of the English government of the time to the events in France.

Positive activism

The period following Waterloo until 1828 was characterised by what we would today describe as 'positive activism'. Following the 'Peterloo' massacre[11] in 1819, in which innocent and peaceful rights protestors were shockingly cut down by British soldiers, the 'Six Acts' were passed, limiting the right to hold public meetings, taxing newspapers in order to keep them from the pocket of the working class, and empowering magistrates to seize 'blasphemous' literature. In the same year, a Working Hours Act limited the number of hours that children aged 9–16 could work to twelve hours a day. Legislation on such matters was seen as interference with parental rights, and their 'right' to send their children into factories for longer periods. The factory owners, who saw this as no business of the government, complained bitterly. But, everywhere, agitation was widespread for reform, for the recognition of deplorable working conditions and for action to be taken to ameliorate those conditions.

The first Reform Act

An 1830 rebellion in the southern counties of England was ruthlessly put down by force, the organisers transported or hanged. In time, however, the Tory government realised that reform was inevitable, and the First Reform Act began its difficult passage through Parliament. Repeal of the Test and Corporation Acts in 1828, admitting Catholics to Parliament for the first time since their expulsion centuries before, may be viewed as a catalyst of reform. The change itself may not have been particularly noteworthy for non-Catholics, but it demonstrated that reforming change was possible and actually could happen.

The Duke of Wellington[12] remarked in 1830 that reform was "unnecessary". This defender of "our perfect democracy" even pretended to be asleep when the parliamentary third reading vote was called. Agitation for social reform, necessary to deal with the chronic conditions of the working classes, and the welfare of children, could no longer be either just acknowledged or ignored. This period is interesting from a Houses of Parliament point of view. Today, we are used to the party system of governance. A 'Labour' or a 'Tory' politician is expected to be answerable to the party whip, and woe betide him or her – and their career – if he or she ignores their 'advice'. This system would not be recognised by late 18th century politicians, for example, Charles Fox[13] and Edmund Burke, sworn parliamentary enemies of the wily William Pitt.

To be a slave to the party line was simply not a part of parliamentary activity; indeed, the individual conscience of the member concerned was a critical part of his armoury as a 'gentleman'. Fox was no parliamentary reformer, and was unshakable in his belief that the MP was a genuine representative of the electorate, although comparatively few voters per constituency existed in his time. It must be remembered that those who elected him were both few in number and often privileged landowners. His brief ministry of 'all the talents' did, however, abolish the slave trade in 1807. Party organisation became increasingly important with the franchise increase of the Second Reform Act of 1867, which expanded the electoral register by almost a million new voters.

This was precisely the problem before 1832 – the number of voters was not representative of the country. Newly industrialised centres such as Manchester, with 250,000 people, had no MP at all, yet the hamlet of Dunwich[14], mostly disappeared under the sea, still returned two members. This frankly ridiculous state of representation could no longer be taken seriously; the clamour for parliamentary reform grew loud and unstoppable. It should be remembered that world population stood at approximately one billion around the time of the French Revolution and it was not to reach two billion until 1918, the end of the First World War. It is a demonstration of the growing confidence of the industrial cities, especially the mill towns, when it is considered that raw cotton overtook sugar as the biggest imported item by 1820.

In 1832, the First Reform Act was finally passed, and limited though it was in terms of franchise extension (the act added almost a quarter of a million voters to the electoral register of nearly half a million), the long 96-year process towards the universal franchise was at least begun. Close inspection of the representative results will demonstrate that the real power still remained in the counties rather than the cities, thus representing the landed classes. In essence, not very much had altered, but 'freedom', in the modern sense of the word, was up and running. Blood had been shed, and disappointment would set in when it dawned upon the majority that precious little had actually changed, hence the rise of the 'Chartist' movement in the 1840s. Lord John Russell[15] played a crucial role in the Reform Act legislation; indeed, he was largely responsible for the framework of the act. His grandson Bertrand Russell[16], born in 1872, who was perhaps one of the finest philosophers and thinkers of the late nineteenth and twentieth centuries, provides a fascinating three-generational link from pre-Victorian times through to his death in 1970, very shortly before the United Kingdom ratified her membership of the Common Market.

2. 1832 – 1875

The beginnings of socialism

This period saw perhaps some of the greatest achievements of the modern era. Queen Victoria[17], from 1837 onwards, would restore enormous respectability to the institution of Monarchy. Her immediate predecessors showed little of her interest or grasp of the challenges to be faced in post-Napoleonic Europe. In many respects due to the training she received from Lord Melbourne[18] on her accession to the throne at the age of eighteen, she quickly and shrewdly judged her politicians. Particularly, she loathed Gladstone[19], adored Disraeli[20], tolerated Palmerston[21], and understood them all. She took her position and responsibility very seriously indeed.

That the working population was becoming increasingly desperate was evidenced by the failure of Robert Owen's[22] Grand National Consolidated Trades Union in the 1830s. Owen, an enlightened industrialist, had realised that better productivity in his factories came from the provision of better working conditions. He also knew that the only way this could be achieved would be as a result of workers organising themselves. He was to coin the expression 'socialism'. His union failed because it could not deliver the expectations of its members, but a valuable lesson had been learned. Workers' leaders began to realise that they needed Members of Parliament to effect real changes. The early seeds of a 'Labour' party had unknowingly been sown.

The Chartists' six points and petition

Meanwhile a mass petition, or charter, was adopted in order to try unignorable persuasion. What is interesting here is that the Chartists' movement was effectively hijacked by impatient enthusiasts, genuinely angry at the failure of the Reform Act and no longer interested in peaceful methods of protest. The movement was to fail, but its aims presented in 1838 have all, with the exception of annual parliaments – an unworkable ambition – now passed into the structures and framework of the constitution. The original twelve members who met at the British Coffee House in June 1837 would be entirely vindicated and, it may be supposed, enormously gratified, to discover that they were ahead of their time.

The aims of the Chartists were summed up in their six-point petition, or 'charter':

A VOTE for every man 21 years of age, of sound mind, and not undergoing punishment for crime.

THE BALLOT, to protect the elector in the exercise of his vote.

NO PROPERTY qualification for Members of Parliament [which had hitherto meant that only property owners could vote] – thus enabling constituencies to return the man of their choice, be he rich or poor.

PAYMENT of Members of Parliament, thus enabling an honest tradesman, working man or other person to serve a constituency, when taken from his business to attend to the interests of the country.

EQUAL constituencies, securing the same amount of representation for the same number of electors – instead of allowing small constituencies to swamp the votes of larger ones.

ANNUAL parliaments, thus presenting the most effectual check to bribery and intimidation, since though a constituency might be bought once in seven years (even with the ballot), no purse could buy a constituency (under a system of universal suffrage) in each ensuing twelve months. Members of Parliament, when elected for a year only, would no longer be able to defy and betray their constituents.

These considered reactions to the failures of the 1832 Act were felt by the Chartists to be a viable remedy to the failure of that act to do little else for them but to transfer their grievances. They had realised their true situation, which was one of:

"Slavery which has been exchanged for an apprenticeship to liberty".

The Act was the first in a line of four extensions to the franchise. It had established the principle that reform was possible and as a result any likelihood of a revolution in the continental style receded. Another long battle was to be fought in order that the labourer might receive at least some proportion of the growing wealth of the country.

The Corn Laws

An event occurred in 1846 which was to have lasting significance on the political landscape – the repeal of the Corn Laws. The Corn Laws protected domestic agriculture in preference to grain importation at lower prices, by placing tariffs on those imports. Given that the agricultural interest represented in the House of Commons was substantial, it was perhaps understandable that those MPs could hardly be expected to vote for a reduction in the income of their estates. Nonetheless, Robert Peel[23], Prime Minister at the time, became determined to repeal the Corn Laws, recognising that protectionism was not a long-term sustainable option. He achieved his aim in 1846, and in doing so bequeathed a bitterly divided Tory party, which was not to achieve a working House of Commons majority again until 1874, nearly 30 years later. Some 60 MPs split from the Conservatives with Peel and became known as the 'Peelites'. William Gladstone was one such member, who was to become one of the two biggest influences of the Victorian political age. The protectionists, led by Bentinck[24] and Disraeli, were outraged by Peel's about turn. In time, they had to concede that protectionism was a dead issue. English agriculture was not destroyed by cheap imported grain, as had been forecasted. The subject was dropped as quietly as possible. Peel died in 1850 as a result of a riding accident.

Further reforms and acts

The Great Exhibition of 1851 celebrated the achievements of British Industry in Paxton's[25] famous Crystal Palace. The age was one of unbounded confidence in Empire and innovation. The Second Reform Act of 1867 widened the franchise substantially, by adding almost one million voters to the existing one million on the electoral register. Serious comment was made during the drafting of the Act on the possibility of granting universal franchise, although nothing was to come of this bold suggestion for another 60 years. The Liberal government of Gladstone from 1868–1874 was directly responsible for much of the judicature as we see it today.

The budget of 1873 was the last recorded time that any serious consideration was given to the elimination of income tax. Had Gladstone won the General Election of 1874, his biographer Morley[26] suggests that he wished to abolish income tax during the next parliament. However, Gladstone lost the 1874 election. Admirers of Disraeli, who won it, must have wondered about this lost fiscal opportunity. In reality, there was little scope to achieve abolition – perhaps Gladstone knew this and was behaving with some mischief ?

During his administration of 1874–1880, Disraeli's Home Secretary, Richard Cross[27], was responsible for the 'permissive' acts such as the Artisans Dwelling Act, which in some local authorities prompted wide scale slum clearance and the building of modern housing. Birmingham was particularly successful in this programme. Cross remains one of the most important, yet unsung, reformers of the period. Extraordinarily, no biography of this important man has been written. Crucially, our path to freedom was enhanced by one important but overlooked domestic act, The Climbing Boys Act of 1875. If your profession was that of chimney sweep, you could only obtain a licence to be a sweep if you did not employ small boys to climb chimneys. Any potentially civilised society could hardly support child employment in this way, and any recollection and compilation of landmark events of that time has to acknowledge the significance of this act. It does give an interesting indication that Victorian society, for all its reputation, did genuinely evolve a positive attitude towards young people, and recognised their value beyond that of a source of cheap labour in order for British industry to remain competitive.

What of freedom during this period? Significant steps in both the personal franchise, and the Second Reform Act, showed important gains for both individual and state. The secret ballot, introduced in 1872, finally weakened the grip of landlords' power over tenants, ensuring that they could no longer influence, through intimidation, how the latter voted. The General Election of 1874 was therefore the first to be held under rules that we might recognise today; the individual vote was an uninterrupted and unhampered process not witnessed or influenced by another person. Wider corruption however, was not tackled until 1883, when the worst excesses were removed by Acts of Parliament. The widening of the voter base ensured that Members of Parliament now had to appeal to a broader section of society, rather than a privileged few.

The British Empire

This second 43-year period might, above all, be described as one of incredible confidence. The British Empire, founded in piracy in the 17th century, owed its strength to policies of robbing the Spanish, beating the French in regular episodes of war, copying The Netherlands' banking methods, and appropriating what it could from India. Britain truly did rule the waves, but the British came late to the concept of Empire. Portugal and Spain demonstrated overseas acquisitive interest long before Britain; they had scoured the known world for natural resources, especially gold, leaving England little fresh opportunity for plunder. Therefore, licensed 'privateering' (individual enterprise involving stealing from others at sea) morphed into government policy, and the English were simply better seamen.

Once established, British sea power and the unrivalled supremacy of the its navy ensured a strong position for the British Empire in international affairs. The politicians used this with varying degrees of both subtlety and success, and the United Kingdom grew in confidence, and territories. The task of managing, and in some cases simply holding on to, British colonial interests was to prove enormously expensive in due course. In retrospect, the confidence of the time was simply incredible. Whoever thought that Great Britain could retain these colonial interests without enormous costs in treasure and manpower? However, a consideration of the idea of liberty was a feature of the colonial legacy.

This period was critical for what was to occur in the following decades, as we will see. Great Britain saw a future and a value in Empire, and all the trading and defence complications that entailed. A unified Germany began consciously to emphasise the importance of domestic manufacturing, but did not entirely neglect its imperial ambitions. Queen Victoria ensured that the European monarchies inter-married wherever possible, as her own large family perfectly demonstrated. Even she could not have envisaged her own family being involved on opposing sides during the Great War of 1914, but that, as we know, is exactly what happened.

Manufacturing and technological decline

The seeds of what would become a dangerous manufacturing decline were sown with the lack of investment in technical education within the United Kingdom. It appears today that we continue to neglect this important aspect of our national education. A Royal Commission was appointed in 1872 to examine the obvious level of neglect into the teaching of science. To this day it remains difficult to convince our society that resources do need to be committed to technical education in order for us to be world-competitive. We claim to acknowledge the ongoing neglect of this perennial problem, but always fail to deal properly with providing the answers. Why is it that some things simply never change, despite the obvious need for action being right under our apparently disinterested and disorganised noses? Could it be that our 'upper class' contempt of those 'in trade' back then ensured our national failure to continue the Industrial Revolution's pace of change, and that vestiges of this prejudice still remain now? Did we honestly think other nations would just sit back and accept our prominent position in world affairs without us having to earn it? Indeed, it seems that we persuaded ourselves that simply being British was quite enough in the superiority league.

Technological ground would be lost to Germany particularly during the last quarter of the century, with lasting repercussions that continue to be apparent to this day, almost 150 years later. As an example of how to neglect international market potential, the United Kingdom of the last half of the 19th century has an unchallenged record of failing to forecast what the nation would need in the longer term. Our decision to follow the path of Empire, as opposed to further developing our manufacturing industries, ensured that sufficient numbers of young talented people were not properly trained for the 20th century and beyond. The number of people needed to run the Empire was astonishingly small. This was not a national vocation designed to contribute anything to the manufacturing economy. Furthermore, we shall see that the Industrial Revolution unwittingly provided an education straight jacket. More importantly, in 1872 the American economy became larger than the UK economy.

3. 1875 – 1918

Protecting the Empire

A completed national railway system, coupled with what had quickly become the most efficient manufacturing base in the world, had given Great Britain an enormous international advantage. Add to this worldwide naval supremacy protecting trade routes to the Empire and we have a picture of true domination. The last quarter of the century, however, exposed Britain's future in unforeseen ways. Imperial and colonial policy certainly ensured that the education system produced men of sufficient calibre to run the Empire, but it may be argued that Germany focused instead on industrial development – and thus the seeds of British decline in the domination of the 'Concert of Europe' were sown.

Disraeli had become Lord Beaconsfield in this era, and the derogatory term of 'Beaconsfieldism' came to refer to any policies seen as lacking moral principle by his opponents. Gladstone regarded Beaconsfieldism in the approach to political issues as profligate and did all he could to reverse Disraeli's policies in his second administration of 1880–1885. During this period, the Third Reform Act of 1884 added a further two million to the electoral register. The cost of Empire protection, and the realisation that overseas territories would be difficult to maintain and retain, led to wars in Afghanistan, South Africa and, ultimately, to the First World War. When the Empire came under threat, the response was swift, brutal and not always successful. The 1899 Boer War in South Africa is such an example. As far more recent history has shown, we continue to be unable to learn from our experiences in Afghanistan.

The legacy of the First World War

With the demise of Queen Victoria and her son, King Edward VII[30], Europe shuddered under the impact of war in 1914. By the time it was over four years later, nine million would be dead in the last war fought on defined fields of battle. Even war itself would change from this point on, and in retrospect the pointless slaughter of millions would be scrutinised closely. Subsequent generations took many years to question the numbers of dead and to ask 'why?'

Despite these war years, enlightened thinking resulted in an overhaul of the educational system, which meant that by 1918, you could at least stay at school until you were 14 years old. In fact, you had to stay there, by law. The role of women in the armaments factories demonstrated their necessary and totally positive contribution to the needs of society. In another ten years, those women over 21 years of age would achieve the franchise.

Unfortunately, the Versailles Treaty[28] of 1918 ensured that future conflict with Germany was a virtual certainty. It also ended a so-called 'golden' era in British history. But how golden was it? Looked at dispassionately, in the aftermath of the Great War we were being forced to recognise overseas national aspirations, and to reappraise our attitude towards the Empire. We would now be obliged to share more equally those assets as a result of nations acquiring their independence. Gladstone, the dominant figure of late Victorian politics, recognised what was coming only too well. His fiscal rectitude was at odds with foreign adventures of Empire; he knew the cost would be prohibitive, and was determined to balance the exchequer. His liberal ideas of a minimalist non-interfering state and fiscal probity seem apposite today. He abhorred waste. Quite what he would make of the 21st century European Union failure to lodge audited accounts we can only imagine. It is worth remembering that 'economic policy' or 'unemployment' as we understand these terms was never a subject of cabinet consideration. The depression of the late 1870s did not provoke fierce cabinet debate; it simply 'was'. The brief advantage of being the first nation to industrialise had passed.

Why was the United Kingdom so effective at colonialism, when other European nations, notably France, Spain and Germany, so conspicuously failed by comparison? Perhaps Britain at the very least pretended to do 'deals' with the target territory, rather than simply steal what they came for and return the plunder to their king or queen simply to fund wars. Indeed, much of the explanation may be found in how war was funded. Credit played a major part, since it became possible to fill banks with promissory notes and manufacture the required millions. Now we fund our peace in a similar fashion, by the method known as 'quantitative easing' or simply issuing government securities. This early credit system was learnt from the Dutch, and subsequently refined. Centuries before, a prominent example of pure plunder was the Spanish appropriation of South American gold under Cortéz[29]. These nationalist overseas attitudes were prevalent throughout the late Victorian era, but the rules would change.

The Soviet Union

This period also saw the overthrow of the imperial Russian royal family, which saw the Tsarist monarchical era finished for good. In England, King George V[31] would feel some guilt for many years that he had refused asylum to his relatives, who were subsequently slaughtered by the revolutionaries in July 1918. The 1917 revolution in Russia heralded the infant Soviet Union; communism was born, and was to influence substantial portions of the geopolitical sphere until the Russian model's effective demise in 1989. Russians would never forget this terminal lie, and those responsible with negotiating with modern-day Russia would do well to remember how keenly many people there feel that they were lied to for more than 70 years. Freedom from serfdom did not mean freedom. Communism truly was an exchange of slavery for a fake apprenticeship in freedom. (It is interesting to note that in the early decades of the 21st century, those remaining communist countries vary hugely in how they apply 'communism', thereby proving the elasticity of the expression. China has recognised the need for some reform, while even Castro's[32] Cuba has done the same. North Korea, at the time of writing, remains a basket case, sadly belligerent on the doorstep of South Korea and Japan. Were China to withdraw its patronage of North Korea the landscape might change. Until then, change of any kind is very unlikely in North Korea).

It is a widely-held view that the world really did change after the First World War. The influential rise in stature of the United States was unquestionable, and for the following 60 years they and the Soviet Union would remain locked in an ideological struggle, both determined to hold sway over as much of the world as was necessary to prevent the influence of the other. By any definition, the Victorian age was finally over. Empire, however, was not.

New empires

What the world map would look like today had the British Empire not existed is a moot point. What the map would look like if another of the imperial conquering powers had achieved military ascendancy is anyone's guess. It has been suggested that the Empire was the nearest thing to a world government. The English language dominated, while liberty, for all the unfortunate coercion too often employed, became a more widely understood idea and an element of common law was introduced in the colonies. Was the British Empire entirely a power-mongering enterprise or has it left any kind of a beneficial legacy?

That Empire continues today is unquestionable, now in the hands of the USA. Whether that is what they wanted or expected is another matter, but it does seem that any examination of history demonstrates powerful dominance by certain nations at certain times. China, Britain and America come mainly to mind, and the United Soviet Socialist Republics (USSR) similarly had specific imperial designs. Empire, in one form or another, is here to stay.

4. 1918 – 1961

Universal franchise

In 1918 women over the age of 30 were entitled to vote and, whilst faintly amusing to modern sensibilities, there was some concern that women might outnumber men were they able to vote at the age of 21. However, in 1928 the universal franchise was finally awarded to everyone, male or female, over the age of 21. This gave an automatic entitlement to a vote at a General Election, a long and hard fought-for privilege. After the First Reform Act of 1832, 96 years later, everyone over the age of 21, regardless of their gender, now had the right to vote. Liberty of political expression, it could be said, was achieved. The ensuing years would issue an unsaid challenge. Would the value of such a vote be maintained in the face of technological change? Would the voting framework remain relevant to the age? Would reforming appetite be maintained, or was the job widely agreed to be 'done'?

The League of Nations

The post-First World War reconstruction of Europe was forced to admit the failures of the 1918 Treaty of Versailles, which, whilst far from perfect, is a document perhaps unfairly traduced. It was pure folly to attempt to extract enormous sums in reparations from Germany; these treaty clauses were in any case never fully enforced. The failure of the 'League of Nations' alliance to deal properly with Germany at this stage should not be laid at the door of Adolf Hitler's[33] subsequent behaviour, tempting though it may be to do so. His unsavoury record must not be allowed to disguise the fact that the military clauses of the Versailles Treaty were evaded by the Germans long before 1933. In much the same way that the 1914–1918 conflict was to have been the 'last of all wars', the crisis of 1921–1922 saw the main Western countries enter what was to have been the 'last of all crises'.

There was little unemployment until 1920. But the onset of a worldwide slump meant that consumers had become too poor to keep up demand, confirming that 'what stops rots'. Whilst few people starved in the West, historical analysis of the period asks the question; is inflation in any way preferable to the systematic deflation of the individual and the personal ongoing tragedy of fruitless job-seeking because the jobs have ceased to exist? This is what troubles the economist of the first years of the 21st century, for the overwhelming consensus seems to be to run the inflationary risk. Nobody is fooled by the current temporary threat of a deflationary period, since fluctuating commodity prices are clearly responsible for a substantial influence on low to near-zero inflation rates. The growing ability of industry to recognise and deal with off-shore manufacturing competition has ensured subdued wage inflation. Economic scenarios seem uncertain. So, post-2008, even inflation is not behaving as expected, nor are interest rates.

The financial crash of 1929

Confidence in the post-war world grew, but this unbounded optimism was unsustainable. The 1929 stock market crash saw an end to the 'peace and prosperity' assumption for the foreseeable future. The economic failures of the 1920s led to discontent on a wide and international scale, and in Europe resulted in another war into which the whole world would be dragged. This time the dead numbered some 60 million – the 2008 population figure of the United Kingdom. The disturbing economic parallels of the first decade of the 21st century and the third decade of the 20th century are striking. What is very different is the reaction of the authorities today to a world of real declining demand.

Nobody wishes to repeat the devastating depression of the 1930s, with enormous unemployment estimated to have been in excess of 50 million worldwide, world production cut by 50% and world trade down to 30% of what it had been prior to the 1929 crash. Nevertheless, there seems to be great and enduring reluctance to address the causes of inflationary asset 'bubbles'. Terrible though the 1930s were in this regard, the problems were at the very least flushed out. In contrast, we appear to be determined to cover up, or maintain, the circumstances that led to the 2008 global financial debacle. We continue to trumpet 'growth' as the ultimate solution to our economic ills. We allow the levels of personal credit to remain high. It is difficult to come to any other conclusion than that we haven't learned our lesson. In too many cases, we refuse to address or acknowledge the real value of balance sheet assets.

The road to fascism

By the end of the 1930s, war seemed to be the inevitable result of both economic failure and the failure to address the problem of mass unemployment. There were two very prominent features of the international scene, of which one became highly visible, whilst the other led to 60 years of ideological international division. Firstly, the Soviet Union, in its infancy, suffered rather less than other developed countries, since it had much less to lose in the first place. Tsarist Russia was not an advanced technological society. Indeed Joseph Stalin[34] warned as early as 1928, as did several Soviet leaders, that a crisis was inevitable and that war would be a result. Secondly, the rise of fascism became practically inevitable too.

This particular lesson should be learned today: neglect truthful politics, and the door is left ajar for a promising 'Strong Man' promising solutions, who will of course be in the pay of, and thus will defend, the interests of the financiers, at least whilst he consolidates his own position. He may be what some might call the 'New World Order' nominee.

When those in charge let the electorate down by destabilising the consistency of circumstances over which their money is held, there is a crisis of confidence. Add to this a significant distrust of the democratic system by those it purports to represent, coupled with a general failure of the elected representatives to actually listen, and a dangerous atmosphere is able to develop, nurtured by the Strong Man. It is difficult not to feel slightly uncomfortable in the second decade of the 21st century as we see some of these elements present once more. Fascism is, though, an episodic tendency.

Two capitalist reactions to crisis

When capitalism goes into a state of crisis as it did in the 1930s, and as it is doing today, it has principally two directions to take. Put simply, it becomes an awful possibility that we might throw everything away which we have laboured to build up over centuries, most especially our real freedom. The direction we decide to take is so crucial, it is hard to over-emphasise how important this particular decision is, and even more important that people know that such a decision is being taken. Nobody honestly would wish for a re-run of 1930s European history, but that is what may be at stake. Our political leaders owe it to all of us, and themselves, to come clean and provide the facts – and therefore the truth. Philosophically, the political theatre must provide the audience with the truth, or we may be in more serious trouble than we yet know.

The two directions usually taken in such circumstances are as follows:

i) The possibility of a fascist reaction: Whilst the lack of direction in managing the vacuum in post-First World War Germany was ultimately exploited by Hitler, it should be kept in mind that fascism is not a tendency or a proclivity shown by any particular nationality or race; it arises from a particular state of capitalist economies at a particular point in time. If money becomes both unsound and unreliable in value, societal foundations are removed and uncertainty prevails. It is easy to think that fascism is generally an Italian, Spanish or German mentality, but that isn't true. It furthermore explains Hitler's pathological hatred of communism and early Bolshevism, which was constantly blamed by both he and General Ludendorff[35] for undermining the morale of German troops and the civilian population during the later stages of the 1914–1918 war.

As dissatisfaction with the political process increases, the tendency for an apparently helpless electorate to vote for fringe political groups rises, helpless because they feel nobody is listening to their core concerns. We see this right now in the UK.

ii) The expansion of the socialist state: In times of financial crisis, the opportunity is almost irresistible for the expansion of the 'socialist' (government-owned, in the name of collectivism) state. It is possible that some form of expanded protectionism is irresistible simply to expand government tax income, severely reduced due to high levels of unemployment and high levels of benefit payments. Post-2008, we saw in the United Kingdom, under a Labour government, the beginnings of exactly this; effectively subsidising some failing banks was potentially just the start. Those of us who remember the less than successful attempts at establishing socialism in Britain in the 1960s and 1970s realise that this simply does not work with any degree of efficiency. We are grown up enough to know that nowadays we ought to be able to buy a newspaper on the day of publication with some degree of certainty that it will be available to buy, or that if we flick a light switch a bulb will ignite to light our way. These functions were not always available to us in the gloomy atmosphere of the 1970s. We ought to remember with great clarity how easy it is for a nation to decline in the hands of awful management. This has historically been anathema to the moneyed classes, since any expansion of the true socialist state has been regarded with horror by financiers.

Similarly, the financiers suppress technological advances where it is in their investment interest to do so. Why let humankind anywhere near low cost energy systems if that threatens their existing income streams? Furthermore, it is in their interest to suppress 'working class' popular movements and retain control of the money supply. In doing so they promise to protect 'rights' and 'freedoms' and generally look after the interests of people not as financially fortunate as are they. This rarely, if ever, happens. In broad terms, this encourages fascism, the control of the national financial assets and, at best, a stable, if ossifying, economy. It is simple to see that as surely as a fascist state is doomed to fail, so is an outright socialist state. The degree of control required ensures that it will be an episode in the life of a nation. Similarly, the socialist state carries enormous control costs which ultimately render the exercise invalid. (It is therefore possible to see why the expression 'The facts of life tend to be Conservative' really means 'take care of the pennies, and the pounds will follow'.)

German territorial ambition

What may be one of the lesser-known origins of the Second World War are Hitler's original thoughts behind German national expansion. He thought it possible, in the atmosphere of the 1920s, that a treaty could perhaps eventually be agreed with Great Britain on the western flanks of Europe, enabling German expansion in the east without interference. Similarly, he felt that Italy might be able to do much the same to the South. Mussolini[36] did, after all, stay in power for more than 20 years beginning in 1922. He ruled by decree, which was playing the game as his predecessors had done for many years, but it was his fault that Italy turned out to be more trouble to Germany than she was worth. Mussolini had re-armed too early in comparison to Germany, which meant an over-reliance on an up to date Germany and a reliance on German raw materials, with an obsolete military capability by comparison. He, therefore, became a virtual prisoner of Hitler's Germany. If Hitler thought he could turn the Italians into the modern equivalent of Roman soldiers, however, nothing could be further from the truth. Whilst Hitler's early 1920s view of Italy's possibilities to the south of Europe never became a serious piece of the German expansion jigsaw puzzle, it is ironic that the challenge posed to NATO in the European east by the Warsaw Pact countries required so much investment in allied time and fiscal effort. The strategic thinking of Hitler was published in his book *Mein Kampf* ('My Struggle')[37] and confirmed his ambitions in eastern Europe and his hatred of the Soviet Union.

The post-war period

In 1945, the Second World War ended. Hitler was dead. Whatever else he was, he was an excellent psychologist, a brilliant actor – and ruthless. His blatant disregard for individual freedom and his almost total disrespect for the individual all round are the classic hallmarks of the dictator. (In future we might look out for the aforementioned Strong Man with answers, who exhibits such qualities). Europe once more needed reconstruction. 1945 saw the election of the first Labour government in Great Britain with a working majority under Clement Attlee[38], who had worked so closely with Winston Churchill[39] during the war years. In 1947, North American money was made available to any European nation for rebuilding purposes. (As French leader General de Gaulle[40] mentioned to Richard Nixon[41] in 1969, "In the Second World War all the nations of Europe lost; two were defeated"). The prime condition imposed by the Americans for this aid was that the recipient nations create a joint organisation to manage these funds and to set up a common economic policy. This was done, and the Organisation for European Economic Cooperation was created. This gave European nations some idea of the complexities of real cooperation, and was to lead to the Treaty of Paris in 1951, signed by six nations, which dealt specifically with pooled coal, iron and steel production. These items were felt to be crucial constituent elements of any war build-up, and this therefore made a repetition of 1939–1945 unlikely. So it has proved.

For their money, America obtained a bulwark against the spread of communism in Europe. This task of sponsored European reconstruction arguably ended the after-effects of the war by around 1960, at which date it may be safely asserted that the conflict, and the trail of economic destruction in its wake, was over. In 1961, the construction of the Berlin Wall across Germany signalled a new era in international politics, which became known as the 'Cold War'. For almost 30 years this 'Iron Curtain', designed to keep the citizens of the Soviet Union in, rather than to keep others out, was a potent symbol of the lack of freedom for those who lived to the east of the wall. It was to divide Europe until 1989. After 1945, it is difficult to over-emphasise just how rabid the fear of communism was in the continental United States. Former US president Richard Nixon, in his book *The Real War*, amply describes in detail just how much of the administration's time and effort was devoted to countering Soviet influence.

Oil and the superpowers

The Soviet Union, together with the United States of America, held 'superpower' status and posed a colossal threat to freedom everywhere. The USA became the international 'free world' defender against the behemoth communist bloc, which was very assuredly pursuing worldwide imperialist ambitions to spread communism where it could, by whatever means possible. In 1961, John F Kennedy[42] was inaugurated President of the United States. Significant though that may have been, another crucial event happened that year. OPEC, the Organisation of Petroleum Exporting Countries, was born. It was to be of huge importance in determining international economic thinking for decades to follow, and since huge reserves of oil lay under the sands of the Middle East, the region would know no lasting peace from thereon. Critically, democracy, as the developed Western world understood the term, was not the system by which the region was organised and governed. Protecting the world oil supply, or a very large part of it, would dominate world politics in some guise or other for years to come. World population numbers had, by 1961, grown to three billion, so the finite supplies of oil would in theory need to be spread around rather more evenly. The quantity of oil that remains is unknown, and therefore the fear of an oil-restricted world is an ever-present concern.

The acquisition of nuclear technology by oil-rich Middle Eastern states remains highly suspicious to many commentators. Why do they wish to acquire such technology, when they effectively float on so much oil? This is to misunderstand three important points, one of which is the export value of their oil reserves. The second – since they know their lack of water may become critical – is nuclear desalination technology. Thirdly, they also fear the impact the huge quantities of shale oil and gas discoveries in the USA is likely to have on oil demand. Any alteration in US foreign policy thinking towards the Middle East as a result of growing domestic energy independence makes any nuclear capability more important to, for example, Saudi Arabia. Iranian nuclear ambitions are a further destabilising influence on Israel's relations with her Arab neighbours.

The organisation then known as the OEEC[43] grew to become the Common Market, fully established by six European member states in 1958. Since the first, almost successful, attempt by the Romans to hold sway over the whole of Europe, Charlemagne[44], Napoleon and Hitler had tried to do the same and failed. Now, the issue was no longer national expansion by conquest, but rather unification by trade, currency, politics and economics in general.

5. 1961 – 2004

Modern history

This period is contemporary and there is little need to summarise events in depth since many of us can recall the significant events of the time or have had it taught to us as modern history. The global community has organised itself into political or trading blocks in order to best participate in growing world economic prosperity, with mixed results. The demise of the Soviet Union, the demolition of the Berlin Wall and the end of the East German state in 1989 meant an end to 50 years of conflict, begun in 1939. The organisation known as the European Economic Community, designed to facilitate wider and free trade between European nations, grew to 25 member states.

The creation of the World Wide Web, the introduction of inexpensive international travel and, of course, the relentless increase in global population to over six billion were significant features of this period. Failure to distribute international assets of basic needs fairly (such as food, water and shelter), with population levels so high as to be impossible to ignore, led to dissatisfaction on an epic scale. This gave rise to wide-scale emigrations and economic asylum-seeking, and presented a big challenge to humankind to manage these and other problems of population shift. It may be argued that failure of even asset distribution has given rise to the no-hope attitude of extremists, which we will explore more in Chapter 3. These years are extraordinary for reasons not seen before.

World War Three and liberalisation

As noted, the post-Second World War years and the exhaustion that always follows war were over by 1960. If you believe that one war must end before the next starts, the USA and USSR had their eye on one another before the 1939–1945 conflict was even over. It may be argued that the dropping of the atomic bombs on Japan was actually a warning to the Soviets of the frightening potential of weapons technology as much as an elimination of Japan from the war. The Americans saw World War Three as a 'work in progress' before the Second was concluded.

The decade that followed saw enormous cultural change. Those born during and after the Second World War experienced a liberalising atmosphere. Experiments in sight and sound were everywhere, musical styles changed and personal styles of dress and behaviour reached new levels of personal expression. The music of Lennon and McCartney[45], the lyrics of Leonard Cohen[46] and Bob Dylan[47] were to be hugely influential for decades to come. The times really were changing. Attitudes to questions of morality were called into debate, both in literature and the theatre. What was, or was not, considered obscene, and the laws supporting controls of obscenity, were increasingly out of touch with prevailing attitudes. The sheer speed of change, on reflection, was breathtaking. In 1960, to have forecast man to be either on the Moon or to be naked on a West End of London theatre stage would have been seen to be truly ridiculous – yet both happened before the end of the decade. Contraception, meanwhile, gave women reliable biological control over their reproductive systems for the first time; and so genuine equality of gender seemed to be a distinct and real possibility.

Attempts by the 'newly vocal and politically knowledgeable' youth to be heard became increasingly sophisticated. Anti-Vietnam War demonstrations in both the United States and Europe left few political leaders in doubt as to exactly how unpopular this South East Asian involvement was. By 1975 the war was finished, with over 58,000 American troops dead, while Vietnam was unified. The United States had failed to bestow any dignity on the conflict by declaring war on North Vietnam. Loss of life on this scale in a pointless and unwinnable conflict today seems incredible. Sadly, technological advances in sophisticated weaponry have not stopped non-combatant loss of life, even if they have enabled greater control over what and who is destroyed. This may have reduced combatant losses and made conflict more 'target-specific', but it hasn't conferred additional authority nor justification to the idea of 'collateral damage'. Personally, I found it unsettling to once eat breakfast in Laos sat in front of a neutralised cluster bomb found "not far from here", with 'made in USA' on the casing. Unexploded American ordnance remains a problem in Laos. My grandmother clearly remembered the first flight made by the Wright brothers[48]. That her grandson flew supersonically in the same century is graphic testament to the pace of change seen during these periods, and the pace continues to quicken.

Communications

Communications industries in these four decades changed out of all recognition. In 1961 the UK boasted two television stations; one state-sponsored and one independent. In 1967 the first colour pictures were transmitted. Forty years later, satellite-enabled technology offered hundreds of options to the viewer. The influence of satellite broadcasting in undermining East European communist countries dominated by the USSR must be acknowledged. Access to Western broadcasts enabled the great communist lie to be undermined, which is an unusual example of a particularly beneficial televised influence. The positive confluence of both terrestrial and satellite television really helping to change the course of history is unlikely to be repeated.

Radio also altered as a result of independently-driven broadcasters. State telephone monopolies ended too. Mobile phone and computer technology costs all reduced to allow individual ownership of hitherto expensive and often bewildering technology. Electronic mail and social networking arrived. All these innovations transformed the way we do business and communicate with one another. The 2004 telecommunications world is unrecognisable when compared with its 1961 predecessor. We have adopted telephones, computers and televisions in ways unforeseen only a few years ago. The results of this wide-scale adoption were not always positive. The beginnings of what some call a 'screenocracy' could be detected quite early on.

'War on Terror' and loss of freedom

In reality, there cannot be a war against 'terror' since terror cannot be a party to a conflict. Since what has become known as 'post-9/11', one sinister effect of extremist behaviour, or 'terrorism' as it is labelled, is the state-sponsored removal of freedom from innocent citizens. Remember, these rights were hard-won. Their withdrawal is invariably made in the name of 'protecting' the citizenry.

This loss of freedom may take the following forms:

1. The possible monitoring of e-mail, social networking and telephone conversations; digital surveillance is cheap.

2. The discussion and possible introduction of identity cards or schemes, including plans for the microchipping of populations.

3. The passing of ill-considered laws under the parliamentary 'guillotine' procedure.

4. Detention without charge times increased.

All these moves work against our individual freedoms, and make a mockery of our so-called democracy (discussed further in Chapter 6).

The failures of democracy mean that our representatives no longer represent properly those who elect them; they have ceased to listen, and it no longer seems to matter to them if they don't. It is catastrophic to anaesthetise the people into meek submission and also for the people to cynically acknowledge...

"I'm only one, I can make no difference" ...

This is impertinent, and constitutionally a dangerous result of continual representational failure, which, unreformed, bodes ill for our future. Must a properly-functioning democracy be measured by the ability of its members to be conned?

6. 2004 – 2047

Six considerations

Since this period is only one quarter completed, we have the luxury of speculating as to what the immediate future might hold. Importantly, we can also consider what the most critical factors might be in deciding how we will successfully maintain our hard-won freedoms during the next years until 2047.

As we have identified, we are concerned with six principal considerations that will affect our global community, and everything living on the planet, regardless of species:

1 – Each individual has 'awareness' responsibility
There must be an awakening of the individual to his/her place in the natural order, the realisation that each of us are a vital part of the whole, dependent on each other, our collective actions, and the realisation that for every action there will be a reaction. This is the ultimate humanist response.

2 – Each elected government has responsibility
There must be a re-establishment of genuine democracy coupled with a reporting of the truth and an elimination of 'off the record' fiscal transactions and technological innovations. There must be no taxation without audited accounts and honest disclosure of where the money goes. There must be skilful but fully accountable management of an integrated global community that is genuinely answerable to the entire community. There must be genuine free trade, not the current obfuscation known as the World Free Trade Order. This simply doesn't work and has become another talking shop. This is world governance? I think not. It is not working properly.

3 – Each of us is responsible for the environment
We must realise and acknowledge that we are an integral cog in the grand design. We may not confound nature, any more than we can 'defeat it' with some idea of dominating it. We must learn to balance our real needs with the needs of the planet, and stop our directionless plunder. We bequeath our successors the results of our treatment of the environment. Nobody can overcome nature, for we are part of it. Furthermore, we will lose our ability to be free if we continue with the pretence of domination.

26th December 2004 saw what might be described as one of the worst natural disasters in modern recorded history, with the devastating tsunami in the Indian Ocean. Thousands died; the energy force of more than

23,000 Hiroshima explosions destroyed lives and property over a huge area bordering the Indian Ocean. For those of us not normally exposed to the extreme forces of nature, this reminder of that force was brought to international attention, happening again with the similar Japanese disaster of 2011. Eleven countries were directly affected in 2004. Unknown numbers remain unaccounted for, but more than 250,000 people died. The international community responded quickly to calls for direct aid to the areas badly hit. This shows that humanitarian concern is alive and well, once again demonstrating that it seems there almost has to be an enormous catastrophe from time to time to waken our sensibilities to those worse off than us, particularly in far away countries. Fourteen islands in the Maldives had to be evacuated, their drinking water permanently contaminated. This low-lying collection of atolls demonstrated all too clearly the vulnerability of near-sea level habitation, and all this without the influence of a melting polar ice cap.

Important issues of the environment are covered in Chapter 9. We all know, or are at least aware of, our obligation to ensure we pass on to our children as few of the consequences of poor global management as possible. Doing nothing is no longer an option (regardless of the actual facts of climate change, upon which scientists seem unable to agree. When our technologies eventually have the potential to interfere with the weather, the impact of any decision will have far-reaching consequences. Management of the HAARP project (the High Altitude Aurora Research Project) and other similar attempts to manipulate the ionosphere (HAARP is reportedly now mothballed but its progeny almost certainly lives on), certainly does need to be subject to far higher levels of international scrutiny. Environmental concerns involve acting now. Nature regularly reminds us of her awesome power, but we should also beware of humans trying to emulate or tap that power.

4 – We must properly educate our young

Article 26 of the United Nations Resolutions of December 1948 clearly states "Higher Education shall be equally available to all on the basis of merit". Quite how this squares with charging tuition fees for higher education is beyond me. How do we structure a system capable of the honest education of our children and grandchildren to be both aware of, and be able to deal with, the real global questions that are coming and which must be answered? Why must current education systems serve the education system itself, and not the best interests of students? This prevailing systematic attitude does nothing for creative future management. Our grandchildren will be in charge soon enough. To not make available to them the necessary intellectual tools to do this in a considered manner is criminal. Academic standards in British schools are plummeting. A 2013 survey undertaken by the Organisation for Economic Cooperation and Development show UK students at the age of 15 faring very poorly in mathematics, at 26th in the global league table. In science we are in 18th place. This is simply not good enough. Chapter 4 covers education in more detail.

5 – We must properly consider the consequences of technological innovation
The impact of technological innovation and our ethical management of the consequences of our inventions is critical. We know that we do not 'keep up' with the full effects of our technological innovations – we are not cautious inventors.

6 – We must continue to recognise the ongoing need for genuine reform
Reforming zeal is more crucial than ever. We must not accept the status quo simply because we are too busy to take an interest. Suggestions for reform in the following chapters propose genuine and lasting change for the benefit of the majority, not simply the vested interest. We have already observed that the current system of democracy is often purported to be the best of a poor list of options. Be that as it may, it's what we have. That it can be improved case by case there is no doubt. I suggest that the Swiss model offers the best system yet of both local and national administration. Detailed suggestions may be found in Chapter 5.

The exportation of democracy as approved by the USA is fraught with difficulty. If Palestinians vote for Hamas[49], and the US doesn't like it, they promptly interfere, with flagrant disregard of the populace's wish.

There are similar examples in South America. Just because something is manufactured in the USA, this doesn't make it instantly exportable or acceptable. This reflects the 'deductivist' behaviour of the US in foreign policy; they appear to react to circumstances on a highly selective basis, without regard for the historical big picture. The 2003 invasion of Iraq is a classic case. Unwittingly perhaps, the USA clearly demonstrates that it is not yet an experienced manager of empire.

SUMMARY

Two and a quarter centuries have passed since the French Revolution arguably laid the foundations of meaningful freedom. There have been several significant attempts to curtail the rights and freedoms of the individual since that time; fortunately, all such attempts seem destined to fail. History is on the side of some form of democracy, but it remains true that in order for democracy to flourish then economic circumstances need to be encouraging enough to warrant changing from other forms of 'government'. Dictators dictate surely enough, but what replaces them we now know needs detailed and pragmatic attention. Democracy is not an exportable package, and interference in another nation's affairs in the name of it is no longer an option.

Misplaced optimism in many parts of the world, coupled with almost non-existent domestic infrastructure, means that young nations are susceptible to disruptive ideologies amongst their young populations, who see little future in their blighted country. This subject is addressed in the following chapter. What to do about it is the huge challenge facing the world community. Nobody can afford to shrug their shoulders and ignore the growing problems of the desperate.

3

THE INCONSISTENCIES OF ECONOMICS, RELIGION AND HOPE

"People are adrift, insecure, cheated and angry".

A climate of fear

Here in the early decades of the 21st century we are faced with an international crisis involving extreme religious opinion and violence. The perpetration of gross acts of inhumanity against people and infrastructure in target countries by extreme and hostile religious groupings has introduced a climate of fear and uncertainty in those countries. Radical groups often claim responsibility, using tactics both incomprehensible and alien to Western defence and response systems.

The emergence of the self-proclaimed 'Islamic State'[1] from the battered remains of the failed states of Iraq and Syria is deeply worrying. The extreme Islamist group 'Boko Haram[2]' is busy destabilising vast swathes of Nigeria and neighbouring African countries. There is ample evidence that the vacuum left by the American-led intervention in Afghanistan to remove the Taliban has been ruthlessly exploited by al-Qaeda and a resurgent Taliban, covertly supported by the Pakistani military. Had the opportunity to rebuild Afghanistan been properly taken, and its fledgling government properly supported, the region might have achieved genuine stability. Instead, extremist groups have utilised weak or non-existent security arrangements to exploit training opportunities on both sides of the Afghan-Pakistan border, with terrible consequences for both local and international communities. Extremist groups are taking, and have taken advantage of, a clear lack of focused Western response as to how to handle this situation. American determination to root out al-Qaeda leaders took precedence over any notion of 'nation building', and they determined that cooperation with the Pakistani military was the most effective way of finding these characters. Evidence that Pakistan actively supported the

Taliban seems to have been overlooked, which, coupled with the financial aid given to Afghan warlords, undermined the government notionally charged with running the country. Put simply, America appears to have funded a Taliban-sympathetic Pakistani military government responsible for tolerating, on their territory, fighters out to kill American service personnel. This bizarre state of affairs demonstrates all too clearly the failure of long-term American planning, or complete lack of it (some conspiracy thinkers have even suggested this might be part of a deliberate and wider destabilisation programme for the Middle East). America eventually lost interest in Afghanistan and turned its attention to Iraq, with disastrous consequences. One suspects Africa is far down the American agenda despite Nigeria's strategic oil reserves. Meanwhile Boko Haram murder, kidnap and enslave, practically unchecked.

The American 'War on Terror' demonstrates an enormous misunderstanding of the law of unintended consequences. Again, since terrorism cannot be party to a conflict, how can there be a war against it? Furthermore, nobody seems to have predicted the reaction to the incredible American statement "why do they hate us?" – which implies that the USA hates back... thereby convincing many Muslims, encouraged by radicalising clerics, that the Americans and other Western nations are out to target Muslim civilisation. Failure to nation-build after war simply confirms this impression.

The shootings in Paris in early 2015 in protest at the satirical lampooning of the prophet Mohammed in the French publication *Charlie Hebdo*[3] appear to have been calculated to provoke anti-immigrant sentiment amongst the indigenous population. Such attacks clearly demonstrate the two distinct *modus operandi* of organised disruption. Complex plots, such as downing passenger aircraft, seem to be preventable in large part. However, small groups intent on suicide missions are far harder to detect and prevent. France possesses the largest Muslim minority in Europe, and also has an organised right wing national political influence. Right wing elements are only too happy to exploit an indigenous lack of broader understanding on the question of immigration, giving rise to further heightening of tension in local communities. Has France been singled out for particularly concentrated attention for this reason? The attacks are in direct contravention of Article 11 of the 1789 *Declaration of the Rights of Man* (see Chapter 2) which clearly states "every citizen may speak, write and print with freedom". Is the objective to stir up greater anti-immigrant sentiment on the European mainland where the largest Muslim population resides? Is this part of a coherent strategy to maintain tension between religious and ethnic groupings, and prove Western society is truly intolerant of the Muslim faith?

In both France and Germany there is active resentment of the Muslim community, which has condemned the attacks in unequivocal terms. In The Netherlands, the mayor of Rotterdam, a Muslim of Moroccan descent, went further, telling his co-religionists on television:

"[Just] because some humorists you don't like are producing a newspaper – you can 'sod off'. The cost of seeing and hearing things you don't like is more than outweighed by the benefit of being able to say anything you want".

That publications may lack a degree of taste in what they publish is quite another question.

Although terrorist groupings may appear to be incoherent, many people are prone to falling into the media-inspired trap of calling all Muslims potential 'terrorists'. If we fall into that trap, we reward the real terrorists' criminality at the tops of our voices. This is not lost on those who seek to drive a wedge through society in the name of Islam. That Islamic State[12] contrives to make al-Qaeda appear a moderate organisation is incredible. That the conditions for its very existence have been allowed to flourish smacks of poor foreign affairs management by the USA, at whose door this problem may be squarely laid. 'Terrorism' has enabled ultra-conservatives in America to broaden their contest with al-Qaeda into an unintended global conflict with Islam, and perceived state sponsors become part of the al-Qaeda network, whether they like it or not.

We are also faced with the unpalatable possibility that 'false-flag' events may be perpetrated by self-serving groups in order to keep populations in a permanent state of 'preparedness' for terrorist atrocities. To experience this atmosphere, to understand how a population lives in almost constant fear and anticipation of an attack of some type, a visit to modern Israel is essential. The feeling of tension is palpable. We discuss the Middle East in detail elsewhere, but there is no better demonstration of a society living in continual fear. It is a deeply unpleasant experience, and one is left to wonder what impact this must have on young people born into this tension, and who know no other way of life. The atmosphere of distrust must have a totally negative effect on any worthwhile 'peace process'. In fact, such a term is a mockery of language.

The corollary of this, of course, is a restriction on personal freedom, which is deemed 'necessary' to remain free. This is an insult to us all. For reasons explored in Chapter 5, the absence of certain truths (facts that we can absolutely rely on) from our political leaders gives rise to an inevitable cynical response to all the information we receive through the media – in other words what we read in newspapers, see on television and hear on radio. Is this 'news' really true? Are these extremists, which is the label given them by the media, really responsible for all these bombings and threats? That a significant number of people are now even asking this question is a damning response to those in charge of our democracy. In short, many of us we feel that our governments may be lying to us. If they are, why?

Government itself has become a problem. People see themselves in an endless competitive struggle and turn against the very thing they have in common to meet their social needs; the governments under which they live. If they are not lying to us, then why are these external extremists perpetrating such outrageous acts in order to gain recognition and world attention? Is the base problem a genuine desire to wield religious influence, or is the real aim a redistribution of global wealth? If the ambition truly is a worldwide caliphate, as promoted by the likes of Islamic State, the only antidote available to the 'infidel' world is an acknowledgement of chronic social and economic shortfalls, and the will to act in order to rectify those problems. There is a lack of will to fight if economic opportunity is available. Western public indifference, or plain disbelief that there really are threats from groups determined to inflict damage to life and property in 'peacetime', is an extraordinary indication of just how much lying the population feel the authorities are capable of, and is further evidence of the erosion of public confidence and mistrust in our elected representatives.

Before September 11th, 2001, various terrorist acts failed to achieve the recognition that the perpetrators hoped for, for example the previous targeting of the World Trade Centre in New York in 1993, American embassies overseas and the bombing of the American warship *USS Cole*. At first sight, it would appear that the extremists recognised the vulnerability of the domestic United States to a much larger and public terror outrage and so a change of tactics was introduced. What became known as '9/11', with the destruction of the World Trade Centre towers in New York, the strike on the Pentagon and the loss of another flight, is all-too well-known. This raised the profile of international violence to unknown peacetime heights, and introduced the War on Terror to a hesitant and shocked international community. Yet people continue to wonder whether the facts concerning this outrage will ever be fully known. Conspiracy theorists speculate that the story is long on obfuscation and it is widely said that factually misleading information has been supplied by the authorities. Questions have been raised that again and again ask:

"Who really were the perpetrators and who was responsible?"

The anomalies are certainly many. Three buildings at the WTC collapsed, yet only two were directly hit, none of them following the usual rules of physics. Many eyewitnesses spoke of unexplained explosions going off in the towers long before they fell, and others are visible *as* they fall. The hole in the Pentagon seems far too small for a Boeing 757, and the expertly-flown plane which supposedly struck was apparently being piloted by one of the worst fliers ever trained by his unwitting instructors. Numerous warnings of the attacks were ignored, no serious effort was made to intercept the flights even once the hijackings were known, and air traffic control transcripts have been suspiciously obfuscated since. The list goes on.

Was there any involvement from within the United States border by domestic nationals? Either way, long on shooting, short on thinking, reaction to 9/11 has frightened the United States into draconian domestic security measures. The War on Terror declarations have often appeared to aggravate the international atmosphere still further. There is little need to list a detailed summary of acts of international violence, suffice to say that declarations of war must involve the honest truth, straight dealing with the nation and a total lack of salesmanship and/or deception by the government. The allied invasion of Iraq was undertaken with doubtful legality, without United Nations agreement and on patently inaccurate intelligence.

"The British Government has learned that Saddam Hussein recently sought significant quantities of uranium from Africa".

These words, which would become the focal point of the controversy that would haunt President Bush and the United States until the election of President Obama[4] in 2009, suggested another approach. It gets worse, for the stupidity in removing an evil dictator without a clear vision of the Iraqi future and without the cooperation of the people, was always unlikely to lead anywhere. Saddam Hussein[5] was indeed an evil leader, but he had nothing to do with the events in New York on 9/11. Furthermore, to heighten the stupidity of this adventure, Hussein held the imbalance of Shia/Sunni regional differences in check; removing him without due care has led to the disasters of Islamic State today. In the wake of Hussein's removal, the American people were susceptible to the false but politically useful suggestion that he *was* responsible for 9/11. The pretext for the invasion was a perfect screen for the Bush administration, and an unjustifiable war began. That area did not need another conflict. For concluding remarks on 9/11, see Chapter 13.

The Balfour Declaration

Sadly, the Middle Eastern Region has been fraught with tension since the creation of the state of Israel. The famous 'Balfour Declaration[6]' in 1917 was the first recognition of Zionist ambition by a major world power; Great Britain. Contained within that declaration is the following sentence which clearly states that:

"It be clearly understood that nothing shall be done which may prejudice the civil and religious rights of existing non-Jewish communities in Palestine, or the rights and political status enjoyed by Jews in any other country".

The words of the Balfour Declaration have come to haunt all efforts at creating a stable Middle Eastern region able to accommodate Arab and Jew. The creation of the state of Israel, surrounded by Arab neighbours, was certain to be a particularly difficult undertaking. With hindsight, it is easy to spot the potential for political difficulties. Blaming the Israeli nation for an inability to integrate regionally, or blaming the Arab nations for failing to accept this new state of affairs, is simplistic. Whichever way the situation is analysed, the Arabs have been asked to accept the Israelis in their midst, and this was never going to be easy.

An impossible union

David Ben-Gurion[7], the first Prime Minister of Israel, was very aware that the Jews were unlikely to be welcome. As he commented in a private conversation:

"Why should the Arabs make peace with us? If I were an Arab leader I would never make terms with Israel. This is natural, we have taken their country. Sure, God promised it to us, but what does that matter to them? Our God is not theirs. We came from Israel, true, but 2000 years ago, and what is that to the Arabs? There has been anti-Semitism, the Nazis, Hitler, Auschwitz, but was that their fault? They see only one thing; we have come here and stolen their country. Why should they accept that?"

Whilst the establishment of the Israeli nation may have suited the post-Holocaust 'real politic', and however much the conscience of the allied victors was salved by the establishment of a Jewish state, this was not a stable or worthy long-term solution. With a seeming disregard for Arab sensibilities, and blatant inequality of territorial asset allocation, lasting peace remains elusive. Nobody may argue the facts, nor the inexcusable behaviour of 1940s Germany. Moreover, any indication of a repetition of such behaviour would never be knowingly tolerated. To stop such behavioural possibilities internationally remains an honest objective of the United Nations, to which all nations must subscribe. But an examination of the United Nations Partition Plan of November 1947 reveals the impossibility of peaceful coexistence between Jew and Arab, and the impossibility of reconciling the thorny issue of Jerusalem. The plan placed Jerusalem in isolation within the proposed Jewish State sector, and bore an uncanny resemblance to the isolated position of Berlin in 1945 partitioned Germany.

Splitting the proposed Arab Palestinian state into three sectors could never be workable, and so it proved. The 1949 armistice map drawn after the First Arab-Israeli war shows an expanded territorial gain by Israel. Gaza was occupied by Egypt, whilst the West Bank was occupied by Jordan. Palestinian autonomy remained out of reach, and remains that way 60 years later.

The 'Six Day War' of 1967, the humiliation of Arab military capability and the vast acquisition of territory by Israel gave ample evidence of the determination of the Jewish nation to remain established and safe. There could no longer be any question of doubting the sincerity, the effort, the historical and religious will of the Jewish people to establish a permanent home for Jews of all nations. Yet, where was Israel expected to locate all the international Jewish people who had the invitational right to enter Israel and take up residence, because they were Jewish? Is it possible that an expansionist rather than preservationist Israeli policy existed prior to 1967? Was the 1967 war something more than a retaliation to Arab aggression?

As the maps show, Israeli territory expanded hugely as the Arab offensive failed, to the Arabs' cost. The unintended consequence of unrestricted immigration to Israel of any Jew who wished to take up residency meant that enormous numbers of homes were needed. Settlements sprang up in occupied territory to accommodate them. Did anyone forecast the future need for so many new homes? Without the territorial gains of the 1967 war, it is difficult to see where the new arrivals could have been accommodated. Was the Israeli nation in purely defensive mode when the Arabs threatened in 1967? Or were they always looking at long-term territorial acquisition if the Arabs did begin a military offensive? If this was the case, such planning is understandable given the nervousness and precarious position of this young country, surrounded as it was by unsympathetic Arab peoples. Israel could not have foreseen, nor did anyone else, the collapse of the USSR, and the immense wave of immigration to Israel that followed. Without the occupied territories, where were these immigrants to be settled? Although the Sinai desert was returned to Egypt in 1982, the West Bank remains occupied and actively populated by incoming settlers. The thorny issue of a partitioned Jerusalem remains.

The truth is that Israel is able to continue settlement building on the West Bank for two reasons: the people need space, and the USA bankrolls the Israeli nation state. Without that money, Israel would probably be finished. This is a fact that any Israeli will acknowledge. The Arabs are well aware of this fact too, and they know that who pays the piper calls the tune. It is easy to see why the US is unpopular within the Middle East.

The resulting flowering of Israeli economic growth is admirable; the high technology industries in which they deal are quality testament to targeted commercial ambition. This is a logical step toward the establishment of a long-term future. To stay competitive in the industrial and economic scene is of paramount national importance. The North Americans implicitly protect this investment. In turn, there is a massive and real long-term problem of envy felt by the disadvantaged Arab neighbours of Israel. The US budget allocation for Israel is massive; it would be fascinating to know the truth of the actual numbers, and how much is given to the Palestinians conditionally on a similar basis? Small wonder that imbalance exists. The Americans feel that Palestine and other countries of instability such as Syria and Lebanon harbour international terror groups such as Hamas and al-Qaeda[8], and must be kept at a disadvantage. The collapse of Syria into civil war and factionalism, with extremist groups unsympathetic to the very idea of coexistence with Israel, further alienates Middle Eastern populations from American foreign policy.

The roots of terror

When does a terror group acquire legitimacy through democratic elections? Menachem Begin[9], a member of the group 'Irgun'[10], subsequently walked the corridors of power, as did Martin McGuinness[11] of the IRA[12]. When Hamas was democratically elected in Palestinian elections in 2005, Israeli leaders voted to withhold millions of dollars in monthly aid. This was an approved election on an internationally-recognised ballot, yet the Americans under George Bush declined to "do business with terrorists". This is hypocrisy, writ very large. The American government cannot afford to upset the powerful Jewish lobby in Congress, yet if they fail to offer balanced alternatives to the one-sided arrangements in place, how can anyone avoid upsetting the Jewish lobby without patient and exhausting negotiation? How shall we ever make progress? American presidential attitudes to this problem could help solve the difficulties for both Jews and Palestinians, keen as every president of the USA is to solve this long-running problem. Yet the status quo is unlikely to alter without radical steps.

Acknowledging the despair of long-term refugees might help us to understand why there appears to be a constant supply of volunteer terrorists. Where there is no hope, what is there to lose? There is no surer confirmation of this than seeing a Palestinian mother giving an interview to a television reporter, saying how proud she is that her 18 year-old son will become a martyr – in Western parlance, blow himself up in an act of terror, taking as many of the 'infidels' with him as possible. To most cultural instincts this is nigh on incredible – giving birth, nurturing one's offspring for almost two decades and then condoning a course of action in which your son or daughter volunteers to die? In this hopeless scenario, the individual has no hope at all, so he or she thinks that they may as well kill themselves with as many of the 'enemy' as they can. The guarantee of a place in paradise seems ludicrous to Western thinking; the fact that religious zealots can successfully peddle this nonsense demonstrates how wide is the gulf in mentality. One may also ask of what use are 72 virgins in paradise to a ten year-old suicide bomber?

However, when your father and grandfather were born in a refugee camp, as you were, and you all still reside there, you might be forgiven for a certain amount of head scratching – what isn't going on here? Small wonder that the youth of Gaza, for example, lose patience, since they see that no progress is evident. It is beyond our comprehension here in the West. Life for most of us has rarely, if ever, been anything like as desperate, pointless or wasteful, so we fail to understand this terrible behaviour. Trying to understand is not to condone. But the complete loss of hope is an invitation to pick up the gun and join the terrorist group, for when you have nothing, you have nothing to lose. This explains the 'reminder rocketry' that finds its way into Israeli territory, to which Israel responds in sheer frustration.

As a general point, there is nothing disruptive about spiritual religion. Dogmatic religion is, however, an enormous and growing problem. How can the dogmatic religionists have their undue influence on societies neutralised and made more representative, with less afterlife 'hope peddling', encouraging anti-social international tension, and worse? Sadly, dogmatic religion is hardly a new disruptive force; potential loss of religious influence is never a popular prospect amongst faith leaders. One cannot blame Islam alone for this.

A possible solution?

It is broadly acknowledged that the Middle East is an intractable problem, one that, so far, has been impossible to solve. The need for a determined third party moderating influence is as strong as ever, a role which the USA alone can fulfil. The current one-sidedness of the US approach has not always been in evidence – during the Suez crisis of 1956 the US was instrumental in forcing the Israelis to evacuate Gaza, which they had shown no sign of doing voluntarily. They responded to a very strong demand from the President to fulfil their obligations to the United Nations. The Palestinians, meanwhile, need a contiguous state worth the name, and a fairer distribution of incoming fiscal resources would be a start. Fresh water, essential infrastructure such as roads, sewers, an airport and electricity are all needs which might give hope for some kind of future. Hopefully, this will be a future which carries something more than refugee status for further decades. A great opportunity exists for the USA to rebuild influence in the region by making significant contributions to these infrastructure projects. This need not upset the Jewish influence in America, and would be an enormous step in achieving a broad and lasting peace. Give hope, stop terror. Youth may be less likely to join military training if opportunities and some hope for a decent future existed.

We are forced to the inevitable conclusion that a more equitable distribution of essential amenities in those countries seemingly in perpetual strife must be helpful in improving and defusing international tension. A 'one nation' solution to the Arab-Israeli situation is not an option. The Israelis are convinced that they have a divine right to their own country, and the Palestinians are similarly convinced of their historical right to their land, so two functioning modern states living alongside one another in as harmonious a manner as possible is the only possible solution, and the US is the only broker able to enforce a just and equitable peace that has any chance of durability. Once again, whether the US likes it or not, it must act in a balanced and equitable manner to solve this – which involves conducting a comprehensive sales operation with the Jewish lobby at home. The most opinionated Jewish lobbyist must eventually see that to continue to deny the Palestinians a decent slice of the material cake can and will be a persistent cause of serious and endless trouble. Change must start with the realisation and creation of a contiguous territory, based initially upon pre-1967 boundaries with agreed variations as agreed to be necessary. Both parties need to recognise modern demographics and be realistic; massive-scale reparations are not going to happen and would solve nothing.

The peace management process needs to be decisive and swift, which is exactly the opposite of what has happened thus far. Incremental alterations consume huge amounts of time, and enable spoiling tactics to be employed by conservative elements who do not see an equitable peace as being in their best interests. This is where a positive and balanced US attitude is so vital. It is well-meaning to use nations such as Norway in the role of international referee, but such nations do not enjoy real enforcement powers; the USA does.

Balanced asset distribution

In order to give ourselves any chance of living in a more balanced international world, some effective distribution of global wealth along more equitable lines is necessary. Commercially, it is often the case that 80% of any company sales come from 20% of its customer account list. So it appears to be in the global wealth ratings – 20% of the world's people control 55% of its resources financially. Money never spoke so loudly. A clear and shocking example of wealth concentration is the fact that 85 individuals hold more wealth than half the world's population, i.e. 3.5 billion people. Aid to poorer nations is seldom the philanthropic gesture it is portrayed to be, so why do its recipients usually fail to make any real economic progress? Is this aid so beset with conditions, obligatory arms sales or interest payments as to make it a highly questionable benefit to the recipient nation, if at all?

We have mentioned the failure of a consistent policy of nation building after belligerent intervention. An American thinktank, 'RAND[13]' (Research ANd Development) estimates that $100 per capita is required to stabilise a country out of conflict. It serves no purpose to simply win a military war and depart the scene; a vacuum is what remains. In Bosnia, over $600 per capita was spent. In Kosovo, over $500 per capita was spent. East Timor, hardly a geopolitical hotspot, was granted $200 per capita. Afghanistan merited slightly over $50. Why? Clearly, the USA supported the Pakistani military government, who convinced them that they were best placed to chase down and capture al-Qaeda leaders, and that the Afghans would not deliver. The Americans simply lost interest and moved on to Iraq, with disastrous consequences. In Iraq, enormous quantities of treasure was expended on construction before any serious degree of stabilisation was achieved. That stability remains elusive to this day. In Afghanistan, the reverse happened; there has been too little spent on rebuilding a shattered country and so stabilisation remains a dream. Too much money spent on dubious relationships with non-government appointee warlords ensured a distrustful populace fed up with years of disruption and corruption. Such an atmosphere virtually guarantees fertility for the Taliban to regain control of the country, financed by their control of almost all of the world's raw heroin production. The opportunity to buy the entire poppy production over a five-year period, simultaneously reducing it by 20% annually and replacing it with regular agriculture was missed.

Free trade worth the name

Genuine free trade tariffs are the only options available to growing economies of the 'third world'. It is quite true that these economies possess several labour advantages – very cheap and plentiful labour supply was, after all, how the UK built its industrial base. There is no point in trying to persuade developing economies to pay 'living wages' within their manufacturing industries. Very often these are cottage or family operations in rural or fringe locations. Until organised economies of scale are created, bringing with it trade union representation, realistic terms and conditions remain an unlikely ambition. It will be enormously difficult to improve, by legislation, those poor labour conditions. We might not like or approve of pay and conditions in parts of India or Bangladesh, but the uncomfortable truth is that only way out of this undesirable state of affairs is for us, the consumer in the 'rich' economies, to buy their products. Consumer boycotts of these manufactured products do not work. What can be done to balance international economic prospects? Developing nations will derive benefits from reforms undertaken in developed nations, where the quality of the decision-making process will then be there for all to see.

How can a more hopeful outlook for the world's growing numbers of young people be achieved? There has to be a genuine free trade opportunity. This, coupled with education opportunities, will raise the standard of living for millions. There will be a peace dividend as a result. There is no question that the freeing of markets created immense personal wealth for some individuals and Britain became richer through more efficient industrial practices. Today, there is no question that the successful future for our world lies in delivering genuine free trade opportunities to all nations. Yet, amongst all the deregulated self-congratulations, UK PLC missed a big opportunity. The money didn't reach enough people, and remained in the hands of a greedy few who seemed to have scant regard for anyone unlucky enough not to have their snouts in the financial trough. We might have had more and lasting prosperity for more people, but instead we allowed the debt monster to develop, which came of age in the financial crash of 2008.

Political promises

If being called to account for failing to deliver on promises ever looks like happening, as it rarely has with trade talks and other solemnly promised initiatives and targets, we can at least *see* a genuine failure to deliver. Oddly, politicians rarely seem to resign their jobs if failure is admitted. Politicians can stay in their jobs regardless of whether they succeed or fail, until their constituents have the opportunity at a General Election to confirm their reappointment or dismissal. Our present leaders speak of solutions using the phrase "We must..." This is laudable, but they should add the caveat 'deliver by' as well, and present a date when these solutions will be delivered and achieved. At least their fine words will become a commitment, which they should not be allowed to forget.

In order to restore any genuine optimism in cooperative affairs once more, and to attempt to mend many of the world's problems, reducing some of the ones that lead to extremism, we need the truth from our politicians, nationally and internationally, and a fairer distribution of wealth.

SUMMARY

It is an inescapable conclusion that the road to tolerance, genuine fair opportunity and economic prosperity lies in the development of real and relevant education. This remains true regardless of national status, whether a country is economically developing, or developed. It is true whatever the national geographic position. If young people see a future in which they can participate, then hate-salesmen in the guise of religious authority will have a far harder field to plough. This places a moral responsibility on the USA, in particular, to be more even-handed in those conflict areas that have been a constant source of unrest, especially the Middle East. Free trade, coupled with a balanced and fair diplomatic attitude, must be preferable to the continual unrest we are forced to witness on a daily basis. If we fail to acknowledge even-handedness in such supervisory roles, the international community will continue to suffer pointless disturbances. We cannot hope to see resolution in the current inconsistencies of economic opportunity, and we cannot hope to relegate religious dogma to the margins without a practical demonstration of fairness today.

4

THE URGENT EDUCATION CHALLENGE

"Education is the most powerful weapon which you can use to change the world".

Education challenges

Are we aware that our educational organisations are not structured to allow the big-picture skills of success, to 'keep things simple', to stay focused and admit to mistakes? We have allowed, even encouraged, our key academic institutions to produce graduates ill-equipped to compete in modern decision-making. As we discuss later in this chapter, these institutions have become self-serving. Future decision-takers are trained in restricting and effectively damaging ways not suited to the present realities, let alone our future. Those who are able to grasp the connection between the huge challenges we face, and who are able to employ an up to date method of disciplined thinking in order to tackle those challenges are our management future.

Perhaps the most important challenge facing us during the next 40 years is the ill-directed education policies for our schools. This vital subject dictates where, how and when our people take their place, or not, in the pantheon of domestic and international influence and responsibility. If we fail to grasp the nettle of proper educational development of our masters we will simply consign ourselves to the coat tails of other nations who take the education of their youth rather more seriously. We will be condemned to follow, not lead. There is little doubt that our apparent insincerity and unwillingness to face facts when talking about this subject is another facet of our 'politically correct' age.

Moral relativism is rampant. Everyone must have a prize, nobody can fail, and deferred success is acceptable, as is the repeated resitting of parts of examinations you fail. Central government has made available enormous sums of money to our schools, and removed direct local control over school management, tinkered constantly with testing arrangements and inflicted curricula on teaching staff, regardless of the mix of pupils under their care. This approach has diluted initiative amongst experienced teachers, who ought, after all, to understand the calibre of child they have in their care. Being a teacher used to be a well-respected position in the local community; increasingly, this is no longer the case. Politically correct laws restrict respect by pupil for teacher. Pupils know that within the law their teacher has little scope for discipline. Parents no longer empathise with the teachers of their offspring, who already have a tough enough job, even when their child causes problems. In this current atmosphere of suspicion and fear, the parent is as likely to visit the school and confront the teacher concerned, in defence of what really should be indefensible. "I know my rights" is often the rejoinder – reducing teaching to crowd control, where the pupil knows a lack of effort meets with indifference from the teaching staff.

Parents all too often effectively subcontract their child's education entirely to school, believing that that is where they are educated, and that they, as parents, have no other necessary contribution to make. Any subsequent lack of achievement thereby becomes entirely the fault of the school; parental conscience remains intact. A misunderstanding of the word 'education' or what it should entail is a sad reflection on a politically correct society. Undoubtedly there used to be some poor behaviour towards children by a number of teaching staff, but the discipline pendulum has swung too far. As we sow, surely we will reap. What do we expect from our education system in such an atmosphere as this? Sadly, the prevailing league table mentality covers the education system as a whole.

Other issues are also problematic. I present here a letter written by Mr Paul Stiles[1], entitled 'The Reduction of The British Mind' to Dr Louise Richardson, Principal and Vice Chancellor of St Andrews University[2], since in my view there can be no better or more eloquent explanation of how advanced education is being handled, or mishandled, with depressing consequences for the future. This is reproduced with Paul's personal permission, and came to my attention when published in *Network Review*, the Scientific and Medical Network magazine[3]:

"I am writing to you to share some thoughts on my experience here at St Andrews over the past 18 months, in the hope that it might do some good as you try to move the university forward. By way of introduction, I am a postgraduate student in Theology. I am also the author of a book on the nature of the market and its impact on American society, Is the American Dream Killing You? *By coincidence we have a few things in common, as I am also a graduate of Harvard, where I studied Government. My comments have to do with the nature of the educational system here. Since I am a mature student, who has 'been round the block', perhaps I will be able to share some things that younger students don't see, or are more unwilling to share. Or perhaps you may know all that I am about to say already, I don't know. But I thought it worthwhile to make the effort.*

The primary thing I would like to convey is that the system here is plagued and even crippled by reductionism. It is not that pulling things apart is wrong, for it is certainly a powerful tool, for it is quite naturally the only way we can see things whole. However, the system here does not think holistically at the present moment, and this is a very deep-rooted problem. First, let me describe the extent to which I see reductionism permeating the educational system in the UK in general. To be frank, it is not really an educational system – it is a sorting system. The first priority is on grades, not on knowledge. As a result, students are viewed as objects in an assembly line, not individual human subjects. We are here to be quantified with a numerical label. This black-and-white approach is most obviously seen in the anonymity of the system, in which professors do not even know the names of the students who write the papers they grade. This is an idea patently hostile to education – how can anyone track your progress or make tailored comments? And the most unnerving part about it is how many people accept it as normal. Yet it is profoundly abnormal. It subtracts the human element from education, creating antiseptic relationships. Instead of a mutual conversation between teacher and student sparking creative insight between them, there is a top-down, one-way flow of information, in which the individual nature of the student, his basic colour, is not considered.

Another by-product of reductionism is the entire system's emphasis on specialisation, which begins even before university. Students are expected to define an academic interest at age 15, a requirement completely at odds with the nature of the human being, with our propensity for curiosity, change, adaption, evolution, for the right and indeed the necessity to expand our minds in new directions. Instead, the populace is shaped into parts of a mechanised system without regard for the whole person and his essential dignity. Interdisciplinary work is frowned upon as contrary to refining the parts of the social machine. So it is that most students graduate from Oxford or Cambridge without having to read a single work of English literature.

The most devastating effect of reductionism is that it strikes a blow at our ability to think properly. As you read these words your mind is performing a holistic integration, one word after another, creating a rolling concept, a meaning so much greater than the sum of its parts. Reductionism cripples that process, so that the larger whole is lost, and with it the whole truth. There is no depth to thought, no deep insights into the nature of things, nor the synthesis of the whole, but rather a superficial focus on accumulating facts. As a result, students are not encouraged to think for themselves, to create new knowledge from what they learn, but to cut and paste facts into papers with an occasional comment, so they can be efficiently graded. The whole process is about error avoidance, rather than intellectual enquiry and creative risk-taking. In the process we lose our ability to think as human beings, and become mere adding machines. A classic example of this occurred in the pages of The Times *last year, when the director of the Royal Shakespeare Company challenged his daughter's low GCSE score in Theatre. He stated that the reason she had achieved such a low score was that he had tutored her himself. In the process he taught her to think deeply about the nature of theatre, which she wrote intelligently about and been graded down, because the GCSE examiners were looking for the student to regurgitate facts from the acceptable handbook. In short, the system did not want her to think deeply or creatively, to use her own ideas and imagination, but merely wished to assess whether she was playing the game well.*

That is not education. It is the ongoing legacy of the Industrial Revolution, with its sublimation of the human being to linear, mechanical principles. In fact, it is now senseless, as what the economy needs is people who can move around with great flexibility, not people who decided at age 15 to be physicists and have done nothing else.

Now I have to admit that, ever since coming to St. Andrews, I have encountered the same problem as that woman in The Times' *article. I have been consistently downgraded for thinking. And that was the last thing I ever expected. I was never downgraded for thinking in the American system. However, I don't want to couch this issue in national terms, as that would be misleading. As the director of the Royal Shakespeare Company would undoubtedly attest, the ability to think properly is a human right, not a cultural attribute. Furthermore, America suffered not too long ago with this very problem. In the 1950s, America was very much a drill and practice environment, and if you have ever seen the architecture of American elementary schools from this period, which look like brick prisons, the philosophy of the buildings were the perfect match for what the system did to the mind of students. America has changed, however, while Britain has not, and as a result American students consistently underperform in exams here, at least at first. When I first encountered this phenomenon, another American student explained to me: 'It took me a year of bad grades on my papers here before I finally figured out what they wanted. They don't want you to think. They don't want you to take the material anywhere. They just want you to prove what you know. So now I just write a running commentary on the reading, and all my grades have gone up'.*

I did not, however, take his advice, primarily because I think it is wrong, and indeed outrageous, to dumb down the educational process in this fashion. And I have to tell you that I have suffered mightily for it. Now I don't want this to sound like sour grapes, so I must say that prior to coming here I published two books with the two largest publishers in the world, Random House and Harper Collins. Is the American Dream Killing You? *is endorsed by Harold Bloom, the leading literary critic in the Western world. I say this only to suggest that the rest of the world seems to think that I have an ability to write at a level much higher than the grading system at St. Andrews reflects. Indeed, recently I received a 13 on a paper that I thought was excellent, so I submitted the paper to the editor of a journal for science and medicine, and he asked to publish it! Not surprisingly,* Network Review *has a conscious focus on holism.*

One of the many problems in addressing reductionism is that it manifests itself in so many ways, some of which are quite subtle, and others less so. What the system wants here is a focus on microscopic detail, that much is obvious. What drives this, however, is fear. There is a danger of being wrong, of taking any form of risk, of opening up one's thoughts to larger ideas. It is so much safer to choose a topic so small that it reduces the risk of criticism. Meanwhile, the search for universal principles, for deep insight, draws condemnation. Time and again I have been criticised for writing in 'too general a fashion', rather than praised for reaching a new and insightful conclusion. Most atrociously, the system has lost its faith in the truth. Holism yields a truth, the whole truth, but reductionism goes on ad infinitum. *So instead of a search for truth, what we have here is a descent into irrelevance, with its associated lack of clarity and use of jargon, a form of thinking that flies in the face of our own intellectual heritage. Here we are, living on the works of Darwin and Einstein, the implication being that we should all try to emulate these greats, while at the same time, forcing ourselves into a box so narrow that neither relativity nor evolution could have survived. In short we are not thinking. Since when is the purpose of the Academy to breed a narrow mind? Since when is there more value in defining some microscopic point, rather than seeing the whole in a new way?*

The best example of all this is what I am experiencing at the moment. I came to the university to pursue a long standing interest in the juncture between religion and science. It is my feeling that visual observation is the link between the two, for it is at once the cornerstone of science, whilst also being integral to all forms of spirituality. You would not believe the difficulty I have had trying to pursue the new idea here. First I am told that the purpose of an M.Litt thesis is not to say anything new and creative and original, but to show I can do research. I have tried to explain that a new idea can be justified by research, to no avail. I am told I must comment primarily upon the works of others. Secondly, I am told that no exceptions can be made to this, even though I have personally shown in my last book, with its 300 footnotes, that I have already done significant published research. The assembly line is not going to budge for anyone. Third, I am told that my thesis topic is too broad for an M.Litt dissertation, effectively ruling out any interdisciplinary topic such as mine – even when I have experts in other fields willing to jointly supervise. The barrier to simply writing down a new idea here is absolutely insurmountable. This leads me to the final manifestation of reductionism at St Andrews, which is the nature of the organisational system. A reductionist system is by nature bureaucratic. It is inflexible, hierarchical, top-down. This means that it is not disposed to reform itself, but to persist at the expense of any potential reformer. In my view it has become, like so many bureaucracies, self-serving. The longer I am here, the more I realise that the system is not set up for students. It is not here to educate us, to improve our minds. It is not here to further the highest ideals of education. It is rather set up for the professors, with the students being a necessary evil. While I am sure that there are important exceptions, there is, in general, little sense that teachers want to know, engage, or care about, the students, but only deal with us because they have to.

Interestingly, a great and unique book has been published by Yale lately that explains virtually everything that I have just said in psychological terms. It is called The Master and his Emissary *and is about the two halves of the brain. The book is the life's work of Iain McGilchrist, a former fellow of All Souls College, Oxford and practising neuropsychiatrist, and has received rave reviews. Using an extraordinary wealth of research, the first half of the book shows that the right brain is the holistic side. The second half then shows that we in the West have moved to an extreme left position, with all kinds of negative repercussions. As Roger Sperry, who won the Nobel Prize for his work on this issue, put it; 'What this comes down to is that modern society discriminates against the right hemisphere of the brain'. The result is a focus on analysis that separates us from the truth and leads to a psychological and social dead end. Moreover, the book explains how it feels for a holistic thinker to participate in a system like this. Basically, it feels like racism. You are being continually downgraded for thinking the way you do, for being yourself, and indeed, for thinking properly. I can think of no more important idea for this university to engage with than the nature and repercussions of reductionism".*

I understand from Paul that the reaction to this was a reductionist one along the lines of people having a differing analysis of the word! If this is happening at centres of excellence, what do we expect from an underpaid, little-respected profession and from under-invested infrastructure and facilities?

Continually, we seem to fail in directing our youngsters, and expect and get too little in return, aside from politically-driven 'targets' of results which are designed to convince parents that their children are somehow actually being educated. There is also scant merit in tolerating disruptive youngsters until the age of sixteen and then discarding them from the system. Similarly, asking the talented to specialise at this age is almost as ridiculous, as Paul's letter makes plain.

What happens next to that individual matters to all of us. We continue to undervalue and under-invest in scientific achievement. As we have seen, this has been true for more than a century. Are we bothered by this? We are when we see skilled job shortages as a direct result of an uncoordinated education system unresponsive to the needs of a technical economy. We continue to be surprised at our surprise at this situation.

Don't lie to the young

What possible use are endless degrees in subjects of no material value? This simply serves to elevate the individual's expectation of a worthwhile future which then fails to materialise. The bitter aftertaste of this experience lasts for years, is of no value to society and destructive to the individual. If, however, it is acknowledged that the law of unintended consequences supports a candidate by demonstrating an ability to complete a course of study, there is some detectable value, but it is an inordinately expensive method of discovering whether somebody is able to 'stick at something'. What possible use is it to a future employer to be faced with potential candidates for a career job, all bearing A+ grades in everything, yet lacking basic human communication skills?

As an employer, I have experience in discovering a chronic lack of literacy in young school leavers; the inability to fill in an A4 sheet asking modest questions such as 'please write down your address' and 'where you were educated' is incredible. I needed a warehouseman with an ability to read, write and count. I received 24 applications: just two were able to complete the A4 form properly and therefore could be considered real possibilities (a mere 8% of the candidates). In a town of full employment, this was dire testament to local education. I was able to employ a real star, as it happened. I know I was lucky. As a result what we are getting is growing social breakdown. There should be bipartisan agreement that the growing costs of policing (up 40% in ten years), prisons and the courts system (up

45%), youth justice (up 45%) and working age benefits (up 25%) are scant reward for such an unenlightened education policy. Yet the government claims success based upon target-driven objectives in education that is failing to provide the skilled adults our industries so obviously need. So therefore the government wishes to keep them in the system a while longer... Why?

The declared government intention to increase university student places *ad infinitum* is ill-thought-out. Really, we need to have evidence of a successful primary and secondary education system before we elevate 'aspirations' under the current arrangements to a university education. Politically expanding higher education availability does not by definition expand the knowledge base, and the question must be asked; are the contributing careers there to satisfy these graduates? There is a moral consideration here too in that the acquisition of a large amount of personal debt to finance further education becomes a muzzle. To leave university encumbered with money owed (and, as we know, this does have to be reimbursed), is to place conventional restrictions on career prospects, and all this before any mortgage, marriage, and children arrive. Student debt is pernicious and can deter potentially fine minds from taking their intellect further with all the benefits that might bestow. It also introduces a streak of conformity and conservatism so you are firmly within the 'system' – therefore under government control. For this reason, a quality education should be available to those who have the real potential to benefit from it. The failure of this fiscal approach will only become apparent when significant debts remain unpaid by those unable to command salaries good enough to pay back their education costs. As Paul Stiles' letter demonstrates all too clearly, what possible benefit can there be to a box-ticking examination method designed to improve the status of the institution, not the creative thinking of the student?

Since the effects of a reformed education system take generations to be felt long-term, we needed to consider this critical question years ago. But it can never be too late to grasp this particular nettle. It is undeniable that there remains in the private schooling sector a governing-class mentality; for this read 'quality'. A quality all-round education produces quality individuals capable of fulfilling their chosen function in life. Why does this have to be the limited privilege of so few? No amount of tinkering with a broken engine will produce one of lasting quality; it will always remain a broken, if slightly repaired, engine. Forge a new one, and you have an engine capable of fulfilling its design function with appropriate maintenance. So it is with the constant changing of the educational system for our youngsters.

Genuine skills forecasting

What can be done? An acknowledgement that the problem exists would be a start. There is an urgent and pressing need for honest recognition of the problem, and a commitment to the creation of genuine central government forecasts able to identify the skills needed. It is imperative that population numbers are coordinated with professional skills requirements; for example the number of doctors needed per 100,000 people. There is no future in producing twice the numbers needed. The surplus will export itself and quality will reduce along with salaries, reducing the attractiveness of the career. We therefore need the highest and most visionary level of forecasting abilities, which have been conspicuously absent in the past. As we shall see in Chapter 5, this central government function is one of three National Assembly policy concerns, and its importance cannot be underestimated.

There needs to be an incorporation of the ability to be flexible and responsive to the ever-changing consequences of technological shift. Communication between business and academic institutions must be of the highest calibre, and this must extend to and be encouraged by central government ministerial contact. So many education reform solutions lie with the genuine return of local education decisions to reformed District Assemblies, elected by the residents of that area. Local accountability in effectively carrying these out is very necessary. For advanced skills requirements, however, national skills forecasting priorities are essential; certainly specialist requirements will become regional concerns too.

The need for reform continues, and becomes more urgent as failure to adapt to our current national and international obligations becomes ever clearer. If we fail to provide the framework whereby our young people can thrive freely and intellectually, and provide relevant thinking to the future problems that absolutely *will* present themselves for solutions, that future must be viewed with great apprehension. Radical solutions must be considered. The benefits of a properly geared education system will be spread beyond national boundaries; more and more nations recognise this, but many more must join this seemingly obvious collective world need. The need for reform was recognised by our Victorian forebears. We have sadly failed to take education reform seriously enough ever since that time. If we continue to fail in this most important of national tasks, we will continue to produce adults whose falsely-elevated ambitions, courtesy of a false education, will remain out of synchronisation with the basic facts. They are, and will continue to be, unemployable. They will be forever at the mercy of government immigration policies; if the skills are not homegrown there are enough folk willing to fill the void from abroad, wherever that might be. Government will undoubtedly manipulate whatever immigration rules are in place at the time in order to solve the skills shortage problem.

It behoves the current management of the education system to ensure that the young receive a relevant, up to date and skills-related start to their adult lives and careers. To not provide this is nothing short of criminal, since there will be other countries more in tune with what is required, and who see value in the provision of modern investigative and thought-provoking education. The box-ticking culture is self-serving and does the system, such as it is, no credit whatsoever. If the young are not encouraged to think, but merely to 'pass' their examination requirements to ensure that their place of learning is high on the achievement league tables, this is self-serving management by the academics. We are forcing students into mediocrity and dysfunctionalism at best, which is a reflection of the condition and antiquated nature of our academic institutions. A place of learning ought to serve the student, not the teacher. Failure to reform this sorry state of affairs should not be tolerated.

The box-ticking culture has made reform harder, since any complaint is duly entered into a box. So the statistics apparently justify the continuing lunacy; since only 'X' are complaining, what's the problem? But 5%

complaining doesn't mean 95% are satisfied. How are we to get anybody's attention? More importantly, how do we get common sense change to the benefit of the students, their future and the nation's future? We cannot afford complacent ignorant attitudes. We must act, somehow. Unless there is genuine local control and accountability, this is unlikely. Once more, radical reform is essential, not merely crucial. This is a critical and urgent problem and we must address it.

SUMMARY

The sheer size of the 'big picture', educationally, is enormous. The first step of central government recognition of the problem must be followed by an acute and accurate forecast of just where the global economy is headed, and what part the nation's government expects to play in that world economy. There is no question that the UK education system is woefully lacking in both quality and direction. We are not producing sufficient graduates in disciplines such as science and engineering; we have known this for more than a century, yet we seem determined to continue to acknowledge and neglect the problem simultaneously, which simply makes no sense. We are therefore forced to conclude, yet again, that genuine and meaningful reform must be a matter of the highest priority. We must admit to our strengths and weaknesses in an atmosphere of honest realism. This is beyond party political wrangling, for failure to deal with this will accelerate an ongoing tragedy failing the greatest asset of all – national youth.

5

HOW TO ALTER THE CULTURAL POVERTY OF POLITICS

"Must any democratic system be likely to lapse into crude power politics and ever-more elaborate means of redress to accommodate the losers?"

A history of modern politics

Folk are wont to ask what the word 'politics' actually means. I understand it to mean the art, or ideal, of social organisation. Yet the overwhelming response to such a question now would be: 'the getting and keeping of power'. There can be no more succinct explanation of the democratic problem faced by the system that has become modern 'politics'.

Governance of the people by the people theoretically indicates that the people elect one of their own to keep the necessary rules of the game in check whilst maintaining a fair and level playing field. As we have seen, the first Reform Act of 1832 began a slow process, culminating in the universal franchise finally awarded in 1928 to all those of majority, regardless of gender, finally fulfilling the democratic wishes of the population. So revolution as seen in continental Europe did not feature in the process of change within the British Isles. However, it remained a possibility to those charged with the governance of the country.

We have seen that the English governments of the Napoleonic period were seriously concerned that social disruption, as witnessed on the other side of the English Channel, remained a contagious possibility, and individual liberties were curtailed accordingly. Men of enormous integrity feature during the Victorian and Edwardian years; Peel, Gladstone, Salisbury[1], Asquith[2] and other figures of robust opportunism. They were nevertheless devoted to the United Kingdom and Empire ethic, as were Disraeli, Palmerston, Churchill and Lloyd-George[3]. None of these men would retrospectively claim to be anything other than the highest servants of crown and country. Their personal approach was of course at variation in style with the others, but all were united in serious acceptance of their responsibilities of the highest offices of a very powerful global power. Their position was, by and large, respected by the electorate. These men, at the very least, were conscious of their position and aware of media importance, but not especially concerned by 'image'. Since television did not exist to expose their presentational shortcomings, they didn't need media managers and teams of sales people. Performing well in the Houses of Parliament was, however, vital. They also knew the immense power of the press and the men who owned the influential titles, and so were not afraid to do business with them.

It should be borne in mind that regular salaries were not available to Members of Parliament until 1911; many parliamentarians were therefore men of independent means. They were not Members of Parliament for the fiscal benefit they might have accrued by way of either legislated salary or expenses. The contrast, 50 years after 1928, could hardly be greater. By 1978 another World War and the results of a series of small majority socialist governments in the 1960s and 70s, a rapidly diminishing influence internationally, and serious domestic inflationary pressures, caused industrial unrest on an unprecedented scale. People had simply endured enough nonsense. Small wonder that the electorate viewed the opinions put before them on polling day, and sighed:

"They are all the same".

"Nothing to choose between any of them".

"They all lie".

"They all raise taxes".

"They all look after themselves first".

The political theatre looked done for – but what fresh 'show' would work? The 1970s were years that the British people would prefer to forget.

The disruption to both householders and businesses caused by overly ambitious and disruptive trades unions demands lost the country much credibility, which is how the United Kingdom became known as the 'sick man of Europe'. The Conservatives won the 1979 election, pledging a return to stable money and to curb the industrial chaos provoked by poor management and union excesses. Admittedly, these were necessary and badly needed.

To undo decades of national mismanagement called for a massive change in the way that the country was run. So bad had the national situation become that common sense seemed almost to be a radical idea. Amongst the solutions to what had come to be institutionalised problems was much wider liberalisation of trade and the deregulation of financial markets. This called for a huge change in thinking by everyone. Unforeseen by many of us, the decade of corporate greed was underway. The beneficial legacy of this liberalisation was to prove an economic success, but occasionally revealed a deceptive illusion. Yes, industrial unrest declined massively. Yes, the value of money at last stabilised. Yes, personal greed ensured the making of financial fortunes not always legitimate. As a newly paid-up member of a far more efficient world economy, Great Britain took to liberalised markets with gusto, and established the country as an important and efficient place to base a business.

As happens with predictable regularity, the electorate becomes bored with the incumbent government after a substantial period of time, and seeks a change because that seems a timely thing to do. The longer an administration holds power, the harder it becomes to maintain any form of successful track record, and the electorate takes revenge. This is how 'New Labour' came into government in 1997, with one Mr Anthony Blair[4] as Prime Minister. There appeared to be no moral or political philosophy other than to get elected, with himself in command and in charge and the Labour party back into power. Once there, who could adequately offer a policy doctrine, code, philosophy, historical obligation, indeed anything, that this collection of opportunists stood for? This was not 'Labour' in a recognisable form, as 'Tory' is a recognisable form – so what was it? In what did they believe? Personal financial enhancement perhaps? The electorate was begged thus on television by Blair in 1997 to the effect of:

"Give us a chance, please, we'll be whiter than white".

Power, glory, world stage, whatever descriptive choice you bestow, there would appear to have been no guiding motivation driving these people, other than a desire to get, and keep, ever-increasing degrees of power over the electorate, a power which is real and heavy with responsibility. As a method of personal enrichment, a political career seemed a sure-fire winner.

Reverse accountability

A serious problem in so-called democratic societies, such as Great Britain and the United States, is 'reverse accountability'. Since the universal franchise (full voting rights) exists in both nations, any action taken by its leaders is claimed by them to carry the weight of the 'silent majority', who are deemed to be the real block reason why such action is both taken and then justified. Millions who protested against the Iraqi occupation by the West in 2003, for instance, were ignored or, worse, their actions poorly reported, if at all. So although actually possessing a vote, we are, or certainly can be, ignored and our leaders acquire a confident ability to do pretty much as they like. To call this democracy is beyond satire. Inherent in the concept of democracy is the idea that ordinary people do, or should, have some mechanism in order keep reasonable control of the decisions that affect their lives. Ideally, the power of those who govern should be limited by safeguards to ensure that citizens can prevent those they elect from abusing their powers.

Subliminal democracy

Failure to reflect the electorate's views in our so-called 'democracies' produces a poverty of politics, which is insincerity on an enormous scale. It bodes ill for a stable future for all of us, unless there is a balancing influence. Since so many are disaffected, why do we tolerate such arrant nonsense? Perhaps because nobody seriously believes that their individual opinion – or vote – is worth the ballot paper it's written on. Too many people have turned their backs on the struggle that is democracy. However, there is much to be said for action over inaction. Here is a dramatic statistic – less than 22% of the eligible voting electorate voted for the Labour party in 2005. Yet the Labour party 'won'. Such is the level of disaffection that reality TV shows now attract more votes than General Elections. Is there a danger that we become 'vote weary', perhaps? – pressing the Red Button NOW is becoming a norm. We are asked, ceaselessly, to vote for this or for that daily, via our 'Smart' phones, 'dumb' phones, digital TV, e-mail, even by fax. Are we being subliminally convinced that our opinion does matter, since it is continually being sought for trivial matters?

Small wonder then, that casting a vote in a General Election no longer feels to be the privilege it once was, and small wonder then, that we get what we didn't wish for. No surprise then, that any individual attempt to communicate with parliamentarians becomes an exercise in "we're looking into it". Nothing actually happens, aside from a small note officially saying "we're looking into it". This means that they have technically responded to a constituent – so, job done! Tick another box, the problem has been solved, statistically. If you have a feeling of *déjà-vu* here, recall our box-ticking exercise in education as described by Paul Stiles.

In the opinion of many, the advance of technology might one day mean everyone, not just MPs, voting on *all* issues via electronic media. But until the entire system is reformed – as I posit and hope it will be – there is little point in creating an electronic voting system that frankly nobody will really trust. The recent General Election of 2015 rather indicated that the young CAN get on board with voting using the current system if sufficiently motivated. I trust 'Jo Citizen', a volunteer, to do the right thing in the counting hall. On a personal note, as we are about to see, I have been present first-hand at such counts and it's hard to criticise the accuracy of the results.

Lobby fodder

I stood as an independent candidate in the General Election of May 2005, in the three-way marginal seat of Falmouth and Camborne in Cornwall, south-western England. All the candidates were asked to attend a meeting in Camborne at which the general public were to be given the opportunity to ask them questions in person; in other words, an old fashioned public debate. In addition to the voting public, reporters from the press were present. The incumbent MP's agent was heard to say beforehand, "she doesn't do debates". However, she was obliged to attend, and it became obvious, as predicted, that she was very poor at debating the issues presented for discussion. She didn't wish to be there, and this was plain for everyone to see – "just give me the power" seemed to be the air of it; to hell with debating national and local community issues. She was a prime example of parliamentary 'lobby fodder', there to keep up Labour Party numbers in Parliament and to ensure the party's majority. She was defeated, although alas not by me.

What can be done? There is evidence that even none other than the 43rd president of the United States, George W. Bush, when Republican Governor of the State of Texas, was an inclusive and bipartisan governor, cooperating with solid democratic representatives in order to manage the State of Texas for Texans. Local government cooperation can be achieved by cross-party agreement on local issues. There doesn't have to be constant party bickering for the sake of political disagreement. Why doesn't this effective and useful approach progress to national representation? Is it proof that power corrupts and that absolute power corrupts absolutely? Or, more realistically, is this evidence that the higher the elected position, the nearer they are to the real seat of power – the financiers – and they become obligated to manage the moneyed interest, with the little taxpayers simply getting in the way of their 'bigger and more important' picture?

What is it about effective local management that can't be taken to the next vital level? There is growing evidence that the United Kingdom is following the United States in possessing a permanent campaign culture as an integral part of the representative process. No longer is there an electoral campaign, followed by governance. Is governance now simply an offshoot of the permanent campaign? The permanent campaign is indicative of the desire to keep power, to sell itself continually to the consumer, as with any advertised product. This leads to constant partisan points scoring and less cross-party cooperation in order to pass positive legislation for all the populace. After all, isn't the governmental objective to be truthful, honest and truly representative of the population?

We are forced to the conclusion that government today is primarily focused on the manipulation of sources of public approval, typically newspapers, television, radio, the Internet, Facebook and Twitter, and that governing and campaigning are indistinguishable. Somehow we have to devise a method whereby government elected to govern actually does this... we need to keep score. A nationally elected government should govern – not rule in whichever way it sees fit.

Protest voting

So how can we turn ballot papers into meaningful documents?

Since any alternative political party presenting itself within the existing format would be obligated to spend years developing its record, and spend enormous amounts of money in trying to establish a 'traditional party' in our current political framework, that route is unworkable. Assuming that the current political status quo is totally unacceptable to you, why would you waste your vote on mediocre policies? That said, if we turn our backs on the democratic process, we unwittingly hand control to others elsewhere, so what might we do to record our displeasure within the law?

There are three main methods of registering a protest vote.

1. By spoiling the ballot paper, or defacing it.

2. By voting for a 'NOTA' candidate, meaning 'None Of The Above'. (This only works within a compulsory voting system.)

3. By simply not voting at all.

Suppose that a substantial body of like-minded folk, enabled to vote at a General Election, 'spoiled' their ballot papers or voted for NOTA, or None Of The Above. If NOTA were to be printed on ballot papers as a voting 'candidate' option, we would be able to log our protest within the system, and send a similar message to that of spoiling our ballot paper. The returning officer must show each spoiled ballot paper to all the candidates at the declaration count in each constituency. The candidates then agree that the ballot paper is indeed 'spoiled'. The numbers of votes cast for candidate NOTA would be reported, as are the votes for actual candidates. Either way, the first two options at least demonstrate participation in the process, since by simply not engaging you will get what you never wished for. Essentially, the same message is sent to government; we're not thrilled with what's going on. If a NOTA candidate, who of course does not exist, is elected in a constituency there could be no clearer indication that the candidates on offer are not acceptable. 'NOTA' was a candidate in the Indian New Delhi elections in December of 2013 – polling a low 0.6%. In a spectacular anti-corruption themed election, this number may be seen as artificially low, since there was an anti-corruption party floating for the first time. India is the largest democracy in the world; the polling numbers for NOTA at its General Election were over six million, or 1.1% of the turnout, an increase over the Delhi percentage.

A low turnout can suggest an element of protest, but it can also just be dismissed as general apathy. The NOTA systems avoids the risk of this interpretation. NOTA, is, encouragingly, a last resort option of a frustrated electorate who see no possibility of change however they vote. India's Delhi elections in February 2015 produced an astonishing result: of the 70 seats contested, 67 were won by the anti-corruption party, the Aam Aadmi Party (AAP), which specifically campaigned on the elimination of graft in the political landscape of New Delhi. The ruling Bharatiya Janata Party (BJP) won three seats, while the Congress party was completely wiped out. This result was a clear rejection of 'slow or no change' politics by an electorate in excess of 13 million voters. Promising though the 2014 election of the BJP party appeared to be, failure to actually implement promised change quickly enough ensured a thrashing at the 2015 poll.

Scottish National Party (SNP) success in the General Election of May 2015 in the UK clearly demonstrates that the electorate are capable of galvanisation on specific important issues. NOTA, a low turnout, or spoiled ballot papers would achieve several key things: the incumbent government would, as always, be forced to undertake a rigorous postmortem of results and acknowledge failure to engage the voters' interest. If elections were reduced to this level of protest voting, it would be a sad indicator of the poor and declining condition of the political process, but might result in the following:

1. Candidates and parties would need to ask themselves *why* is this happening? *Who* are these people? *Why* are they so obviously unsatisfied?

2. It would visibly show all candidates just how many people are not prepared to let the status quo continue, undermining the 'winner'. This is not a game.

3. It would shake the confidence of both existing and incoming administrations to the core.

4. It would take inordinate amounts of polling at night time, thereby disrupting television schedules and massively slowing constituency results.

Were sufficient numbers of people to do this, a government might be forced once more to take its responsibilities as a legislature far more seriously than they appear to do at present. Entering political life should not be regarded as a one-way ticket to personal prosperity. There are responsible local individuals who are not corrupt and self-serving and who have reputation and standing within their communities, and who are quite capable of managing local affairs. There is, it must be admitted, an enormous challenge to be faced; how to properly remunerate, attract and recruit top quality administrators of sufficient calibre, for example? But it can be done and it must be done. It will only be done when a proper and respected organisation is created that is worth working for.

This could, and should, have the faster desired effect of elected officials having to consider voters once more, and not simply selling their way into power after negative and undignified 'slanging' match election procedures. This may help to move the urgent need for parliamentary reform into forward motion. Commercially, it is always negative selling to belittle the opposition. Aggressively rude comments do not enhance one offer over another. It is hard to see a more coherent manner of getting the attention of the legislature before the voting public totally surrender their interest. It appears to be impossible to obtain truth and honesty from within the current representative system in a reasonable timeframe.

Sufficient voters effectively registering their discontent might have a deleterious effect on parliamentary management. Parliamentarians would be forced to consider a further worse scenario at local level; governance would become hard work but, finally, accountable in real terms. The truth might finally become a valuable sales tool; the 'product' might be less ephemeral, more substantial. The people standing for election might finally be called to genuine account for their genuine beliefs, and deliver genuine results for their constituents. There should not be a return to the days of parliamentary unaccountability by individual members.

As we shall see, the reform proposals that follow would ensure that a political nominee genuinely reflected the opinions of those voters who elect them in all three tiers of government. If a Regional Assembly member stands for the National Assembly, he or she may be certain that since they possess real and valid reasons for wanting the job, they will be accountable. After all, social inertia and the selfish motivations of a few individuals who benefit from the existing regime make systematic reform an extremely challenging prospect to say the least. Such attention-seeking behaviour by disaffected constituents is no less extreme than the outrageous Members of Parliament expenses scandal of 2009. We have an urgent constitutional problem of disconnection between representatives and constituents. This calls for an urgent response of an active but non-violent nature. It also calls for meaningful and genuine reform, at local, regional and national level.

It has for many years been apparent that to lead a democracy, such as exists within the United Kingdom, is becoming very much harder as a result of media management of the news. 24-hour news channels with constant and unyielding pressure to 'perform' in the public domain inevitably creates leaders (using the term loosely), who are able to think quickly and be photogenic. Blair and Clement Attlee (Prime Minister in the Labour government of 1945) might bear comparison as extreme examples; Attlee would conspicuously fail in the media today, whereas Blair conspicuously succeeded in media-handling terms. Thus policy content becomes rather less critical than performance before the camera or microphone. What can be done, aside from bringing current voter dissatisfaction to the attention of those in power? If we fail to address the problem realistically, voters will turn to somebody whom they see as 'one of us' and who actually seems to listen to their concerns. UKIP's (United Kingdom Independence Party) high polling results in the European elections of 2014, and general rise to prominence since, demonstrate this perfectly.

A clear demonstration of voter concern emerged in the results of the UK General Election in 2015, when UKIP managed 13% of the vote and the SNP received 50% of the vote in Scotland. It may be convincingly argued that the principal reason for voting UKIP was unrest over levels of immigration, and in the case of the SNP in Scotland an upsurge of nationalism in response to enormous dissatisfaction with the Labour party, who for many years took their Scottish vote for granted. For both these parties, major and meaningful issues persuaded voters to back their offered policies.

Our national political institutions need urgent reform, reform designed to re-engage the voter in meaningful participation in local and national affairs. How can this be achieved?

Democratic example of Switzerland

The nearest example we have to a democratic system that works, within the borders of Europe, is Switzerland. This country, numerically small by comparison to her larger neighbours, with some eight million people, is consistently held to be an example of true democracy through its system of communes and cantons. There are some 2,600 communes, and 26 cantons. A central government links the cantons into unification and controls only those areas which are of concern to all the cantons; foreign policy and the currency being prime examples. Each of the 26 cantons has its own parliament and constitution – designed for its own particular requirements. German-speaking Zurich and French-speaking Geneva, for example, almost certainly have differing needs and constitutional frameworks. This system seems to work particularly well for varied ethnic groups, which in Switzerland are represented principally by French, Germans and Italians. Canton and commune government is elected by those citizens resident within those areas.

Examine this organisation and it begins to be obvious where the benefits of such a system lie. Each commune is able to become closely involved in the actual decisions that affect them, and therefore to support those policies which work for them in their local area. A voter may elect to live in a canton which closely represents his views and interests, such are the true policy variations amongst the cantons. There is a constitutional right to referendums and initiatives, and important decisions are made by people at a local level. People thus can reject proposed laws but, more importantly, they can propose new measures which, to them, make more sense. This method effectively prevents the abuse of unlimited power, since voter or citizen participation more, rather than less, ensures the removal of unpopular law makers and unpopular legislation.

Local and national government reform

Here is a way in which the British system could be easily transformed:

For commune, read parish council, to become a District Assembly.

For canton, read county council, to become a Regional Assembly.

For federal government, read Houses of Parliament, to become a National Assembly.

Today, in Great Britain, we actually have the potential organisation for such a system under our feet. We have the direct means to control local issues of concern through voter participation, possibly along similar lines to those used by the Swiss. “Ah yes,” say our incumbent power brokers, “but there are 60 million of us; Switzerland has a population of only 13% of the UK, so it would be harder to deal with”.

Why?

Simply turning our attention to such a project will reveal the fabulous possibilities in which to engage people at local level, make our county halls genuinely representative of the parish councils and, very importantly, make a real link between county halls and Parliament. Our current system of constituency representation stands at around 94,000 per constituency; 646 Members of Parliament representing the United Kingdom population of almost 61 million (England, Scotland, Wales and Northern Ireland). If this branch of the legislature is to be principally concerned with foreign policy and matters of national concern to all constituencies, then some reduction in Westminster numbers is called for.

Since local government could be responsible for actually governing people, we do not need 646 representatives at national level. A reasonable number of constituents to represent for the national issues would be nearer 500,000. We could thereby eliminate over 500 members of Parliament, with their concomitant costs of salary, expenses, attendance allowances and of course 'cast iron' pension arrangements. We could run the legislature with no more than 125 sitting members of Parliament, a substantial saving in every way.

It is worth noting that, internationally, only France and Italy amongst the Western democracies have similar representation levels to those of the UK. Other major democracies elect one representative responsible for dealing with many more constituents. Job description is critical – once more, are they senior social workers or are they legislators? It is rarely obvious where the demarcation line is drawn. This needs clarification, which in turn demands specific and clear function of local and regional government. How do we create such a system?

The suggestions are as follows:

250 District Assemblies of 250,000 population:

These assemblies would be elected much as they are now, by local people electing local people to run their locale, exercising their enfranchised right, and they would have the right to raise a local 'land tax' as set by the Regional Assembly. This assembly would be answerable to the Regional Assembly for results. [Referendum call to be 10% of the electorate, entitled to progress to Regional Assembly for consideration. Three National Assembly functions may not fall within the referendum remit.]

125 Regional Assemblies of 500,000 population:

These assemblies would be elected by a franchise vote; two members each representing 250,000 population. These members may not hold office in both assemblies simultaneously, but may be elected having served on District Assemblies. This assembly would be answerable to the National Assembly, and have the obligation to set regional land tax. Representation number: 250 members. [Referendum call to be 10% of the electorate, entitled to progress to National Assembly for consideration. Three National Assembly functions may not fall within the referendum remit.]

One National Assembly representing the UK population:

This assembly would be elected from the Regional Assembly members, one member per 500,000 population, and be able to determine a national 'residency tax' sufficient to cover the expense of administering the three supra-national functions. Since the Assembly would be unconcerned with the direct management of local government, and only concerned with supra-national issues, this need not be a 'full time' occupation. Representation number: 125 members. [Referendum call to be 10% of the UK electorate. Referenda may be referred from Regional Assemblies only, unless the question pertains to the three supra-national considerations; Currency, Security and Skills Forecasts.]

District Assembly

Local, or District Assembly, becomes a far more serious affair, since the next tier of government is a direct reflection of both local and regionally-influenced opinion, and is answerable for results or the lack of them. It would have direct control of locally-raised taxation and run local services, including education and policing. The only central government involvement to be borne in mind is the central direction of the education system, and the occupational skills the nation will need in the future.

Regional Assembly

Regional Assembly is a serious opportunity to have greater and more effective representation of entire regions of cultural and economic circumstances. Since one member from an assembly region may be elected to the National Assembly, the ablest individual available to represent 500,000 people bears a very real responsibility for results regionally. As we have observed, National Assembly considers only supra-national issues, principally the issuance of currency, foreign policy and occupational skills-requirements forecasts. This assembly calls for the very ablest people of the highest management calibre and is obligated to set regional land tax administered by local assemblies.

Reorganisation

A reorganisation of the constituency maps of the United Kingdom based upon this reduced number would ensure a more accurate distribution of seats, based as it would be upon population numbers, not geography alone. Some constituencies would be geographically immense, for example, the sparsely-populated regions of Scotland or Wales. This would not disadvantage local folk at national level in any way. Similarly, the devolved assemblies of Scotland, Wales and Northern Ireland would be no longer either necessary or viable, unless voted for specifically by their populations, who would clearly understand that they, and they alone, would be footing the bill by local taxation. They would in effect become 'super counties'. In any case, these regional Westminster representatives would only be concerned with three supra-national issues; skills forecasting, currency and foreign policy. Were England to possess a devolved assembly, it is apparent that yet another tier of supervisory management would be required to deal with the old United Kingdom national concerns of security, and so it would grow, with wasteful costs to the taxpayer.

Under a referendum system, it will be rapidly obvious that this extra tier of bureaucracy is unnecessary and pointless – and expensive. There are several methods of ensuring that the referendum system is not abused. The Swiss ask for a signature petition of some 100,000 in order for a referendum to be called. The country can be run, given the will, by *people* accountable at local level – and by calling them *District* Assemblies we dispose of the discredited word 'council'. Those assemblies would be directly elected by local people, and would not be of prescribed individual size. The assemblies would be geographically contained within *Regional* Assemblies, again directly elected by the residents of that region. There could be 125 such Regional Assemblies, each looking after 500,000 people. (There must be a sufficient quantity of existing council debating chambers already available under our existing framework?)

National Assembly

The *National* Assembly, elected under a system of proportional representation, would be made up from one member from each Regional Assembly. Again, we dispense with the discredited word 'parliament'.

Political poverty could then be ended and legislative dignity of purpose restored. This would reduce the current unaccountability of those elected, since at every level the local people would have been consulted. Any national 'MP' would be representing 500,000 constituents. Any failure to deliver policy promises to the electorate would be plain for all to see. Well-thought-out governance is a likely consequence of this arrangement, which I offer as a possible working alternative to the existing tired and worn out verbal jousting match we are forced to accept as our national Parliament. This debating method transmitted through television coverage of the Houses of Parliament has bemused our European colleagues. It is as though we have not realised the limitations of partisan politics and that it simply isn't working well anymore. This coverage has reduced our parliamentarians to poorly performing, well-fed, ill-regarded actors in the theatre we are suffered to observe.

We discussed in Chapter 2, 1918–1961, the very real possibility that a skilled and ruthless individual (Hitler was an example) might exploit the 'truth vacuum', one who promises to take care of business, to 'look after' the people, to offer jobs, and who has the oratorical and sales skill to present 'solutions' in a convincing manner, particularly in harsh economic periods. We have ample evidence of the disastrous effects wrought by peddlers of what must be described as fascism. We ought to be aware of this vacuum, which is dangerous and a cancer to the democratic body. If this observation seems to be politically incorrect, it proves the point. It is no longer safe enough to say "the English won't fall for that, it isn't their way". Don't bet on it.

With these suggested reforms, our consistent national trait of 'moaning and complaining' about the way government works, hitherto with good reason (which is why we moan), would finally be dealt with. If we don't like the way we are being governed, we would be able to change those policies which worry us, because an agreed mechanism would exist to effect the change for which PEOPLE have consciously voted.

Properly-considered law

Consequently, I suggest that such changes would immediately alter the negative and complaining culture that undoubtedly exists in the United Kingdom, since if any individual felt so strongly about an issue, he or she would simply have to find 25,000 like-minded folk in order to begin the referendum process enshrined within the framework. This alone is very difficult, but safeguards unnecessary and unpopular attempts to usurp the authority of clearly thought-through law. A successful referendum call would at the very least ensure a full, serious and deep consideration of all aspects of the nominated issue by the very people who stand to be affected by the proposals.

It is evident that reform is as necessary now as it was in the 1820s. The situation is urgent. Today, it is imperative that we begin the process of real reform to reflect our national requirements. But how do we start the procedure in a credible manner? Our problem might be that too many people simply can't be bothered; their lives are generally satisfactory, or they are too distracted, and in any case nobody listens to them. Too many figures in positions of current influence, meanwhile, have much to lose from lasting reform.

Have we advanced so little since 1832? Do we really have to take to the barricades in order to begin the process of reform? Must a huge number of people be pushed to physical demonstration in order to be heard? Change must be possible. Much of the rapidly developing world teaches us that, historically, younger countries, unencumbered by outmoded traditions are more 'on the ball'. Their educational infrastructures are more likely to reflect the current needs of their populace. Their ability to realise exactly where they stand internationally helps them to develop policy needs to enhance and improve their position. Our rich industrial and political heritage should not hold us back from radical and far-reaching peaceful reform. Any change we desire must be reflected in the national workings of governance. There is always talk of reform, but there is seldom anything meaningful in the way of actual real and radical change. It remains just talk. So on we go, and nothing really alters, when it should.

Local government mismanagement

The enormous financial resources consumed by 'local government' together with the sheer numbers of people employed in local government non-jobs is worrying. Often these jobs are in 'enforcement positions', for example, overseeing gender quotas. I was at school with someone who subsequently became a local government 'No Smoking Officer'. All such posts carry with them pension rights of which the private sector can only dream, and often resent. Both national and local government know these jobs and these pension rights are nonsense. The council tax payers also know it, and therefore increasingly resent a substantial portion of their monthly council tax going directly to support council employee pension funds. In times of uncertain employment prospects, it must be tempting for graduates to apply for the only remaining 'jobs for life' opportunities offered by local government offices.

The best brains are in something of a quandary here. Do they elect to take an uncertain career in the private sector with all the variables and risk associated with it, or do they opt for what looks to be a job for life? (Strenuously though such local authorities might deny that this is the case.) A motivating factor in times of fiscal challenges is waste. The lack of quality in governmental decisions, particularly in information technology programmes, means enormous cost over-runs and a poor procurement process. We must acknowledge that our councillors are not always good managers of organisations. We need good efficient management of all our affairs, local, regional and national. An enhanced, restored and fully accountable system of voting procedures would ensure quality services for people at a price all agree to be fair.

If proposals outlined in this chapter were to be implemented, quality of services would certainly improve and local taxpayers would demand proper and true fiscal accountability in all departments. Parents would, rightly, demand the highest standards of education for their children. In this system everyone benefits, quality rises all around and the appropriate calibre of local government employee would be responsible to see that quality is maintained. As we have observed, we ought to be able to rely on our elected politicians to tell the truth. Does anyone know what they really stand for? Even more importantly, the nation gains too when the truth is told. Why these changes are so difficult to even consider is mystifying. We have the solution, the infrastructure and the sure knowledge that the existing system is a failure.

Inflated 'compensation'

The number of executive positions in local government-paid salaries in excess of £100,000 per year continues to amaze. This is local taxpayers' money. We are not in receipt of sufficient quality of performance to justify these salary levels. The time has long passed when an individual chose a safe, risk free but averagely-paid job in local government in the safe knowledge that he or she would receive a two-thirds of final salary pension on reaching retirement age. Local government salaries are no longer meagre or average, nor are the associated pension rights. There is discussion enough now about why it is that local government employees enjoy effectively concrete pension rights, when the rest of us, unfortunate enough to have been raised in private enterprise, have no such privileges.

There are reforming proposals concerning the current Ponzi[5] scheme (a pyramid-selling scam) under government control which is amusingly called a National Pension Scheme. The existing arrangements are unaffordable, unworkable, inadequate and simply unfair. It is to be hoped that fresh plans in the second decade of the 21st century are properly thought-through and costed accurately. We must be very wary as the track record of waste beggars belief. The return of true financial control to properly elected local authorities will end the opaque government control over local authority spending. Many people are simply unaware that some 75% of local monies spent are rebated from Westminster. Paying council tax to your local authority does not mean they have all that money under their control; therefore, neither do you.

The electorate must insist on politicians' individual accountability while they still can. This must begin at a personal level, and each of us must continually remind them of their mandate, which is to represent us and our collective interest as a society, not to rule us as they see fit. It is certain that without individuals demanding their real rights as human beings, honest and lasting positive change is unlikely. We do not need quick fixes and hollow promises from politicians in order for them to win an election. There is a need to recognise that at present the majority of people are seemingly content with, or tolerant of, the status quo, and see no real problem worth the effort of reform. Such people are not particularly fertile material for change, since a change-feeling starts from within. However, when enough people say 'enough', the motivation for change will be assembled. It is impossible to forecast a critical number, or when it will be of sufficient mass to begin the change.

How to restore confidence?

The terrible scandal concerning the expenses of Members of Parliament in 2009 has without doubt made many people aware that the 'system' is self-serving and rotten to the core. The results of the 2015 General Election in the UK delivered unexpected and genuinely astonishing results. Established 'safe' parliamentary seats are no longer a given. There is every indication that those elected MPs are aware that voter loyalty is no longer to be taken for granted, and that their votes must be earned. The two scenarios we have mentioned resulting in enormous numbers of votes for the SNP and UKIP parties served notice that the status quo is now fragile. At the very least we might expect detailed attention to those problems of voter concern. As we have discussed, it is tempting to vote tactically on occasion, and in 2015 many voters did, just in order to obtain an appropriate reaction. How would you feel if the government really was your true representative, fair, honest and accountable? Do you care? Here, we do have a problem, since it appears that growing numbers really do not care. Why is this? Modern-day slavery, it might be argued, is responsible. What do I mean by such a provocative statement? There are two main methods of ensuring that a big percentage of the populace is enslaved. One is fiscal; keep them in some form of DEBT and this will keep their heads down and working to pay for past consumption. The second is astonishing in its simplicity; COMMUNICATIONS. We will examine these themes in the next chapter.

Politicians should not assume that they speak for such a majority without a clear mandate. Current political apathy is dangerous, therefore we need to dispense with cynically-held views about politicians such as "they are all the same". Reform is vital. Discussion on the subject of House of Lords reform is a century old. It should be remembered that the Lords always sends back all ill-thought-out legislation to the House of Commons. Any reform of the Lords, however constituted, must continue to be able to hold the Commons to account. We do not need yet another elected chamber of more 'placemen'. This is an enormous challenge, and a challenge we must not neglect or fail to take seriously.

Sadly, the establishment has much to lose by real reform, which has usually been the case, historically. Unless this is properly undertaken, and not simply a cosmetic media fix, there is unlikely to be much to hope for in terms of future improvements to the democratic process.

SUMMARY

'Government' is in a mess, yet, as we acknowledge, it is what we all have in common. It is held in scant regard and tolerated as a seemingly necessary cross we all have to bear. We grudgingly pay local taxes, not at all convinced that we are getting any real positive value for this hard-earned money.

We distrust it and feel it is inefficient, even when on occasion this may be untrue. We know it is wasteful of tax income and we know we are historically loathe to do much to alter this. All parliamentary reform has been reluctantly conceded, and local government organisational change has been unwieldy at best. Patently, the reform required should be major; no more 'incremental creep' fixation. The will to modernise has to be present. Perhaps the will to take very big steps is present, but the means of expressing it is not. There appears to be an atmosphere of resignation and inevitability about the current arrangements that is depressingly dead. The truth is that people are too tired to care; they don't trust any outcome of yet more tinkering with the system, while enthusiasm for the subject of local government is nil. Until such time as local people feel a genuine connection with a properly functioning system, there is bound to be resentment and ill-will towards a poorly administered and poorly financed 'local' authority.

The harsh truth is that bipartisan politics at local level is necessary. There simply is not the scope for anything other than skilfully administered local services, funded locally and locally accountable. This is above party politics. The truth is that the current 'system' doesn't work in this age.

6

IS THERE A TECHNOLOGICAL DIVIDE?

"If we are to find our way in a world we no longer understand, we need to pay it special attention".

Changing mediums

We are now presented with new technologies which, by their very nature, threaten to disrupt society in unforeseen ways. Some of these very popular technologies, television for example, have already become entertainment options that occupy significant segments of our available leisure hours. Often, we surrender our decision-making process and let 'the box' take us where it will. We are tired, so what the hell... rare is the person who turns on a television to watch one particular programme and then turns it off again to do something else. Technology cannot prioritise, it cannot decide without your input. You will always be the final piece in the technology puzzle. Without you, it's pointless. But many young folk have decided, it seems, that television is "so yesterday" and instead prefer to watch what they choose on YouTube[1], a Google[2] company. This may be a sounder approach, and ensures a far higher degree of specific interest engagement. The way in which we apply these technologies calls into question our motives, and these affect us on two fronts; one is personal, the other is both national and international.

There is a strong possibility that we will shortly face what might become known as the 'technological divide', consisting of either 'good technology', with which we are happy to cooperate, or 'bad technology' which we fail to see can have anything positive to contribute to our wellbeing, personally or as a society. We also need to recognise the potential for possible unrest in society, which will grow if we fail to identify the difference between the two, and the resultant misallocation of tax monies will be called into question. Whether we embrace technological innovations quickly or not usually depends upon how we as individuals are directly affected by the introduction of an invention. It also depends upon whether we are allowed, or not, to participate in technology that for whatever reason, usually that of power and control, is suppressed by government. Inventions either make an impact on our lives, or they do not. The imagination and genius displayed is often incredible to us, and we wonder how we used to do without, for example, electronic mail. The effects of technological improvement have often divided society until the envisaged benefits that prompted the invention become obvious and useful to the majority of people.

The so-called Industrial Revolution began in England in the 18th century, and was to change both the landscape and population demographics forever. Employment on the land, which had been the principal occupation for the majority of the working populace, began to decline and people moved into the towns and cities to look for work. As mechanical inventions altered production methods, the number of workers needed in the factories declined. These innovative processes did not seem to have any benefits for the impoverished worker of the 18th and 19th centuries. This provoked a backlash by the displaced unemployed, who saw all too clearly that these new mechanical devices caused a thinning out of the job market. The authorities' response to that backlash was punitive. An opportunity to distribute evenly the wealth created was lost. The failure to take seriously Ricardo's apt concept of 'Economic Rent' is considered in Chapter 7.

However, few commentators would seriously argue against technological progress in its all-embracing form, and the process continues today. Much as the wheel dramatically altered the daily regimen of its creator(s), the internal combustion engine, the telephone and the microchip have changed our daily lives in ways quite unforeseeable a century ago. Life expectancy has risen as a direct result of research-driven technological breakthrough, and near-space programmes, such as satellites, have given us improvements and innovations that are now part of our every day experience.

Hidden technology

It is imperative to point out that unacknowledged deep space programmes, said to be run by black operations departments of the United States government, are reported to have covered up significant inventions to which the general populace have not been allowed access. These include so called 'free energy' systems and more elaborate claims of reverse-engineered technologies as a result of cooperation with 'external' intelligences. We are told by whistleblowers that the reason for the suppression of such information is this: "We couldn't cope with it". We love the science fiction genre, in literature and film; we can't get enough of it. Is this because it is just that, fiction? If this subject were non-fiction, however, we'd be forced to examine some troubling questions raised outside the scientific norm. We examine this in greater detail in Chapter 12.

Details of such programmes and collaborations are available on the Internet, and I strongly urge detailed examination of this data. Mainstream media will never report what you will find there, as vested interests exist to deny us access to what has unknowingly been financed by taxpayers, the adoption of which would assist us in our quest for international cooperation and sensible employment of environmentally-friendly technologies. It would seem, for instance, that we have no real need of petroleum-based energy. As can be imagined, the implications for the promoters of those technologies is enormous and damaging to their interests. This 'off-account' military-industrial complex expenditure would be faintly understandable if significant sections of humanity were not hungry, thirsty and killing each other. It is unforgivable when technology this advanced is denied humankind lacking in basic needs as internationally defined by the UN. Revelations of these hitherto hidden technical capabilities might make a re-evaluation of what constitutes a 'good' or a 'bad' technology, always assuming of course, that we could "cope with it".

Domestic functionality

Good technologies, which include equipment in domestic use, have transformed household tasks such as cleaning, washing and cooking. These functions have not vanished; they simply take less time to achieve. Those unpleasant and time-consuming tasks are simplified by the washing machine, the vacuum cleaner, the tumble drier and the halogen hob. These items have been instrumental in freeing our time. Some of us might remember those confident 1960s predictions of the 20-hour working week. It was predicted that by now we would have so much leisure on our hands we wouldn't have a clue how to use all the resulting spare time. As we all know, this simply didn't happen. The time saved for us by using these efficient machines has given us the time to work harder at other tasks. Supposedly, we do this to buy more things, to raise our standard of living, but have these additional work hours devalued our effort by actually lowering our quality of life? So we need to evaluate what it is we are working for, and consider if it is worth the extra effort. If the work we are required to do in order to achieve this 'improvement' in our living standards means more and more hours spent working, and perhaps commuting too, are we any happier? It is important not to confuse activity with accomplishment.

We might care to consider how our 'need' became converted to a 'desire' and how useful this conversion is for our wellbeing. Has unnecessary consumption of our time, effort and resources been worthwhile? As we have seen, advertising strategists the world over are overjoyed with our over-consumption, as a result of our participation in their promotional campaigns. If we increase sales of the products their client employs them to promote, they become so successful that they are employed to devise ever-more imaginative ways to persuade us to part with our money. If we become conscious and deliberate consumers, we will have thought hard about each capital equipment purchase that we make. Perhaps we don't need to work quite so hard? Time is not always money. We are, of course, all entitled to spend our earned money as we fit. If we wish to work all the hours God sends then that is our choice. If we have decided that we are directing our lives and working for our own clearly defined future, and that we 'need' an item of equipment in order to make our lives either more 'productive' or 'easier', then that is a right of choice. Technology can be of enormous assistance, but working endlessly to enable us to pay for it must be to ask the question: do we *really* need it?

Are we beginning to invent the unnecessary in order to make even more money? We are truly enchanted with gadgetry. Take satellite navigation as an example, which appears to have replaced the map. If we are going to an unfamiliar destination, we can get there by simply looking at a map, following the information we read and using road signs. We could even ask another enlightened human being, if we can find one, for directions. Instead, we have decided that in order to get somewhere, in fact to boldly go where everyone has been before, using a map is no longer the best method. Indeed many of us may no longer be capable of reading a map. The invention of satellite navigation has been adopted with enthusiasm, but any navigation system that can persuade the driver of a forty-ton truck to use a remote country lane, which is totally unable to accommodate the vehicle, has missed the point. As our urban centres expand, a navigation system which is increasingly now an inherent part of the motor car and must be constantly updated is a golden sales opportunity. Mobile technologies appeal to us and satisfy our sense of movement and freedom.

Once more, communication via space has superseded communication on the ground. How do we decide whether to adopt an invention or not? Does it improve our lives? Does technology, when applied to us as individuals, free us or enslave us? Does buying an item increase our fiscal obligations, and enslave us further? We adopt new devices with enormous enthusiasm. They engage and fascinate us – but are they necessary for our wellbeing?

The answers may be found in a considered personal evaluation of our circumstances. Since we appear to have boundless innovative creativity, this ought to be matched by a higher understanding of our collective ethical responsibility. The technological strides now being taken require us to be both practical and vigilant – to eliminate the 'desire' element and assess each offering based upon what improvement, real and considered, it will actually deliver to us. We should refuse to consider buying anything that we do not see as an improvement to our lives by turning our backs on the blandishments of the salesmen. The more we have, the more we worry about how we have to look after what we have purchased. However, the insurance companies will be thrilled to talk to you about protection against loss. Naturally enough, this will involve a fee. So round we go again!

The more we have, the higher our fear of loss, and the higher our cost of protecting it all is. We need to be aware of the necessity of being a truly educated consumer. So much for technology and the 'consuming' individual. This is only one side of the techno-coin; the obverse is equally important, and it relates directly to our personal identity and freedom.

Bad technology?

What of the potential for bad technologies, and the national and international repercussions? There is another potentially enormous threat to our freedoms from technology itself. The very mention of identity cards, or, worse, impending human microchipping schemes, now being pioneered in more than one country, raises concerns everywhere. Because technology makes these schemes possible, this does not mean we have to agree to their use. Those who apparently do not object to carrying a biometric identity card are often heard to remark:

"We carry credit cards, we have photo driving licences and a host of other plastic cards which clearly show who should be carrying them – what's the difficulty?"

However, those with this view forget that the carrying of these cards is currently entirely voluntary, whilst they seem to be unaware that the carrying of an official identity is likely to be compulsory soon enough. Claims that the highest security can be accorded to the public as a result of carrying ID cards are nonsense. Yes, knowing the identity of an individual can be useful, but it is not the highest security concern by any means.

Fortunately, an ID card scheme was abandoned in the UK in 2010. Let's hope it stays abandoned. We need to be ultra-vigilant in future to prevent the reintroduction of the programme in any form. If the same diligence and concern is devoted to more efficient controls of national borders, and points of entry from overseas, a large element of such security concerns are dealt with, at much less cost.

How did these cards propose to protect individual liberties? The answer was that not only would they fail to do so on any account, but that they would actually have done the reverse. Protestations by government that the carrying of these cards would be entirely voluntary were worthless, for how long would that happy scenario have lasted? It would become all too easy for the authority of the day to concoct a terror conspiracy, and rush through Parliament yet another ill-considered bill to make the carrying of your ID card compulsory. Is anyone happy with yet another 'Defence of the Realm Act' amendment?

Initial cost estimates for this project were huge. The salesmen of such technology would have pocketed billions, and indeed the UK project cancellation fees were substantial. It would have been practical to double estimates of final costs, and double the time quoted for the project to go live. An examination of many government spending programmes show that many prior financial estimates are grossly inaccurate.

Do we ever learn?

Government experience of continual costly blunders in information technology in the NHS alone must surely give pause for thought. The security requirements in themselves ensure that those in control of such projects will be blind to the eventual cost liability. We have become inured to our tax revenues being squandered; we are used to enormous sums of money being wasted by central government. We can be pretty sure that the costs involved in an ID scheme would be stratospheric, uncontrolled and, worst of all, unlikely to deliver any real security benefit to any of us. This is divisive technology which is ill-thought-through and likely to be introduced without the assent of those it will affect most. Guess who gets to pay for all this?

We can, however, be very sure that sufficient thought and detailed planning will have been given to what controlling use an ID system might be put. Identity schemes are an example of bad technology, the introduction of which we ought not to trust, for the possibilities of their misuse and abuse of freedom are legion. The idea of a population policed by embedded microchips risks an even bigger nightmare.

Once again, we are asked to believe the nonsense that the country will be made more secure if we carry identity tags. This is a direct attack upon the liberty of the population. If you have not read *Nineteen Eighty-Four*, by Eric Blair, otherwise known as George Orwell[3], I recommend you consider doing so. The parallels are sinister. We must ensure that technology does not divide our society any more than it already has.

2047 and beyond...

Just imagine: world population is nine billion, with everyone fed, clean water accessible by all, rudimentary health care available to all, armaments industries neutered or redeployed, nuclear weapons decommissioned, genuine global free trade, clean air, and freedom from religious persecution. All is overseen by an elected government representing each nation with a sufficient international mandate to ensure that disputes do not degenerate into war. Impossible? Yes, if the lack of creative imagination and vested interest in the status quo remains. No, if we collectively will it. See Chapter 11 for anti-war legislation suggestions.

The prospect is challenging. So, what do periods of modern history really tell us, and show us? Are we doomed to repeat some of those mistakes we can now so clearly see with hindsight? Can we deal with the responsibility that we have managed to award ourselves – the capability to elect and dismiss our leaders – in an informed, educated and responsible manner?

These periods tell us that historically we were not free, but that the power of Church and Monarch was not absolute. They tell us that although technology liberated us and enabled the spread of the written word, this took a very long time. They tell us that as we grow numerically, and become cleverer at what we invent, we bring intellectual demands of which we show little sign of serious and timely recognition. We fail to address the UN's 'basic needs' requirements of much of the planet's human population. We have seen attempts at European conquest bring two 20th century World Wars, with at least 70 million dead as a direct result. It may be argued that we have avoided a major European war for more than 70 years, and that this must be as a result of closer European trade ties and the formation of the European Economic Community. It is true that a major internal Euro-war today looks unlikely; 500 million people are now tied into trade and other lifestyle arrangements in some 27 countries. But do the maths of maintaining this, and the assumptions about the technological means of holding it all together, actually make sense?

The absurd cost of peace?

The appalling problems of bureaucratic waste and inefficiency at national level have been repeated in our European Economic Area bureaucracy, graphically proven by the failure to 'sign off' European area accounts for the last how-many years. It appears that we are prepared to tolerate this waste as the price of peace.

I was told, in a conversation with a German national whilst on holiday in Turkey during 2008, that "if the wastage/inefficiency ratio is a 20% loss, it is worth the cost". This is an out of date mentality, and dooms the European Union to inflated costs of organisation and social welfare. It seems that we need to re-learn our basic method of adding up: 100 now equals 125. This must be questioned. (Take 20% from 125, and you will get 100). Many industries can only dream of a 20% profit margin, but we appear willing to accept this built-in EU cost as simply a price to pay in avoiding traditional conflicts of national interest. It would appear that greed, corruption and self-serving government has no accountable cost.

In 2014, German Chancellor Angela Merkel's favourite statistic was said to be that the European Union has 7% of the world's population, 25% of its GDP, and 50% of its social spending. There can be no better summary of the ludicrous set of circumstances that the expansion of the welfare state has manifest.

Society that sets out to reduce individual rights in favour of social rights, such as welfare, cannot be shocked at those who wish to move to Europe in order to receive handouts. Liberty is founded on individual rights and becalming the mighty ship of state. Do we care? Give enough people enough handouts and the quality of the democratic process is further reduced. The system must reflect personal contributions... if you don't put in, you don't get out. This encourages effort, enterprise and hard work. If Europe fails to get this message then the countries of Asia, particularly, which don't have these enormous bloated social welfare systems, will overtake European commerce and leave it trailing in their wake.

Digital communications

Unquestionably, examination of the last 200 years must be tempered with the realisation that modern technologies, of communication particularly, have shrunk all boundaries. National interests are inextricably tied to other national interests, for very few economies could adopt a totally protectionist stance in the current age. Yet protectionism is politically seductive in difficult economic times. It increases the amount of tax 'take' in the economy for a period of time. We need each other, and to fool ourselves otherwise is pointless.

We can now talk to somebody else on the other side of the world by telephone, but often we don't. We e-mail, we Skype, Viber, or send a Facebook message instead. The insidious slide into personal communications failure began with the fax machine. No longer was it necessary to pick up the phone and make a conscious effort to talk to the individual of our choice. We could put our information on paper, and send that instead; a letter, sent by another means. Real one-to-one conversation as the first default was doomed. The seeds of indifferent communication were sown. We could communicate when we wanted to without considering the other party's ability to participate at the time of our choosing. This was particularly true in the business community, for long-developed relationships in the 'supply chain' began to wither. No longer could you rely on whom you knew at the other end. E-mail simply proved a faster and more efficient method of faxing. We 'communicate' more, but we COMMUNICATE less.

Our machines talk to each other and sometimes even have the capacity to make each other unwell, whilst our backs are turned. By using e-mails we are not communicating with a face-to-face awareness of each other, yet as most of us know, we do need, on occasion, to see the whites of someone's eyes.

The question of the responsible management of social media has to be considered. Inevitably, this will reflect personal education levels and the ability to understand what actions or postings might return to haunt you in the distant, or not-too-distant future. Once more, the importance of education cannot be overlooked. I detect, however, encouraging signs that the young are well aware of the power of the advertising industry... they fully understand the 'brand' game. That a car might be a method of transport as opposed to a lusted-after coveted status symbol they well understand. To have a nice car is apparently fine, but hardly critical to their lives. Why does this matter? In my view it clearly demonstrates an ability to prioritise when it comes to needs, wants and desires, which must be a good sign. The longevity of certain social media formats remains to be tested. Without question, young people particularly have adopted social media with enthusiasm. As an advertising medium, the potential revenue streams seem to be huge. Until there is evidence to the contrary, corporate investment seems assured as a result.

It remains to be seen how significant the Internet will become in the 'distant learning' aspect of education. There could be many benefits in the implementation of web-based education, with cost of delivery and flexibility of time and place prominent among them. The success of the long established Open University[4] in the UK has demonstrated that there is an appetite for a flexible approach to the acquisition of additional qualifications. It seems logical that there might be a positive role for web-based instruction at secondary school levels.

Political failure to deliver

As individuals, then, we no longer enjoy a close community relationship, and neither do nations. These periods in history tell us of expansionist failures, expensive wars and deluded ambition. Consistent disappointment in the failure of our politicians to deliver we covered earlier in Chapter 5, but there is change that they *could* introduce with some success immediately, and at zero cost. Consistent central government failure to properly consider large-scale technology projects appears to be an ingrained feature of UK policy – whatever is a published forecast is probably undercosted by 50% and the delivery time is probably optimistic by 100%. In short, the real scenario is double the cost and double the time.

Candidates must offer policies to the potential voter with truthful and honest expectation of both performance and delivery. Then, if elected, it should be obligatory to provide a progress report on what was a manifesto promise. Election manifestos are currently worthless. When the policy is revised, tell the 'buyer' (the voter and the taxpayer) about the change so that he/she continually knows what to expect.

A classic case of technology sales failure must be the British National Health Service. The original concept in 1948 was a no-upfront-cost consultation with a doctor, so that a General Practitioner would be available to those who needed one to discuss their health problems. The NHS never set out to be the cure-all organisation that seems to be expected of it today. In other words, successive governments have strategically failed to update the population with what they might expect from the NHS. Is it any surprise that this expensive institution, which is what it has become, is beaten over the head and ridiculed for failing to deliver? Deliver what exactly? That there has been tremendous technological progress in the health care sector is not in doubt, but we know that the population demographic is inadequately reflected in the infrastructure. The costs of healthcare are enormous, and growing. Government must explain with care and precision exactly what measures are scheduled for implementation in order to take care of this growing demand, which will not go away. Once more, the requirement for accurate forecasting is imperative.

Effectively, health care professionals are simply not being publicly supported, since the infrastructure within which they operate is, quite literally, not capable of delivering what the public erroneously expects of it, which is a 'cure all ills' expectation. This is an insult to those who work within the NHS, who know that increasing fiscal budgets is not a complete answer, since the supporting managerial organisation to supervise these budgets costs enormous sums of money. This managerial organisation is solely concerned with fulfilling publicised operation numbers in order to satisfy central government demands, which need to fulfil politically-promised targets and have little to do with taking care of ill people. If you know anyone who has needed NHS help with a life-threatening and urgent ailment, there could be unstinting praise from that person in the quality of timely care that they received. This must tell us something. Is it necessary to have been at death's door in order to praise the care you received? That there are, or seem to be, more managers than nurses should raise an alarm. This is not people-centred health care, and wastes money in morale-sapping attempts to become 'more accountable'. Headline-grabbing initiatives such as 'a paperless NHS by such and such a date' mean nothing to ill folk. They are only interested in a properly functioning system of care that helps them to get well. The many and alarming tales of a breakdown in the nursing system highlights the ethical dilemma here, and I would ask this question of the NHS planners: what is the point of technological excellence if the patient's basic needs are not addressed properly?

Degree-qualified nurses do not necessarily fulfil vocational caring criteria. An obviously caring nurse of a kind disposition who is simply unable to aspire to a degree-standard of academic achievement, but who is otherwise eminently qualified, is lost potential. This is a ridiculous waste. Our history shows us plainly what we require of our hospital nursing system.

A job description for the National Health Service would make for an interesting read... and it is unlikely to be forthcoming. We ought not to forget the necessary marriage of human and machine, but nor should we allow any idea of technical qualification to be superior to a caring and knowledgeable individual at the hospital bedside.

Personal rights over digital data

The preservation of individual rights of freedom in a numerically ever-growing world is a challenge, not least because we will be told that 'it is to preserve your freedom that we have to take it away'. Since 1789, the populace hasn't bought that argument, and nor should it. Finally the age of cooperation is just beginning. We have no other choice. Failure to grasp this fact and to recognise that the removal of freedom *must not be an option* will be nothing less than a catastrophe. There is evidence to demonstrate that the younger generation are not especially alarmed at the current quantity of their data held by the technology of which they are so fond. Seemingly, what is a potential loss of freedom threat to an older generation is of no threatening consequence to the young, who have developed with, and in many cases invented, devices in order to respond to their communication requirements, which are often very different to those of their parents.

Will they have cause to regret this? Not if they manage to keep a critical eye on what develops around them, and ensure that there is not rampant misuse of the data.

SUMMARY

The inescapable conclusion must be that technology has liberated and elevated a large proportion of the human race beyond mere 'survival' mode. Similarly, for this process to continue the need for non-scientific considerations of opportunity, education and trade must be properly addressed. We know we are capable of extraordinary technical achievement, but we also know that the fruits of this achievement are not spread well. The poor get poorer, the rich get richer, as always. Good technology that benefits humankind will find its way to where it is suitable and needed if the circumstances are allowed to flourish. Mobile phone technology in Africa is a case in point.

As always, the law of unintended consequences means more diligent ethical research is necessarily worthy of increased consideration. Raising living standards for many more folk who are yet to have their basic needs met is a management issue. The benefits of technological progress must spread, any divide must be broken down by both education and free trade, nations must abolish subsidy mentalities and let their societies develop for the modern age. This applies to so-called 'developed' nations too; there remains too much protectionism, which does not help developing nations face the commercial facts of life.

7

AN ETHICAL DILEMMA

"Man had no clear indication that he could use wisely the power that already lay at his command; to multiply that power hundreds or thousands of times over by scientific and technological means, without concomitant growth in wisdom, would be to make the world a far more dangerous place than it had been in a less enlightened time".

Ethical questions

That our apparent unbounded ability to accelerate our material world by way of innovative achievement does raise philosophical questions we must acknowledge. Sooner or later, and it seems that sooner is more likely, we will be faced with the fact that we have plundered our natural resources too far and too fast. It is no exaggeration to say that when we are finally faced with a global catastrophe of some description, it is then that we are likely to finally decide to properly cooperate with one another. We will have no choice but to do so. It might be wise of us to begin to structure ourselves beforehand in order to avoid being forced by lack of time into temporary, albeit necessary, solutions to our problems.

Here are some important questions we should ask ourselves:

Do we have the will to apply an ethical approach to global management?

Do we acknowledge a 'fair play' requirement in human needs resource distribution?

How do we stop the abuse of position that colossal sums of money confer?

Do we need to ensure a sensible implementation of scientific discovery?

Do we need and are we able to appoint an ethics committee?

This utopian wish list is all very well, of course. It calls for what appears to be an impossibly high degree of humanity towards man. There we have it, the division of humankind into two distinct groupings: the 'left brainers', those who embrace the material world and all it entails, and the 'right brainers', those who consider themselves to be consciously elevated and energetically aware. (The aforementioned seminal work by Iain McGilchrist[6], *The Master and his Emissary: The Divided Brain and the Making of the Western World*, is an essential book on the subject). This latter group are open to questioning the status quo; it is these people who demand change and who are less susceptible to institutional propaganda. Once again, we see that we are unable to grow our wisdom quotient at anything like the pace with which we invent new and often life-enhancing technologies.

Natural resource plunder is the result of growing population, growing prosperity in terms of demand and, of course, greed. The growth of industrial communities based in ever-expanding cities across the globe has supplied labour for increasingly efficient industries, and in turn has been catered for by them. These massive industrial organisations have achieved a global reach, covering established nations and the growing nations emerging as industrial heavyweights.

The law of unintended consequences reigns supreme, or so it appears. "We didn't consider the implications fully enough" is, sadly, no answer. To regulate after the event, when the unforeseen abuse of the technology horse has already bolted, is simple failure to do the homework. Few would disagree that a proper and serious global approach by all of us toward problems of waste disposal, energy conservation and consumption, pollution and food distribution is long overdue. We are effectively being asked deep ethical questions applicable to all the world's population. Is it right to continually procrastinate? Of course not. Is it right to perpetually ignore, by effectively failing to deal with it, the problem of world hunger? Of course not. We acknowledge the existence of the problem, and then do nothing. Why? Because our leaders do nothing, and we let them orchestrate media-satisfying deals that do nothing at all to actually deliver a solution to the problem.

We need to consider seriously the social consequences of four industries, since they are truly global and managed by comparatively few hands. The management and influence of these commercial structures are of significant interest to all our futures. Their policies and business activities affect everyone. They all call into question our ethical approach to those significant expenditure areas that in one form or another concern each and every one of us:

1. Armaments
   (The Killing Business)

2. Pharmaceuticals
   (The Health Business)

3. Food
   (The Survival Business)

4. Banking
   (The Money Business)

i) Armaments

Nuclear issues

Since 1945, when the Los Alamos scientists' work on atomic fusion provided ample proof of our self-destructive capabilities, our principal challenge as a species has been to detect and adequately deal with the misuse of what we have in some cases created so brilliantly. We also laid the foundations for enormous expansion of the armaments industry based upon 'superpower' influence at one end of the political spectrum, and nationalism at the other. Any discussion on ethics does, to me, have to include discovery and invention.

The nuclear programme is a source of endless debate. The salient point is that nuclear science post-1945 very quickly seemed to become a hugely complex subject – and vastly expensive. An ethical question arises; what was the funding authority actually expecting from this project long-term? Was there any serious analytical forecast of the consequences beyond the anticipated military application? Did it, at that point, expect the nuclear programme to have peacetime benefits? If so, why has nuclear technology remained such an uncertain proposition for so many nations? The inability to credibly establish this technology for secure use in either military or civil application is a blunder of global magnitude. We are convinced militarily, we are unconvinced otherwise. Has the civil use of nuclear technology been one giant unplanned result of the law of unintended consequences after all? We know it 'works', but therein lies the problem. It will never stop working. Radioactive waste remains active for millennia. There is no 'Stop' button.

Take a country like France, which generates more than 70% of its domestic power consumption from nuclear fission; will such dependence be essential in order to protect the surface environment, since we no longer wish to burn fossil fuel? But who takes the decisions on spent material with a half-life of thousands of years? Can we develop the technology to deal *properly* with this waste? Who decides that aspiring members of the nuclear 'club' are of honest and peaceful intent? Has the law of unintended consequences been considered, debated and understood? Are there hidden, therefore suppressed, technologies from which humankind could easily benefit, as is claimed by so many? This asks us serious ethical questions which should have been considered prior to the implementation of a nuclear programme.

So many questions, yet there are so few real and honest answers. The developed Western nations, particularly the USA, feel a nationalist need to maintain military capabilities in order to defend their territorial interests. They also maintain them in order to extend their sphere of international influence. Much of this capability would appear to be 'off budgetary control', known as 'black' in conspiracy theory parlance. As has been suggested, what we have been told by people involved in these projects means that not only are these projects Above Top Secret, but it follows that we haven't the slightest notion, officially, what technologies have either been discovered or are in use. So much for democratic accountability.

The larger Eastern nations, including Russia, also maintain large military capabilities, and their objectives may broadly be considered to be similar. These war-making organisations are extremely costly; indeed, that the Soviet Union is no more (for all Vladimir Putin's nationalistic revival) is in some way due to cost. Maintaining such a huge military establishment was exhausting economically. As with any manufactured product, the more you make, the lower the individual unit will cost. If your production capability exceeds your needs, sell the surplus. This is business. Be sure to stay technologically ahead of your competitors. Sell last year's model to those nations, or organisations, who feel a need for weapons for whatever reason, and whilst you do so hope that they won't be used against you. Never forget to ensure that the ideological compliance of the customer is in accordance with your own ambitions. Once more, the common weapons sales business plan is obvious.

A classic case of a deal returning to haunt the supplier must be the United States selling arms to Saddam Hussein in Iraq. They then decided he was expendable, and by effectively withdrawing support for him they removed their one anti-Iranian guarantee in the region, and their previously supplied weaponry found its way into the hands of insurgents, determined to be rid of the American presence in their country. Sadly, this is by no means an isolated example. The fall of Gaddafi[1] in Libya with the consequent arms 'loss' into neighbouring territories is guaranteed to provide future armed conflict. Imagine for a moment if the material discussed here was of nuclear origin? It may be possible technologically to keep a lid on sophisticated systems, but for how long? This does raise some ethical questions in addition to the more practical problem of how to restrict proliferation.

The cost of maintaining the nuclear deterrent far exceeds its theoretical use or, as we fervently hope does not happen, its practical misuse. The cost of ensuring that the nuclear club does not expand permanently is enormous both in fiscal and in political effort. The cost of maintaining an ageing nuclear arsenal, along with the motivation to look after such a deteriorating 'asset', is very worrying.

Western superpower capability is also shared by Russia, China and India, but the likes of Pakistan being a smaller nuclear power presents a particular challenge, bordering, as it does, Afghanistan. Realistically, there is every reason to assume that Pakistan represents one of the next real cauldrons of international tension. The Taliban[2] will continue to expand their realm of influence within Afghanistan, based as they are in the no-go tribal areas of Pakistan, from where they remain in many respects protected. As Pakistan is a nuclear state, we have, therefore, to be highly concerned that should the Taliban gain effective control of Pakistan, these weapons could fall into the ideological hands of extremists. We must be grateful that the Pakistani Taliban is currently different from the more extreme Afghan Taliban, and there is less chance that Pakistan will adopt the more extreme version, despite American provocation to the contrary. American policy however, particularly in relation to unmanned drone aircraft, is pushing Pakistani sentiment away from conditional alliance against the Afghan Taliban. That the Pakistan military is generally sympathetic to the Taliban is now regarded internationally as more than an open question. By reputation, the large standing Pakistani army is efficient and seems determined that Pakistan will not become "another Afghanistan". This has not prevented the USA coming into serious conflict with Pakistan over the methods used in attempting to control the Taliban in the northern border areas of Pakistan, and the use of drone aircraft is extremely unpopular with the population they are intended to protect.

This brings India and China into a difficult equation, since neither country would wish to see a Taliban-controlled government on their borders, especially one equipped with weapons of mass destruction. India particularly has a problem here; their population does not care for the sometimes wayward behaviour of Western tourists within their boundaries. It is interesting that the 'tourist dollar' has its limits. In Indian Goa, locals no longer care for the lax attitudes of indolent tourists. Having witnessed this type of louche behaviour, I cannot say I entirely blame them. Poor manners by Westerners, and their inconsideration for the sensitivities of local populations, have combined to ensure that they are tolerated at best. At worst, their decadent displays are exploited by the fundamentalist media, who offer them as an example of just how far Western society has declined. Fertile propaganda for the Taliban is not what the North West frontier of India needs. This poor behaviour by visiting tourists is, to a neutral observer, unthinking at best, rude and inconsiderate at worst. It supplies confirmatory evidence to the extremists that the decadence of both developed and developing societies is there for all to witness.

Such observations also help to fuel the likes of Islamic State and other Jihadist groups. One can only fervently hope that the current Middle Eastern instability doesn't one day result in such forces gaining access to weapons of mass destruction there either.

Rebirth of nationalism

The demise of the Soviet Union gave rebirth to nationalism from the Baltic to the Balkans, as countries with their identities suppressed under Soviet control surfaced to breathe independent air for the first time in decades. The shrinking of the Soviet Red Army created an international arms bazaar, the effects of which will be with us for many years to come. As can be the way after decades of suppression, neighbour fought neighbour, which in turn required weapons. There appears to be no shortage of arms salesmen across the spheres of political influence. After all, if required, who supplies the export certificates for arms shipments?

The proliferation of weapons availability has filtered down to our neighbourhood streets, especially in our big cities. The destabilisation of society that this availability brings in its wake is chronic. Often linked to the illegal drug supply trade, weapons-related crime may become the epidemic we all fear, bringing with it a myriad of social problems which are expensive to solve. All of this affects local community. Once again, if enough people can say "enough is enough", perhaps we can begin to address why all this is so out of control. As has been stated elsewhere, when people are insecure, adrift, cheated and angry, and hope has gone, picking up a gun may appear to become the easiest option to solve problems.

Sometimes the side effects of inventions may be unintended and unforeseen. It is not fanciful to propose that the two 1945 nuclear explosions over Japan were a watershed in technological and philosophical activity, with lasting consequences for us all. The rights or wrongs of the detonations have been extensively debated. We were led to believe that we could invest in weapons of human removal. Subsequently, questions relating to the value of humankind were raised, with assurances given by our leaders, who boldly declared that 'Mutually Assured Destruction' (MAD, aptly) would prevent either Superpower America or Superpower Soviet Union from pressing the 'Go' button. A good idea in principal, perhaps, but flawed. This MAD idea assumed that both sides valued their populations equally – which was not the case. The Soviet Politburo's concern for the individual was non-existent. America, however, gave rather more credence to the individual, since democracy rather than gerontology elected the decision-makers. However, these two differing ideologies did not prevent the establishment of enormous and ever-expanding nuclear arsenals on both sides, despite the blindingly obvious fact that you can only destroy the world once, with far less weaponry than was held by either side.

Oddly, the ultimate irony lies underneath the oceans. In the event of a totally destructive nuclear exchange, it seems that the Prime Minister of Great Britain has handwritten letters carried by the commanders of the nuclear submarine fleet: 'Letters of Last Resort'. On receipt of news that catastrophe has occurred, it would seem that at the very last, one human being, a serviceman who happens to command a nuclear submarine, might have the final word as to whether he is minded to give the order to retaliate, or not. Knowing that his family is in all probability dead, is he able to make a balanced and rational decision? This brings the entire subject back to human instinct. The contents of these letters are destroyed with the change of Prime Minister; nobody knows apart from the author what it is that these letters actually say, and past Prime Ministers are not saying.

As post-USSR Eastern Bloc countries join the 'free' world, wasn't it all rather pointless? That question/answer depends upon your personal study of events in the 1945–1989 period. There is little doubt that the enormous expenditures on nuclear weapons were both excessive and largely unnecessary. There were more than enough warheads deployed to destroy everything many times over. By any measure this was ridiculous. Nuclear power, its uses and misuses, clearly defines boundaries of imaginative finite invention and the dealing with intended consequences. Einstein and the

Los Alamos scientists would appear to have confirmed the laws of nuclear physics, but, given their moment once more, would they voluntarily repeat what they had created? As we shall see, this *appearance* of the laws of physics was not all it seemed.

In 1955, a press conference was given by philosopher Bertrand Russell at Caxton Hall, Westminster. This was called in order to make public a statement signed by a number of scientists on the significance of nuclear warfare. Einstein and Russell began this collaboration, and Einstein's signature was given in the last week of his life. Russell's was annotated:

"Bringing the warning pronounced by the scientific signatories to the notice of all the powerful governments of the world in the earnest hope that they may agree to allow their citizens to survive".

There is evidence to suggest that Einstein regretted his part in the discovery and creation of nuclear energy. If we were able to ask him "would you repeat this research?", the answer would almost certainly be a qualified "No". But you cannot un-invent anything. The very least that can be said of nuclear power is that it has, very decidedly, gained our collective attention. How we solve our future energy requirements without the nuclear option has set the inventor and the scientific community a colossal challenge. The United States and Saudi Arabia signed a nuclear cooperation treaty in 2008, ostensibly to allow Saudi Arabia to acquire nuclear desalination technology. Might we have sufficient confidence to believe that brief summary, or must we be faintly cynical and wonder how many branches there might ultimately prove be on this particular tree?

I have yet to hear an informed defence of any research into sophisticated weaponry. We are usually fobbed off with the old chestnut "this is a part of space research", or something similar. The 'Smart bomb', with the potential of reducing civilian incidental death around claimed military installations is an insult. Reduce does not mean eliminate. The aggressive dictator promptly shrouds such installations with hospital or school cover, swiftly cancelling out the 'smart' advantage. When a genuine hospital is hit, smart isn't a word I'd use, with the resulting negative propaganda a dictator's dream. Pilotless drone aircraft fulfil the same criteria, which negatively impact on US foreign policy and reputation.

Any national economy based heavily upon armaments production must eventually be faced with deep consideration of ethical questions. The sale of training jets to Gulf States, which happen to be situated over a seemingly endless supply of oil, is a case in point. How such a deal is transacted, given the geopolitical situation of the customer, is not as straightforward as any similar deal might be to another Western country. Does the supplier ignore 'commission' payments (which are bribes to you and me) over and above the quoted price, or simply build such a payment into the quotation? (This is a big bonus to the profitability of the transaction if the bribe is not actually sought, but a bigger risk that the quotation will be uncompetitive). The country that supplies the product will pay, of course, via the taxpayer, who has no clear idea of how much was paid to whom or where the money went. To even consider such a commercial proposition in the United Kingdom is against the law, but our government seems effectively to turn a blind eye to these questionable deals. Within the current international arms trading bazaar, this seems to work, but ethically this cannot be right. The circumstances surrounding such commercial arrangements surprise nobody; the lies told in justifying them, however, do. As night follows day, arms deals are fertile ground for bribes, backhanders, call them what you will.

We are able to build both advanced weaponry and advanced life-saving medical technology with bewildering speed. It almost appears to the casual observer that a guilty conscience is being assuaged here. We can almost hear an insouciant sales presentation developing, along the lines of 'such and such a medical product is the side result of technology developed for military solution X'. That will convince everyone that in order to do the surviving, we also have to do the killing. Governments then tell the taxpayer the 'killing kit' is where the beneficial technology really comes from, thus validating the need to develop killing systems first, without which the research and development won't be there for the important 'living stuff'. It also justifies the tax expenditure used on these projects, if the project is ever admitted to in the first place. How convincing is this? Actually, it is an insult to our personal intelligence and our pockets. Fortunately, some bolder members of our scientific community object to such blatant governmental interference. They leave weapons considerations to be explained by the career politicians, followed by the whistleblowers, if they can manage to stay with us.

ii) & iii) Pharmaceuticals and Food

A compensating culture

Huge, brilliant and enhancing developments have taken place in many fields of practical research, giving increased opportunities to many who would otherwise founder. However, every smart, new, fine, life-enhancing drug introduced at boggling cost seems to raise ethical questions. When it comes to health, government appears not to be 'for' the people, but appears instead to be for the pharmaceutical industry, indeed often at the expense of the people. As an example, diabetes is a condition affecting ever greater numbers. Why? Is this a self-inflicted result of abusing our system, our own body? Is our food chain contaminated? Shouldn't we know why the numbers are growing so fast? At the very least, if we were told we'd be able to inform people, truthfully, as to how to improve their chances of staying free of conditions such as this.

We know overconsumption of refined sugar is a prime cause of obesity. We appear to have a compensating culture active here; consume sugar to get fat, then swallow pills to deal with the health problems caused by its over-consumption and the myriad of other health problems caused by inactivity and poor diet. Thus, it is reasonable to consider these two industries in harness. It is invariably an astonishing experience to queue at a supermarket checkout and glance at the purchases of the next-in-line customer. The lack of nutritional value in what we class as 'junk' food and ready-made meals, which are both expensive and synthetic-tasting, beggars belief. Potatoes vie with gold when the price of a processed 'oven ready' chip is compared with the humble virgin potato. Crisp packets the size of garden compost bags do not offer much contribution to a healthy existence. The pharmaceutical industry is waiting outside, though; no problem, we'll sort you out. Surely they will, but you will pay, financially and with poor health to boot.

Where is the real educative influence on nutrition values? How can we expect folk to understand what constitutes a balanced food intake, when television promotes sugar-loaded 'food'? How can we inform people that foods containing large volumes of processed sugar are effectively lethal? The body eventually says "enough", and diabetes becomes the epidemic we see today. Our problem now is one of rights. How do you answer "it's my right" or "it's my body" when people are challenged on unhealthy lifestyles? When big people statistically become significant they acquire a political dynamic, and the problem actually goes away when it becomes politically unwise to disturb it. To be frank, this is a case of 'follow the votes'. The food industry cannot even agree on an obvious and easy way for the consumer to understand a common labelling system. If a product contains 50% refined sugar, we should at least be told that it does. We have a new 'SS' here: Salt and Sugar.

Convenience foods and carbonated drinks

There ought to be proper clarification and understanding of those foods that are frankly lethal to the consumer if eaten or drunk in regular unrestrained volume. Carbonated sugary drinks should carry the strongest health warnings, at least as virulently nauseating as those warnings carried on cigarette packets. These drinks, in many cases, have zero nutritional value, and simply make the consumer fat. In the interest of plain language we might consider using the word 'fat' once more to describe those people who have abused themselves by overeating. In recent years, to describe somebody as 'fat' implied just this; that it is a self-inflicted condition. Some return to being embarrassed by being fat may be a lesson to young consumers who have missed the point. It has been said that the average North American consumer sinks 800 cans of fizzy drinks annually – and we then express surprise at the rise in diabetes-type conditions. That quantity of refined sugar intake is unnecessary and dangerous. I discussed the *a posteriori* question of 2 + 2 = 4 in the Introduction. If ever the evidence became proof, surely this is it? If we value the health of the nation, these problems need some attention, rather than folding in face of the vested interest, which is, as usual, considerable. Having examined the evidence, something ought to be done rather than simply 'taking note' or taking 'on board' the facts. Raising the price of carbonated dynamite in cans, and passing the revenue to the maintenance of the hospital estate, might assist mightily in bridging the funding gap.

The health problems created by the growing inability to cook anything in the domestic kitchen is a concern to many people. Opening the microwave door and placing a ready-meal inside it is not cooking, yet this is as near as many people get to it in their busy lives. Sales of ready-meals have enjoyed massive growth in recent years, while portions have grown substantially. Despite clearer labelling telling the consumer what is actually inside the confection, the time-saving element nullifies any concerns regarding the contents. A large packet containing, for example, a lasagne does what it says on the packet; heat me up for 30 minutes and I'm all yours. The fact that a decent meal involving meat, potatoes and vegetables can be constructed in the same time doesn't matter if you can't be bothered or you simply don't know how.

Wellbeing education

Education rears its head once more when we are unable to escape the conclusion that we need to communicate the well-researched benefits of a particular course of culinary action. The price mechanism could be used to encourage this but, again, there is much talk and precious little action. If you want to eat inferior but easier food, then fine – but the reality is that you pay, first financially and then subsequently when your health fails and you pay again. It seems we need to give serious attention to the realities of our diet. Once more, the truth needs to be told. If we are effectively poisoning ourselves to death, and those who are unable to grasp the enormity of the problem refuse to accept the realities, they may simply need to be priced out of their behaviour pattern. This is not Big Brother telling folk what to do: it is making these products so expensive that people are practically forced to wonder why they are so expensive, and pay if they insist on buying them. The wallet, as always, has the last word.

We seem able to pin certain cancers onto cigarette consumption, directly and indirectly. The resources for the financing of lung cancer research are totally inadequate, however, and a dire insult to those afflicted who never in their life smoked. It is not a true governmental answer to respond with "It's too difficult to register the numbers". How come the government moves with alacrity on matters of security, with astonishing swiftness and highly detailed attention to closed circuit television cameras, speed cameras, identity issues and customs and revenue income? 'Numbers' is something government can do extremely well when it suits them. In short, the government can provide us with supposedly accurate information when they so choose, particularly in support of an unpopular policy. So we need to demand accurate and truthful information for our community, not just accept punitive controlling supervision. The price mechanism has been used to tax-raising effect in the tobacco industry; you want to smoke, then fine, but you pay, first financially and again subsequently when your health collapses. The same logic must be applied to damaging foods intake. Some devastating logic on the subject of health comes from the east:

"Calling for a doctor when you are ill is like having to dig a well when you are thirsty".

Advances in medical technology are accomplishing some amazing things. Are we, however, in danger of losing the human face of medicine? An oft-used metaphor says our fascination with the car might lead us to forget the driver. The driverless car is already being developed, almost proving the point. A profound invention, one with the capacity to change forever our current living order, depends, after patent award, on the ideology of the creator to use it positively or otherwise. The ability to tax any item with enormous regular consumptive throughput by any population is at the top of any government wish list – this is a problem they can swiftly solve. As we have seen, this explains why government, in thrall to the vested interest, appear to be uninterested in so-called free energy. How would they tax it? The answer is: with difficulty. But it would be easy enough to devise a taxation system to operate a revised 'free' economy. If such energy were made commercially available, the implications for the eradication of poverty are almost without end, with concomitant improvements in global health.

All political colours of government, democratic or autocratic, need money to fund their grip on power. Make no mistake, if free energy technology and other advances have been suppressed then this is all about power in the final analysis.

iv) Banking

Fiscal stupidity

The events of 2008, the result of an enormous and unsustainable asset 'bubble' market created around the world, called a halt to the greatest accumulation of collective fiscal stupidity not seen since 1929. Lehman Brothers bank collapsed, and governments felt it necessary to step in to support the global financial system. I do not propose to repeat published data on this crisis; the bibliography is substantial enough. These events are still recent enough for almost all of us to have been affected by the 'credit crunch' in some way or other, or we are being affected still. The harsh truth is that governments surrendered control of the money supply to the banking system. I am convinced that elected, and therefore accountable, governments alone should issue currency, and that their respective banks should simply handle the money as they and their confident customers see fit. Fractional Reserve banking – the creation of Commercial Money as opposed to central Bank Money – becomes dangerously out of control when coupled with poor lending decisions. The danger of a 'run' on banks, which is essentially what happens when depositors want to withdraw their money *en-bloc* in response to a crisis of some description, when that money is no longer actually there in the bank but tied up in speculations elsewhere, is acute and exposes a system which is not designed to withstand such behaviour. Extremely low percentages of overall deposits held by banks in developed countries is all very well in certain (positive) economic conditions, but when times are tough the system requires more fluidity than may be available

– which is when cash becomes king. This creation of money is ethically questionable, encouraging as it does casino-type speculative behaviour in times of confidence. The limitations become all too clear when sentiment is less optimistic. There is a case for substantially raising the minimum percentages of real deposited money the banks must hold.

Quantitative easing

Faced with a fiscal crisis of enormous proportions, the response of central government in both the UK and the USA is to 'quantitatively ease' our way out of the manufactured crisis without causing the mayhem seen in the early 20th century. This actually preserves the system and involves central bank purchases of government securities from the markets. This is done in order to lower interest rates and increase the money supply. It does this by swamping financial institutions with invented capital in an attempt to increase both liquidity and lending. This type of policy does not involve the printing of new banknotes, and is usually an option only when short-term interest rates are near zero. This policy buys time without really changing anything. In the UK £375 billion has been issued at the time of writing. This is a colossal amount of money, unsupported by any form of manufactured product, and which doesn't find its way into the credit system. There are risks in the implementation of such a policy, however, when interest rates remain low and the economy stubbornly refuses to respond to such stimuli. As the Governor of the Bank of England has admitted, nobody knows if this strategy will ultimately work. There are evident downsides to it, even if the upsides remain elusive. Because government buys bonds, short-term interest rates remain low, savings attract what is in effect a negative interest rate, and the money supply is lifted. But if this is not administered under tight control, inflation remains a threat. Pension fund income is correspondingly reduced.

So, interest rates are at an all-time low and the results for savers are catastrophic beyond satire. Pension funds lose their investment advantage in the market, thereby eroding confidence further. The ability of the pensions industry to deliver awful results has been breathtaking. Our willingness to not understand this industry is mystifying. To cap it all, the government of the day exhorts us all, with no sense of irony whatsoever, to "save for our retirement". How this advice squares with the 2015 decision to allow unfettered access to personal pension funds before retirement age is nothing short of extraordinary. We can expect to see some inventive and fraudulent schemes designed to persuade the vulnerable to part with their funds in "too good to believe" high-return schemes. Small wonder that there is no real appetite amongst the population to throw more good money away. Yet the problem is acute and we are not providing for our retirement at anything like an adequate level. Again, the problem remains one of truth and confidence. The banks have abused their customers and the system within which they operate. We no longer trust them.

Banking failures, were they fully allowed to happen, would do wonders for panic and confidence in the money supply. The real financial position may only be ever known if failures are permitted to happen and governments do not continue to prop up the banks. The 'easing' method may be doomed anyway, for it involves increasing the money supply and runs the risk of an inflationary reaction. Everyone knows that the system is effectively corrupt; the self-interested behaviour of some bankers is a disgrace. The results in the case of failure would be nothing short of catastrophic. However, it is humane to at least try to avoid the resulting human misery of *not* trying this method of fixation. If QE does actually work – let's be positive, if not a little sceptical – then it is to be hoped that subsequent attitudes towards risk and lending will be somewhat more intelligent than in the recent past. The incurred debts will have to be paid at sometime by either us (unlikely, since there is so much of it, although taxes will rise to be seen to attempt it) or our children, or their children. There is a growing realisation that as the debt pile grows, the possibility that it will never be repaid is becoming a real possibility. What happens then is anyone's guess. 'Austerity' is a no-growth no-fix situation too. All this policy does is to prevent a further explosion in spending rather than seriously reducing debt levels.

When this fundamentally unsound idea fails, and when the state finally loses control over the money supply, its real value will be in tatters, savings will be ravaged and inflation will take hold as it does, and the stage will be set for the Strong Man to step in, offering solutions to the problems.

Increasing the money supply is by all means a disaster; it must in time be inflationary and simply delays the required correct solution to the problem. This isn't pretty and the suffering is immense. Fascism is a fertile and seductive creed in such circumstances. We need to understand the danger that democracy faces, and the loss of freedom which always follows. It may be cathartic, meanwhile, for most of us to rant at the sheer iniquity of the entire banking industry. The insane salary levels, amusingly called 'compensation', paid to those we know are responsible for appallingly lax ethical behaviour amounting to outright criminality, is frankly obscene. Just where has all this money come from?

It would appear to be self-evident that whatever financial instruments that are being passed around the banking system contain an incredible degree of margin – which the customer must pay at some point. That doesn't deal with the rank manipulation of inter-bank lending rates, the wholesale selling of utterly inappropriate 'insurance' instruments, and the complete failure to understand that in any business the customer has to get what he or she needs first. Then, as the 'supplier', the bank gets what it needs; all this has been forgotten. What other industry is bailed out of failure by the taxpayer? What other industry is deemed too big to fail?

A telling observation here is to call your bank and listen to the automated phone systems one now has to go through. "Press button one for...", etc. This tells you, loud and clearly, that they have way too many customers. Each of us is beyond attention, as the quality press will confirm on any weekend examination of the financial section. How many tales of exasperation and total lack of consideration to the customer and their problems do we read every weekend? Some of these sad stories are resolved, but only after the forensic intervention of the journalist. The only conclusion must be that had the journalist not become involved, the customer would be left helpless and without remedy. Again, in every case, the company is "sorry for the inconvenience caused to Mr & Mrs H. Enough, and we have retrained our staff, sorted our system, painted the ceiling, etc., to ensure this doesn't happen again". So that's fine then; only it isn't. The same stories emerge each week with a different financial organisation. This industry has the reputation it deserves. Once again, the truth will out.

The value of locality

To consider truly useful banking it is necessary to do so in the context of locality. International banking is beyond realistic democratic control and of no direct interest to local communities. How retail banks should relate to community is important, since 'the bank', along with the Manager, used to be a vital part of the local economy, and this should be revitalised. This means the issuance of credit should be, as it once was, at the behest of someone who knows their locality, their local businesses and the players involved. The current system of credit-scoring, box-ticking and other nefarious methods designed to remove all risk from the proposition are counterproductive, and contrary to the very idea of locale and community. You are more likely to have your local bank branch close down than to see a manager with authority to lend to you as his/her own decision. Everybody understands that there are limitations in lending policy which are concerned with national performance in the economy. Nobody understands impersonal corporate-style rejections that are unconvincing, seem poorly considered and feel inhuman.

We should not be surprised at the steady closure of local retail businesses, as there is little chance of an idea being financially supported by a local bank, managed by somebody who knows the town and the person with the idea. True, the Internet is a growing feature in household expenditure, and items such as books, compact discs, DVDs and other small shipping-friendly items are obvious candidates for online expenditure. You cannot blame anyone for buying competitively online; most folk do. This type of consumer behaviour ensures budding entrepreneurs consider their proposition with even greater care if they feel the high street is somewhere they wish to locate their business. Local banks with a meaningful decision-making structure would at the very least assist local communities by being intimately aware of local business conditions.

A reality check

There is a persistent problem connected with banking that will not go away, and that is the supply of credit. Since 2008, money has become, despite record-low interest rates of 0.50%, expensive and difficult to obtain. This is a problem for business, but there is evidence to show that businesses are reluctant to borrow for both cost and confidence reasons. Government media people continue to talk about the problems of 'growth'. The real situation for many people is that they are mortgaged to the hilt, are constantly at or around their credit card limits, and have no appetite for debt-financed consumption. For years, growth has come courtesy of cheap borrowed money, which is cheap no longer.

I submit that the current period of low growth is in fact a reality check – if we do not have access to cheap credit we fail to consume at anything like the same levels we did when money was easily available and inexpensive. In short, what we have now is a more normal reflection of where we really are in terms of 'natural' demand. We tend to consume less, become more discerning and more reluctant to commit to unnecessary expenditure, especially if we haven't got the money. How many sofas do we need to sit on, especially as we've been given a 'nothing to pay for four years' deal? This is an insult to the collective intelligence, yet it seems to work.

Credit card abolition

Credit cards deserve their place alongside heavily sugared fizzy drinks as a social menace. I propose their steady abolition; by this definition I mean their phasing out over a period of time. As a personal financial instrument they are fine if the amount owed is paid in full each month. Thus they become a 30-day deferred or collective payment card, not a credit card. However, as an instrument of credit/debt, they are anti-social in both rates of interest charged and as an encouragement to over-commitment financially. An apt demonstration is provided by the card companies themselves. If you ring to enquire at what level your current balance is, you will be told that you have £££ to spend – calculated as your credit limit less your outstanding debt. This isn't your money, but they are happy to lend it to you, at interest of course. These are questionable ethics too.

'Payday' loan companies have succeeded in giving credit card interest rates a degree of respectability by charging astronomic rates of interest, as opposed to simply excessive. To abolish credit cards, a period of grace to write down one's debt to zero could be envisaged. Ten years might be seen as reasonable. Once this period expires, the debt could be converted to a bank loan at an interest rate nationally agreed, when we can rely on debit cards only. In other words, if you don't have the collateral, you cannot have the goods. This will rebalance the economy and eliminate ridiculous and damaging levels of personal debt, often encouraged by those organisations that should exist to manage money, not provoke consumers into poor fiscal positions that ultimately threaten them, if for some reason they fail to keep pace with repayments.

Lest there be any accusations of Big Brotherdom here, I feel we are already there. Modern slavery is present in two forms, and one of them is debt. I highlight the other elsewhere. To bear no personal debt is freedom, and the banks have a responsibility in helping the right people with the right fiscal proposition. Were we to have an economy not predicated on personal debt, I suggest we would have a healthier social community too; there would be rather less for folk to worry about, and less worry about where the next meal is coming from financially.

There has been much talk of banks dividing their operations into retail and investment divisions, the retail division being entirely separate and accounted for separately. Customer deposits would be ring-fenced from smart accountants with money-making plans most of us simply don't understand. It transpires that many fiscal instruments in the City of London were hardly understood by the players themselves. If that is the case, what chance do the rest of us have in following this particular game of poker? We know who always wins that game.

We discuss elsewhere that the central state should have three main functions: foreign policy/national security, the issuance of currency, and skills forecasting. Banking means handling money and therefore comes under the national remit. I repeat: money supply should belong to central government. Leave the banks, under supervision, to deal with the issuance of money and to whom they issue it.

Inertia selling

How often have we checked our bank statement to find a 'DD' (direct debit) gone through against our expectations? This is inertia selling if we forget from one year to another and it's gone through our account and been paid again. It is too much bother to try to recover the payment and retrieve our money. We promise ourselves we will deal with it before it is due to be paid again. Therefore we paid for something we no longer needed. The ultimate banking insult can be to try to cancel a direct debit – we can be told later that they can "find no record of such an instruction" but, sure enough, the next statement conclusively proves the money has been deducted from our account anyway.

Do we read our energy supply meters whenever we receive an estimated bill? There is no need to 'bank' with our energy suppliers by paying them in advance; they don't pay us interest and they can use our excess money to earn themselves interest on the short-term money markets. This amounts to a surcharge on our basic needs. Not everyone maintains their financial affairs with the diligence necessary to keep these bank account plunderers at bay. We ought to be one step ahead of this nonsense. What can we do? To avoid these situations, we can thoroughly check our commitments, and cancel those that we no longer need.

Life insurance is another tap over whose flow we appear to have little control. We should from time to time check our policies to ensure that they are still what we really need. Our circumstances do alter, and so should our attention to the supporting paperwork. Insurance is, after all, a fear payment.

There are, of course, circumstances where insurance is mandatory and simply sensible. But banks and insurance companies also offer us identity theft insurance. If we are reasonably certain we won't forget who we are, why would we want to be a part of this balance sheet-improving wheeze? It is far cheaper to buy a shredder and recycle the minced results. Indeed, the banks have been guilty of mis-selling various financial products on an epic scale, and have been fined for their poor conduct.

An analysis of needs, wants and desires

"An addictive, insatiable craving for ever more material goods to fill the inner emptiness is producing a manic techno-consumerism that is cannibalising the planet".

We may not have conducted a recent audit examining how we consume in any one day in our lives. Much of what we do may be habitual; after all it's 'what we do'. We have plenty of 24-hour periods in our lives, and there is always tomorrow. But perhaps it is worth asking ourselves what food have we eaten and what food have we thrown away? How was that food packaged? From where did the food originate? What other products did we buy that day and why did we buy them? To respond "I needed them" doesn't necessarily answer this, as we shall see. How much water have we used? How far did we drive in our car(s) and why? How much television did we watch? (How long the set was on for is a different matter). Some people are conscious consumers – however, many of us are *habitual* consumers.

Detailed analysis of one's personal circumstances might help with the practical realisation of what might be personally possible. This is not an appraisal of our material position in life, but an assessment of who we are, where we are and how we are. Do we know ourselves? Would we, under any circumstances, consider ourselves wise? Wisdom is not simply the acquisition of gray hair. It is a deep question to ask of oneself a levelling and inquiring question of honesty. Just what did you expect from your choices? In answering this question truthfully, you acknowledge a deep degree of understanding. It also turns a sense of 'want' into reality; its relationship with real need therefore enables us to ask the important question – is what we propose to acquire necessary or just an item on a flippant wish list? Although we think we are an evolved species, many of us seem quite capable of robotically repeating today what we did yesterday, without questioning why. The purpose of honest personal answers to these questions is to dissect what is a 'need', what is a 'want' and what is a 'desire'. All three of these simple words help to clarify our actions and our responses to external stimuli.

Do we need it?

Let's take 'need' first. We need air, water and food to enable us to survive. Our part as one seven-billionth of humanity can assist change by asking whether we also really 'need' the other things sold to us as 'must-haves'.

Car advertising on television, for instance, has been of such intensity that one wonders how much advertising money there is invested in each vehicle sold. The figure of £800 has been mentioned. The extraordinary things that we are being asked to believe will be ours when we buy these machines are embarrassing. We are exhorted to, amongst other things, "Move your mind", or "Enjoy the freedom of the open road", and incredibly, acquire "Auto Emocion", whatever this might be... Do you need it? Perhaps you do, but only if you understand the relationship between your emotions and the internal combustion engine. Why do you need a new car? There ought to be a good reason, a real reason to buy another car.

There are many ways to reduce unnecessary consumption – by asking ourselves all the time, "is this item really necessary?" Do we actually need what we are thinking of buying? In doing this, we retake an element of control in our lives by denying the peddlers of greener grass. Have you noticed, it's never for free?

Do we want it?

Let us look at 'want'. Want differs significantly from need in that needs are life requirements, without which the species fails as a collective and as individuals. 'Want' is also clearly different from 'desire', both of which do not have to be species-threatening. This is where the 'hidden persuaders'[3] of advertising come into consideration, an industry increasing in sophistication all the time, an industry merciless in its skill at targeting and identifying potential consumers, an industry at the forefront of technology.

Occasionally, it is useful to be told of a product's existence that will make our lives very much easier. How many times have you heard that word of mouth is the best reference? This is because if we feel strongly enough about how successful an item or service has been for us, we can hardly wait to tell others. We simply love to be seen as good judges. This is not necessarily evidence of how great the product is, but how great we were in finding it in the first place. However, word of mouth doesn't help corporate branded product sales and marketing corporations grow big enough, quickly enough. Why is this? Quick returns required by corporate investors mean that profitable results are wanted by companies *now*. The phrase 'Return on Net Tangible Asset', or RONTA accounting, often means 'sweat the assets' – and so every avenue is explored in order to sell more products. Satisfying shareholders before customers..?

Do we desire it?

Thirdly, we must consider 'desires'. Primarily, we are concerned with material desires. Those desires that are fundamentally acquisitive and particularly obtained at the expense of the wellbeing of others are spiritually damaging. Add in an element of self-aggrandisement and we have a downward spiral of almost inevitable dissatisfaction. Not all desire is negative, but material desire is fraught with spiritual difficulty, and we know how temporary the feeling of wellbeing is after acquiring something we have 'shopped' for. If this acquisition is funded by increased debt, it is further enslavement.

It has been said that luxury is what everyone wants and nobody needs. Desire is often imagination run riot, with no logical foundation of ideas upon which to build. It is not pure fancy to conclude that the elimination of desire is a source of freedom. We must acknowledge the differentiation of 'desires' here and further examine the doctrine that all desire is to be eliminated. The Buddhist viewpoint is quite clear that this is the case, which is an interesting and common sense analysis. However, the pure desires of creative impulse do not involve materialism but contribute positively to spiritual development. So to take the Buddhist view too literally is a mistake, and is not realistic in the current spiritual climate. Desire born of real love and generosity of spirit is reverential in the extreme, and is further common sense confirmation of the power of love. Desire born of love cannot be wrong; desire born of lust is wrong since the emotions are not balanced.

Why waste your intellectual time lusting after impossible dreams? We ought to be continually aware of the increasingly sophisticated ways in which companies are able to target each of us as potential customers. Their objective is to make us aware of a desire we didn't know we possessed, to persuade us into yet more targeted consumption. So-called 'loyalty' cards are essentially tracking devices. Technology ensures that our spending patterns are monitored. We are then told that this is for our benefit, since these suppliers claim that we no longer have the time or the inclination to trawl through endless information. Instead we can have the right information we need with greater accuracy and even greater speed. They apparently need to arrive at this conclusion without talking to us.

Data analysis is grotesquely sophisticated. These companies know we have a declining wish to discuss anything, or even have the time. A conversation? Sorry, no time for that. I'm sure that I speak for many people when I say that I am more than capable at deciding for myself what it is that I desire. The danger lies in unscrupulously-directed marketing at those on the financial margins who do not need this type of 'assistance'. Converting a want into a hardcore must-have desire always leads to a wasteland. Dreaming brings us inevitably to the external stimuli of desire creation; the advertising industry. Let us consider company advertising campaigns, with all their subliminal psychological dexterity, targeted marketing and ruthless creation of 'desire'. Years ago, we wondered "where did the yellow go?" in toothpaste ads; now we are expected to marvel at a car "shaking its ass". This is all very well, and most of us can laugh and forget we have seen the 'message'. But *have* we forgotten?

Branded goods

It is fascinating to witness the number of folk prepared to wear clothes in public that advertise a particular brand, with writing displayed all over what they are wearing. Shouldn't the brand owner be paying the wearer to wear their clothes? Isn't this free advertising for the manufacturer? Are we unable to create our own image to the extent that we must pay others to do so for us? This would have been unthinkable even 30 years ago. As a sunglass salesman in the 1970s, I was regularly asked whether it was possible to remove the engraved brand name from sunglass lenses. Opticians, to whom I was trying to sell the product, felt the engraving was too prominently displayed for their customers'/patients' taste. Now, the same sunglasses would be unsaleable if they *didn't* have the brand name prominently visible on the lenses. This is an obvious reflection on how consumer tastes change.

The ability to forget the message is not so easy when a financial product in the form of a credit card is sold to an inappropriate audience, who may have seen this card as an opportunity to spend virtual money they did not possess. This ruthless pushing of expensive credit to people who did not have the necessary financial acumen to manage that credit was not in any way solving customer problems. Instead, it created them. Offering mortgages to those people who had no hope of ever dealing with their repayments was a root cause of the 'toxic asset' problems originating in the USA. Transferring debt from one card to another to obtain an 'interest holiday' does not solve the problem; it merely delays it. Whilst card transfer fees information is legally presented, these 'partially visible fees' do not make zero-interest holidays the great deal the card company would have you believe.

Devaluation of gold

I recall very clearly in the early 1980s buying petrol and using a gold credit card. This elicited a "wow, you must earn loads" from the cashier. Now, not an eyebrow would be raised. The banks missed a brilliant opportunity, confirming that, in their industry, when gold means nothing then nothing can be relied upon anymore.

I recall trying to hand back to the American Express company a platinum card in order to trade back down to the original green card. This proved a card too far; the bank simply could not understand why anybody would want to become a financial heretic. There was no system whatsoever to allow me to trade downwards and issue me with a basic, no-frills, green card, so I ended with no American Express card at all; or at least until I recently received one that I hadn't even asked for. (Not platinum, not gold, not green – but grey).

Gold in any form, plastic or otherwise, should be an indication of high value, and the banks have played fast with the commodity commercially. To cheapen gold in any way is an error, which has led them on to platinum, and, in the case of American Express, black, which now bizarrely represents their highest value credit rating.

Is resistance futile?

So how can we change this pointless and relentless march of consumption? Make no mistake, you are being aggressively targeted to consume. Television, radio, newspapers, junk mail, e-mail and websites are the obvious conduits, and, of course, we must not forget the ever-present 'survey'. We have all heard this type of opening gambit:

"Could you spend a few minutes of your time filling this out please, Sir?"

"Would you mind answering a few questions, it won't take long?"

If a company offering a product is so certain of their product's efficacy, why do they keep asking questions? If the product is on the market, there must be a reason *why* it is on the market. Why do potential customers have to confirm that reason all the time? To electronically pin you down is the real answer. If the product is not selling in the volumes envisaged, hard luck on the companies; their homework may have been faulty, or they may simply be a poor judge of the potential market. But the truth of the real need for surveys is the ongoing constant refinement of the analysis of your spending habits, like it or not. Telephone marketing is an invasion of privacy. Under any circumstances, we do not have to play any part in this unwanted intrusion. These people simply want to sell more, and they don't care where or to whom, as long as they sell more products.

Creating a business from a bursting need to 'make money' is a hollow ambition, but creating a business dedicated to solving customer problems and thereby *enabling* one to make money is entirely different. A business becomes legitimate when it can provide answers to problems. If no problem is solved for a customer, then a business does nothing other than try to make money. It is not a blueprint for lasting success. This is why many me-too businesses fail. Any business idea created with the sole objective of making money is a business idea built on sand.

Nothing is 'free'

Offers that pretend to give you something for free such as "two for one" or "buy one, get one free" should be treated with both caution and disdain. To those who are unaware of exactly how this works, here's what 'free' really means. For example, when you buy a pair of glasses with a simple prescription for £100, and get another pair 'free', the cost of goods for the second pair or the cost to the seller of the second pair in offering this miraculous deal might be just £10. You are being convinced that you are getting £200 value for £100. Don't forget, the first pair cost £10 too, so effectively the seller gets your £100 for a total cost of £20. £80 is a great sales margin, but £90 is even better if you only buy one pair. Would you have gone into the store if the advertising hadn't persuaded you of the brilliance of this deal? Wouldn't it be honest and more transparent to offer one pair for £50 and get another for the same money if you needed it? You'd still part with £100. Let us suppose that you don't want or need the second pair, as you already have another pair – so where you see a "buy one get one free" offer, why not ask for just the one pair for £50? You don't want a free pair, just the one you came in for. You'll find this is not acceptable, for no spectacles seller will let you get away with this option. So are you really getting one for free? You decide. The unused glasses stock held by the spectacle-wearing public is enormous. This is especially galling since many opticians decline to fit new lenses to these 'freeway' frames if your prescription changes. It is waste creation once again.

Steady state economics

One title I considered for this book was *A Ricardian Sunrise*. There are two contrasting indicators that amply demonstrate both ends of the common sense spectrum. The first is David Ricardo[6] (1772–1823), who wrote *On the Principles of Political Economy and Taxation*, published in 1821. Ricardo deserves his place amongst the greats of economic theory, for he advocated the comparative advantages of free trade and gave precision to the concept of 'Economic Rent', of which more later. Free trade is the cornerstone of world prosperity; protectionism in the UK, as we have seen, was a dead-and-buried issue by the early 1850s. As an early proponent of free trade, Ricardo saw clearly how trade could be conducted to mutual advantage. Protectionism remains a temptation to cash-strapped governments in times of economic uncertainty, and is, as it always has been, a distorting influence.

At the other end of the spectrum, we have the 'Ricardian Equivalence Proposition', which demonstrates a level of creativity we have come to expect in the fiscal climate of today; in other words, unintelligible. I find the

Ricardian Equivalence Proposition so emblematic of the current age, being apparently bizarre and seemingly at odds with both facts and common sense. This hypothesis borders on the truly fantastic. It holds that:

"Consumers think about, or internalise, how the government will be able to pay for tax cuts".

As a result, the timing of any tax change does not affect their level of spending. This demonstrates the ludicrous and silly extent to which economists are capable of theorising. Is this proposition actually saying that the population is in some way in internal synchronisation with government fiscal policy, and empathises with it regardless? Are we so subliminally compliant? Does it mean that we fully confirm the twin law of taxation and death being as inevitable as each other? This proposition implies an extraordinary level of compliance and rationality, which is both fantastic and unlikely. On a less invisible level, the idea that the public will save any excess money to pay for future tax increases is wishful thinking. Put another way, consumers are happy to justify anything to themselves in order to continue spending. They'll find the money somehow. The assumption that individuals would even consider saving for a future tax increase is fanciful.

There is a suggestion that, as a result, it doesn't matter whether the government funds its spending with tax increases or with debt, because the effect on demand in the economy is the same. The government is therefore complicit in the continuation of analytical distortion and the continuance of a manipulated and increasingly worthless currency. The need to be re-elected is paramount – shirking the responsibility for a timely and real decision, or delaying it at best. Government needs to reassume control over interest rates to cool down an overheated economy. The banking system has clearly demonstrated its inability to do anything more than think of its own balance sheet. Collective failure of catastrophic lending policies have resulted in a credit squeeze and an urgent rebuilding of shattered balance sheets at the taxpayers' expense. The lunatics appear to be in complete control of the asylum after all.

True, consumers will go to many lengths to maintain their lifestyles, and will make all reasonable attempts to handle tax increases imposed on them. We therefore accept taxation with representation more or less regardless of individual impact, because we adjust to the current tax regime. Any increase in personal taxation, if not funded by a corresponding increase in income, must reduce discretionary spending, unless additional credit is allowed. We have discussed the increase of the money supply, quantitative easing, and its likely inflationary effect. If government defends demand by these methods it delays the inevitable recalibration of the economy and the acceptance of reduced levels of economic activity. This is tantamount to a blatant refusal to accept the facts of life. Furthermore, current demand levels are false indicators; we no longer know the reality of the economic situation. We no longer *know*.

Is this our Ricardian Sunrise? If we are asked to accept hypotheses such as these, we remove ourselves yet further from genuine and fairly straightforward transactional economics that we are able to understand. This is yet another delaying tactic in the support of an overheated and unsustainable world economic mess based upon financial instruments that benefit the few. David Ricardo, on the other hand, shows us a practical, genuine and common sense method of conducting trade. The contrasts are stark.

Real needs

We need to re-establish what our *real* needs are. In turn, eventually our real economy will be a reflection of the true demand of products and services that are needed. If we refuse to be drawn into nonsensical 'deals' that do not enhance our lives, our suppliers will have to offer products that we are prepared to buy. It is self-evident that any economy must eventually settle down over a sustained period of time in response to genuine needs-based demand. We have to admit that we have lived beyond our means for so long that a quick solution is unlikely to succeed in correcting an enormous debt problem. Essential products in any market will provide proper solutions to real problems; those necessary products will then sell, since they have a real reason to be in the market in the first place.

The fake recession

In the second decade of the 21st century, we are reaping the consequences of the banking profligacy of the first decade. It is stated that we were "in a recession". We were not. What we were and are in is a more real reflection of the true economic position, which *seemed* to be a recession but it is in actual fact where we really ought to be, rather than in a situation where we are rushing headlong into ever-increasing levels of pointless consumption we call 'growth'. The consequences of disintegrating interest in how we are governed has allowed mismanagement of our affairs. We are now able to see quite clearly the awful results of decades spending money we did not have. Does anyone seriously think we can avoid paying the price for this profligate behaviour? Does anyone think we cannot pay the bill and should therefore declare ourselves bankrupt? This is not an option, nor should it be.

Why we need a debt-free economy

A debt-free economy is based upon balanced income and expenditure. For us to incur debt there should be a worthwhile and genuine reason for us to do so. As a country, we have forgotten this obvious and basic truth. As a first correctional step, we should bring manufacturing more into a genuine needs-based reflection of consumption. This should cut down on big quantities of waste, extend product lifetimes and reduce product disposal problems. We are running out of places to incarcerate our unwanted materials, or, to put it less delicately, our rubbish. Rising standards of technology in manufacturing means more reliable product, with cars a classic example of rising quality standards of engineering. Yet again, this would confirm the real value and nature of the true economy, not based on the questionable issue of credit.

Encouragingly, we see the automotive industry beginning to address the problems created by unwanted quantities of cars destined for the scrap heap. More and more components used in new cars are recyclable. The car manufacturers know that they will eventually be legally obligated to build a recycling requirement into their new models, and they are doing this in response to that knowledge before they are forced into doing so. It should be a short step to extend this ecological requirement to other consumer durable products. One clearly obvious result of computerised robotic mass production is much more precise manufacturing quality, which results in much greater product performance and much increased reliability. You have now an implied right to expect better technical performance from what you buy. Nevertheless, always resist becoming a habitual early adopter of the latest gadget by honestly asking yourself "do I really need it?"

Constant spending to keep the economy afloat

An interesting observation which supports the continual growth idea in the economy and 'Continual Consumer Spending Theory' is that this constant consumer spending is necessary to keep the national industrial wheels turning. It is suggested that if we fail to keep spending, unemployment levels are at risk and living standards will decline. Lack of constant growth in personal income is said to cause a degree of nervousness about spending. Spending what we have is sensible; borrowing someone else's money to spend might not be so smart. When we worry about our future prospects this means that we stop or slow down our spending; we delay house moves, we delay buying the next car, and we stop eating out quite so often, which has devastating consequences for the economy. This personal reaction to uncertain individual circumstances is natural and sensible. However, the logical results of this hesitant consumer behaviour are truly devastating to an indebted economy, as immediate post-2008 consumer behaviour in the world economy clearly showed. Families can keep their existing car for another year and probably don't need to move house unless it is necessary for employment purposes. An overseas holiday may not be high on the domestic agenda in such straightened times. If income is down, we can tighten our belts a little, since we probably feel a loss of confidence in our ability to pay our way. Indebtedness is a result of overspending. We need to return to the old method of being able to pay for what we buy, at the very time we buy.

The collective consequence of a deeply-indebted population is catastrophic to the economy, which is now so finely balanced that any movement in interest rates ceases to have much effect, until, that is, rates move towards a more 'natural' 5% level. However, these low interest rates enable the banks to rebuild their shattered balance sheets by refusing to link their lending rates to national interest rates. The economy grinds to a hesitating halt when the consumer (you and me) stops spending money. Whilst tax revenues fall, increasing levels of unemployment benefit must continue to be financed centrally from a depleted treasury, and the nation goes further into debt, which at some point should, morally and strategically, be repaid. National debt is hardcore debt; it's been there for years.

Does anyone care anymore? It is unlikely that many do care, but we should. Cash-rich countries ultimately wield as much power as cash-rich individuals. It is always better to have some money to loan to others, than to borrow it. The words 'piper' and 'tune' come to mind. So nervous has government become that the slightest sign of consumer belt-tightening brings a response from the fiscal authorities, who *reduce* interest rates to keep the production machine going despite clear evidence that people realise they have reached their limit of personal fiscal responsibility; in other words, they have no more borrowing capacity. This explains why interest rates in the United Kingdom remained at the post-1688 low level of 0.5% for more than six years, a situation unheard of in the last three centuries. Something is amiss.

Does this interest rate manipulation deal with the 'under-consumption' problem? Government is not the only manipulator of interest rates, as we have seen – the banking system is guilty too. If money is less expensive via low interest rates, people will borrow if they are confident and able to convince their bank that they will repay the debt as scheduled. In the early 21st century, banks were intent on rebuilding their negative balance sheets, and placed strict criteria on consumer and industrial lending. This strict lending policy by the banks has ensured that national economic recovery will be slow. Real interest rates (those rates charged to the person or organisation taking the loan) are high, even if they are able to obtain the money. If money is scarce because banks refuse to lend it, under-consumption remains a fact and demand is low. However, this really means demand might be where it should be, and financed from money that is available and not via debt.

The problems that small businesses experience trying to obtain credit from reluctant-to-lend banks are legion. Since these businesses employ enormous numbers of working people, this policy becomes strangulatory and the economy as a whole continues to struggle. And so it may be many years before we reach a steady and real position of financial stability. We must remember that these circumstances have arisen because of the appalling and greedy behaviour of the banks. Since nobody is keen to pick up the next person's debt through higher taxation, we need to keep our spending within the limits available to us. Fortunately, some spenders know when to stop, or when they should stop but, as always, those taxpayers who have any money left will pick up the pieces. Eventually we will see the advent of an era which might be classified as a beginning of a well-thought-through consumer-buying process.

The age of practical consumption

This corrected balance of demand would be the major contributor to 'steady state economics'. Buying only what is necessary cuts waste, locally and internationally. The faintly lavatorial-sounding phrase 'quantitative easing' is an attempt by national fiscal authorities to pump billions and even trillions of dollars, pounds, or euros into their economies in an uncertain attempt to prop up a continuation of bad spending habits at a personal level, and failing fiscal systems at a national level. Whilst discussing this point, it is worth observing that no longer is there any attempt at numerical unity, even amongst scientists and mathematicians, as to exactly how many noughts, zeros, whatever your preference, that make up a billion or a trillion. (Stephen Hawking[4], in his book *A Brief History of Time*, felt that it was necessary to write the words "million after million after million" rather than try to use noughts, when describing stellar distance. He knew how meaningless so many noughts may appear when read.) Were this money ever to be printed in the form of banknotes, a government order for the printing of a trillion pounds might induce some shop floor head scratching. Who turns off the money printing press and at what number?

The result of quantitative easing is uncertain, since nobody knows, or will admit to knowing, whether or not this massive issuance of securities is going to work. So we have a major financial management figure, the Governor of the Bank of England, admitting that a £375 billion *experiment* is underway. How can it work without being chronically inflationary? How can it work without eroding the savings of the very people who might be persuaded to spend money (the retired)? How can it work without eroding the quality of pension funds? Can we run the risk of leaving an enormous national debt to be paid by our children and their children?

It is incredible that we might, after all, have something to learn from Robert Mugabe's[5] handling of the Zimbabwean treasury. Mugabe issued enormous amounts of the Zimbabwean currency by simply printing it, with the predictable results of soaring and chronic inflation. The reckless creation of £375 billion and the Bank of England Governor's confession that he had "no idea if this would work" was playing a *Monopoly*-type of game with the pound sterling, and is exactly the type of financial irresponsibility that could be expected of a banana republic, and as such would be publicly derided by financial commentators. Yet our government chose, on our behalf, to expand the money supply and mortgage our children's futures. This irresponsible inflationary decision reeks of political expediency. It was, and is, a refusal to face facts.

There is a further complication that arises from the expansion of the money supply. Interest rates in one of the developed economies, the UK, are at an all-time low. Investors look overseas for a better return on their money, which is a natural reaction. What happens when interest rates rise in the issuing country? It may become more attractive for the investor to repatriate his money and leave the country where his money was invested short of liquidity for its own investment purposes. This must lead to a devaluation of the overseas currency in question, and threatens the stability of that country. The central authorities of the USA Federal Reserve have only to indicate that they will reduce the quantity of 'easing', which means reducing the monthly securities volume issued, to induce money to return home for higher returns. It should be borne in mind that the Federal Reserve is a privately-owned organisation apparently subject to Congressional oversight, whatever this loose expression truly means. This activity morphs into currency manipulation – in 2013 it rather looked as though a trial run took place, and it 'worked'. Currencies such as the Indian rupee fell. Subsequent announcements were made to the effect that 'tapering' the reduction of the extra dollars issued would not be as aggressive as originally intended, so up went the rupee once more. The developing countries – now half the world economy – have enormous amounts of international money invested from developed countries. A reduction in overseas currency values is a reduction in pension fund investments, further complicating the picture.

All this also confirms to those holding the purse strings that they have total control over the world's money supply, and they know how to manipulate it.

Post-2008 banking 'crisis'

The 2008-onwards era demonstrated just how nervous the world's financial authorities were. With interest rates approaching zero, the willingness of the consumer to borrow remained at best muted. The lending agencies, notably the high street banks, were wary of lending indiscriminately again in the sure knowledge that the resulting criticism would be at best difficult to justify. They also failed to offer loans at rates that even approximated to the National Interest Rate, preferring instead to rebuild their embarrassingly poor balance sheets, often at the expense of their new shareholders – the taxpayers. The major economies refused to isolate debt-laden toxic assets, preferring instead to resort to quantitative easing in order to either "keep things going" or to "restore last year's borrowing levels". This steadfast refusal to face economic facts was staggering. There seemed to be a firm refusal to deal properly with poor quality debt and chronic debt levels, (i.e. to write them down or off). The government failed to properly penalise those institutions which got the handling of their product so wrong. This failure to face facts is to prop up and maintain ongoing corporate failure. Why support ailing banks, who lent to un-creditworthy individuals and companies?

The answer was, of course, political. Everybody knows this aid shouldn't have been given, and only the major players could hope to benefit. The small-player businesses slipped away, unnoticed and unmourned. No government wants to be seen to deliberately place millions out of work if any other solution is available. Not a word was heard in recognition of those industries which successfully weathered this particular economic blizzard. Were they being penalised for their success by the subsidy of less able companies in worn out industries – the banks? They almost certainly were, since the climate of low willingness to spend money clouded the economic horizon for most manufacturers and sellers regardless of what they were making or selling.

What needs to happen

The consequences of a second large-scale commercial closure programme in 40 years would be catastrophic – however, there are far fewer obvious candidates for closure; the 1980s saw to that. The 'easing' programme is an attempt at fending off another era of commercial failure. If these motives are sincere, as they appear to be, that is admirable. But costs of rescue packages will have to be paid, as will unemployment benefits if rescue does not succeed. The 1930s demonstrated too clearly what happens to inflated asset values. The period of adjustment is long, as the higher inflated values need to come down to some type of accepted realistic value. The consumer decides when that will be. The grim facts are not being faced. Re-engineering attempts to deal with grossly over-inflated values, toxic balance sheets, defaulting borrowers and low consumer confidence will not work. The isolation of 'toxic debt' must take place to understand the true scale of the problem.

Central government may finally realise that efforts to keep the country operational, with near-zero interest rates and exhortations to continue to borrow and spend, are doomed to fail. Confidence is a precious commodity, so when it is in short supply there is no incentive to spend beyond personal means. At some point, debt must be paid by nations and also by individuals. Nobody knows if good money will become bad money supporting existing bad money. The cost will be huge because the standard of living will decline, but the situation must be faced if we are to learn anything from this state of fiscal chaos. The lesson seems to be obvious once again: live within our means. To discover what those means truly are will take both time, determination and a willingness to face unpleasant truths. When money is borrowed, from wherever and whoever, sooner or later the lender or lenders are going to want it back. The previous party is well and truly over. Let's look forward to the next party – prepaid. We need a debt-free economy because we need debt-free people. Debt-free people are truly free to make considered decisions in their own time.

Tax reform

The current system of taxation is massively complex, and rewards luck as much as any other endeavour. Inadequate and mired in voluminous hard-to-understand fiscal law, taxation logic is beyond normal levels of understanding and it needs radical overhauling. Enormous sums of money are forcibly removed from individual earnings by central government, and where that money goes is buried in accounting systems few seem to properly understand. We know we don't have enough money to achieve our social obligations as a society; further, we have to admit the yawning gap between the haves and the have-nots is growing ever wider. This must eventually lead to social unrest. We have discussed the potential framework for the reorganisation of three tiers of national government, so let's see how we might pay for current expenditure and future liabilities such as pension provision. We need to rediscover David Ricardo's concept of Economic Rent. We have seen that 1873 was the last seriously considered (Gladstone was a serious man) date for the abolition of income tax, a hated imposition. We need to recognise that this outdated and unjustified method of taxation was only meant to be a temporary way of raising money, but became permanent and loved by central government the world over.

Economic Rent

Economic Rent is not what we negotiate on a lease to become a tenant of a landlord. It is the difference between costs of production that an enterprise must pay, and the revenue of that enterprise. Economic Rent is the difference between the two, and is what could be contributed to funding our social liabilities for the *use of land*. The same applies to individuals, and their capital gain on property. Economic Rent is therefore the surplus income over the minimum amount of money on which people need to live. Since government seems able to determine the amount on which a pensioner needs to live, for example, there ought to be a consensus on just what constitutes a 'minimum subsistence' figure.

Howls of outrage are premature... since it is entirely possible under such arrangements to eliminate nationally-imposed income tax and have a land taxation system administered by our District Assemblies, as explored in Chapter 5. Land is thoughtfully provided by nature, and some of us make enormous unintended gains as a result of our stake in the 'housing market'. What of those who pay rent by way of a lease? They will never enjoy such gains, and society thereby seems destined to become ever more divided, unequal and unjust.

For a well-argued and up to date interpretation of Ricardo's Law, examination of Fred Harrison's[7] book on the subject, *Ricardo's Law: House Prices and the Great Tax Clawback Scam*, is rewarding. Harrison presents interesting examples of how we can set about reconstructing and replacing our overly-complex and outdated tax laws. His thesis is neither fanciful nor impossible, and deals frankly with issues of the failing state.

As a starting point for overhauling our unfair and divisive method of raising taxes, the concept fits neatly with the reduction of the Centrist State and the return of power to local people. Just because Ricardo was a late-Georgian 'almost-Victorian' does not disqualify him. On the contrary, an opportunity was missed deliberately by the politicians of the age, because of their vested interest. This is not to argue for any degree of socialism; it is a proposition aimed squarely at a more equal and honest distribution of wealth. Those lucky enough to gain financially simply by living in their homes and paying nothing for the privilege enjoy a massive advantage over those who have no such stake in land. This cannot be described as fair in any way. Crucially, the wider this gap becomes, the more exposed society is to a highly divisive future. Unreformed, this situation is not sustainable and we are all aware of this.

SUMMARY

It is extremely difficult to conclude otherwise that our standards of behaviour and consideration towards each other leave much to be desired. We manipulate, we fix, we lie, we cheat, we take quick inconsiderate decisions to the detriment of each other and the planet. We possess a phenomenal ability to forge our own path at the expense of others. Our ability to view the 'big picture' is blinkered to the point of insanity. Weapons, drugs, money and food drive the world economy for the financial benefit of a very few. Undeniably, it is questionable to state that banking has bestowed significant benefits on the people as a whole; indeed, the rush to 'globalise' has been instrumental in helping to destroy locality. There can be no defence of the armaments industry; we know well the justifications of the spin-off benefits from weaponry. This is unethical and frankly insulting to those who have no empathy with killing. The knowledge that historically national economies have been lifted out of recession by the armaments industry – Germany in the 1930s comes to mind – should serve to incentivise us to think of a better way to handle our economic problems. We address the organisation question in Chapter 10.

We must handle forecasting and education in a more practical manner; we need to know what our society expects from those charged with management of the economy, and we need to have an informed and educated pool of talent from which to draw these skills. We have some legacies of poor decisions to address – for example, how do we deal with our nuclear residues? It is no answer to continually delay investment in examining these questions. We may even obtain significant benefit from researching the solutions. The handling and issuance of money would appear to be an increasingly sophisticated business which few are able to comprehend. Again, elected central government must be responsible for the issuance of currency, and then let the banks handle it. Currency should be subject to electoral oversight, not be the subject of speculative gain by those who already have enormous amounts of it. That the rich get richer and the poor get poorer is well-known, but this does not mean it has to be an endlessly-

propagated self-extending truth. We ought at the very least to address our organisations to effectively deal with United Nations-recognised needs. It is not acceptable that the gap between those that have and those that have not gets ever wider; it is an admission that we have failed at the top of our voices. Ethics is ideal conduct. We all of us know that it is not an ideal world; however, it is us that make it even less ideal. We must acknowledge that change is not just an option, but that it is vitally necessary. Too often, it seems, we are in this life together to exploit the next person in a spirit of self-advantage that is beyond ethical standards of decent behaviour which ought, by education, to be widely understood as automatically 'not on'.

8

A CONSIDERATION OF WORLD POPULATION

"In every nation is the mystery of all nations".

Overcrowding

A world population in excess of seven billion presents us with a variety of problems. Living together in ever-closer proximity means that we need to understand how to deal with the practicalities of constantly growing populations. This is an enormous strain on the infrastructure of so many countries, which did not envisage having to accommodate so many people.

70% of the world population is now said to live in cities, and the associated behavioural consequences of such high concentrations of humanity tend to be complex. Economic consequences are the reason for why people congregate in these cities; this is where they are able to find work. This huge redeployment of humanity worldwide from the agrarian to the industrial economy has been underway since the Industrial Revolution, resulting in the development of the modern consumer society, providing the economic nourishment to feed individual ambitions, those of their families, and their dreams of prosperity.

One highly visible result of the expanded world population is the growth of the 'super-city'. It also brings highly visible confirmation of there being 'too many rats in the trap'. The conurbation of London, metropolitan New York and the growing cities of Asia and South America are all good examples of population overcrowding. The move to such areas is far from complete, particularly in the developing world, which is proving to be chaotic, and since we have such a poor record of planning for future urban requirements doing nothing is no longer a realistic option. Can this go on unchecked? Should it go on unchecked? What of the consequences of unfettered expansion? Do we leave the status quo as it is and deal with the negative consequences of crowded city populations as and when they occur? Unchecked movement of this kind has led to these overcrowded super cities. What might happen if and when industrial demand declines and the jobs no longer exist?

China and India

China and India in the 2000s may amply demonstrate what could follow as a result of falling industrial production. Together, these nations constitute almost 50% of the world's population. In both countries there remains a large agrarian sector in their economy, but could this reabsorb large numbers of people previously employed by industry? This is highly unlikely. There has never been a reversal of the drift away from the land in the last 200 years. Given their experience of the 2000s, if orders for goods to be exported begin to decline it will be interesting to analyse in years to come what happens to China and India's traditional export markets. China alone is responsible for 70% of the world's iron ore consumption. Those countries which supply the huge Chinese appetite for raw materials are vulnerable to downturns in demand. Australia is particularly at risk of a Chinese reduction in raw material consumption. If overseas demand collapses, trying to replace that demand in their underdeveloped domestic markets would be an enormous problem. The Chinese and Indian consumer does not yet have sufficient money to replace export-led demand. As their middle classes expand, the inevitable corollary is higher labour costs, which must reduce the attractiveness of both nations as manufacturing bases from which to export. The results of rapid growth in these countries place enormous strain on urban infrastructure. Just supplying fresh water and electricity to ever-expanding populations is a challenge. If demand-led consumption does fall, and leads to unemployment on a huge scale, the social challenge will be a serious problem. Small wonder, for the numbers defy belief. 22 million people in New Delhi alone demonstrate the colossal scale of the problem. There is almost an implied requirement to keep employment 'going' in the fullest sense, and such numbers carry an urgency of solution provision. This is a bipartisan human needs situation in which bickering politicians are unhelpful.

As salary levels remain static in the West, the tendency to bring overseas manufacturers 'home' or 'on-shore' becomes a viable option as domestic costs begin to come into line with overseas manufacturing operational costs. Freight costs and order lead times don't help the equation for the importer. Even so, the move into the super-cities seems likely to continue. As a dominant emerging power in the East, India has growing power and influence. What it chooses to do with this influence has yet to be made apparent, but it is unquestionably currently tied to their growing economic influence and links with Western markets, especially the USA. India realises full well the importance of economic cooperation with her Asian neighbours, and with the USA. The populations of India and China are numerically similar, but they face different challenges. India has pursued a different industrial growth strategy, a more 'value-added' policy. Nonetheless, the growth of the middle class in both countries is adding pressures to inadequate infrastructures, water supplies and communications. Quality expectations are high. India faces a changing political environment too: the weak and corrupt nature of all levels of government is finally exasperating the voters. The infrastructure cannot cope any longer and corruption ensures that nothing is done without additional payments. The voters have had enough. Waste disposal is chronically inadequate and pollution is horrendous. Failure to address these problems is resulting in stagnating investment levels and is stalling growth. There are encouraging signs from the Modi-led BJP government elected in 2014 that this may be beginning to change. India has every possibility of being the next major genuine growth economy; one hopes its people get to share in the created wealth.

Middle class expansion

Personal and recent experience in India (2007–2008 and 2013–2015) showed the burgeoning middle class in a somewhat negative light. Conspicuous consumption is something quite common in so-called affluent societies, but in India it has been elevated to new levels. It seems to an outside observer that the Indians can hardly believe their luck. The recently acquired visible symbols of wealth are particularly obvious when they appear alongside systematic and chronic poverty, which is prevalent in India. Whilst the caste system remains, poverty will continue to be institutionalised. What is less savoury is the newly-wealthy peoples' attitude to the poor:

"They are our poor, they are used to it; don't worry about it, it's our problem".

This widespread and rapid adoption of middle class Western culture and values does not presuppose a sympathetic attitude to others less fortunate. The Indian advertising industry also finds a huge and willing fresh audience upon which to peddle its 'creativity'; this audience is flush with new money and an urgent individual desire to show everyone that they have that money. The true tale of an Indian entrepreneur visiting a Ferrari dealership with a suitcase full of cash money and who wished to buy his father a car for his birthday is typical. He was informed that cars are built to order and that it would take six months to complete manufacturing. He was disappointed that he could not take a car away there and then, and immediately lost interest. So there is every possibility that over 40% of the world's population is, or is about to be, made ready for a re-run of unfettered Western consumerism. Those products that they fail to supply for themselves will be readily available from elsewhere. Exports to India and China are an identified priority amongst Western corporations. The potential is huge and so, of course, is the resulting demand on natural resources. Yet the Indian and Chinese economic approach is different. China has become the workshop of the world; if you need 10 million of any product you discuss your requirements with China, not India. India has decided that following China in volume-related industries is a poor idea. It has instead pursued value-added industries, hence their substantial investment in technology projects. Simply put, value-added products are those that require higher quality specification which command higher prices and therefore offer improved profit margins. Since the price required is higher, it follows that production volumes are lower. An example of this might be the comparison between newsprint paper and magazine-quality paper.

India is the largest democracy on the planet and appears to recognise the futility of competing with low-margin mass-producing competitors. This is smart thinking, since the mass producers eventually have to share the fiscal spoils with their workers, wages then rise, competitiveness declines and the cycle begins again elsewhere. By virtue of this value-added policy, India has spawned an enormous burgeoning middle class intent on earning and consuming in the Western idiom. Interestingly, this huge country with ancient and rich historical traditions older than the West is quite happy to adopt the Coca-Cola culture completely, and their young are quite happy to dress in the branded manner and be 'cool'. Young folk the world over do this, and why this is doesn't matter here. This type of behaviour isn't unusual and their actions mirror our own Western way of doing things. What does matter are the social consequences of increasing middle class wealth, and the fact that we have an exciting opportunity to examine today what happens to a society where this growth in modernism occurs. In other words, what are the side effects or, more properly, the direct effects of this behaviour?

Problems in addressing population problems

If we care enough to address the answers to the problems of there being so many people, then we have to pay real attention to the major problems faced by the deprived people of what we patronisingly call the 'third world'. The problems of millions of people not having sufficient food, clean water and shelter are damning enough. The dilemma facing the rest of us is, on the other hand, quite simple; reduce general demand and the need for production declines or ceases. Overall prosperity will decline and the quantity of money available for 'noble' causes (charity for the poor in the developing world) reduces or disappears. This economic fact of less production will happen when there are fewer markets (less people) to buy and therefore less money is available. Let's go several stages further: whole industries may no longer have any reason to exist.

What if the consensus forecast for 2050 is inaccurate, and we double the 2004 population figure to 12 billion? We'd be wrong by 25%, which is an enormous miscalculation and one for which there is a political unwillingness to plan. However, experience shows such planning might be sensible. Unless a convincing case for a radical slowdown in the growth of the numbers can be demonstrated, this could turn out to be a realistic worse-case scenario situation and should at the very least be the subject of a contingency plan. Let us suppose that the world actually ran out of oil, and that the introduction of free energy is in fact not viable or not 'permitted'. The economic consequences would be enormous since job losses alone would run into the millions and all the associated industries that are reliant on their relationship with the provision of oil would suffer appropriate levels of pain. Global travel would decline massively. Without pushing the dire consequences too far, this isn't going to happen without drastic and severe social repercussions.

Mass-production depends upon a mass of population and an awful lot of production, which is necessary to be able to play 'pass the parcel'. This means that we each make something and the other buys it, and vice versa. We are all involved in this game. Any significant reduction of economic activity mirrors the population number it serves. There is no point in making anything if there is nobody in a position to buy it.

The controversial neo-conservative 'Project for The New American Century' (PNAC) reportedly had as one of its aims a world population reduction to 500 million. Quite how this was to be achieved was not divulged. This aim is not verifiable, but has been espoused by conspiracy theorists. Population reduction of this kind would be, we can safely assume, a technical contribution from the pharmaceutical industry, almost certainly in the form of viral control. PNAC, essentially a thinktank, is said to have been wound down today, but there is little doubt that this collection of luminaries were, and probably still are, taken very seriously.

Aside from the Chinese authorities' failed efforts to restrict the numbers of births by decree (which has created huge gender imbalance in Chinese society), are we to assume that perhaps our world population may keep growing? Have we any room for manoeuvre as to how we deal with this? Yes, we have. We must change the imbalances we have introduced on our planet for the benefit of all species which live on it. Failure to address fundamental behavioural change means that we will have an uncertain future.

If we can't be bothered to change our views, or fail to recognise the necessity for changed behaviour by everyone, the results hardly bear thinking about.

We must admit that a proper and considered international solution to this problem will require a level of thinking not yet demonstrated by our national governments. See Chapter 10 for reform suggestions on World Government. Nothing short of a huge shift in resources away from armaments and bloated militaries, phoney aid programmes and dubious patronising attempts at health management in 'third world' economies will suffice. It remains extraordinary that in order to exist in peace, humankind must devote massive fiscal resources to instruments of war. It remains extraordinary that children and adults go hungry in a world where all agree that there is enough food to eat. It remains extraordinary that we are able to devote resources to investigate our planetary origins, yet remain unable to provide clean water to many who don't have access to such a definitive need. It is time we all objected, loudly and more loudly, and more loudly still, until the powers that be actually take some notice of our objections to this stupid state of affairs. United Nations declarations clearly state what is required. Why is the will to implement the declaration so lacking? Since it is transparently evident that our current political system is not prepared to address these critical concerns with anything other than platitudes, pressure of a kind hitherto untried must be actively considered to elevate these and other concerns. These are not 'issues' – they are PROBLEMS.

Should we fail to recognise and manage this most pressing of international problems, the consequences are unimaginable. There simply has to be a programme of global reform based upon the real needs of the world's people, and this means all of us, regardless of colour, wealth, creed and geographical location. We briefly considered the results of our current national education system in the 2004–2047 section of Chapter 2, and more fully in Chapter 4. Let us presuppose that we achieve some success in altering this situation by 2047. We cannot leave to mere hope that a more enlightened and useful way of producing educated people will result in an international system which is designed to provide the skills and understanding that humanity needs in the numbers required. This means an expansion of the 'middle classes', which by today's definition means the broad mass of working folk with an acquisitive but educated material dynamic, perhaps property ownership and a job that reflects the degree of educational and skilled achievement shown by the individual.

As we have seen, China and India alone represent almost 50% of the planet's population. These two countries have not been slow to recognise their skills requirements; they have tuned their educational and vocational systems to reflect their national needs. It is worth considering why it is that these countries seem to possess keener foresight on their national skills requirements than the 'developed' Western economies have displayed.

China remains a communist country, with a benevolent attitude to business development. India was until recently more or less closed as a country in which to do international business. Russia must also be mentioned here too. Formerly a communist superpower, Russia is now nominally, if debatably, democratic. The three countries differ hugely in population numbers; Russia is empty of people, with just 140 million, in comparison with China and India. But they all share one thing, which is a lack of democratic tradition in pre-Second World War modern history. Is this an advantage on some levels? It would appear to be just that, since an ability to instigate the necessary education programmes, to anticipate what is needed and to act upon it has produced an educated middle class, and quickly. All three countries' populations appear to condone a 'tough and strong' attitude at the top of the governmental tree and, especially in China, people just want to be left alone to make money. The individual vote seems not to be cherished to quite the degree it is supposed to be cherished in developed democracies. This important distinction really needs to be understood by Western policy makers, particularly the USA. If there is any appetite for democratic reform in these countries, it will be made apparent by local populations at a time of their choosing. Interference by outside forces *a la* 'Empire', deciding what might be good for their own national interests, is outdated and always fails in the long term, as has been demonstrated too often by the USA, ever keen to export its own brand of democracy without proper forethought. Personal growth will eventually be reflected nationally, but the time this may take could be decades.

Urban congestion

The motor car is now synonymous with over-population and the car is an ever-present expensive item in the lives of many of us. There are also millions of them. We rarely congregate *en-masse* without our cars. One of these problems is highly visible, and that is the overcrowding of our transport systems. We tolerate the endless frustration of yet another delayed journey, of having to reschedule appointments, and of losing control over the way we spend our time. The vehicle in which we endure this inconvenience might be described as a technical miracle. It can offer us ever-increasing reliability, and we can now assume we will actually arrive at our destination, which as recently as 30 years ago was not a given fact. We sit, immobile on the tarmac, in a comfortable seat at a cabin temperature we have set, listening to music or speech radio, where the news can confirm what we already know; that we are stuck in a seemingly endless traffic jam. We are no longer able to cross London with any more haste than the Victorians, but we can do it in some style and in rather more fragrant surroundings. This is not to argue for the return of the horse, or for the mechanised jam to be replaced by a four-legged bad-tempered equivalent. Trains and aeroplanes offer as much inconvenience as travelling by car.

We appear to accept this classic example of overcrowding as part of our day to day existence. We do not, however, accept this personal inconvenience when on holiday. The prospect of spending several hours in traffic jams on holiday would be seen as a waste of our holiday time. Yet we seem to accept unquestioningly the consequences of overcrowding for the rest of the year. We may feel that we have no choice, but we do – by looking seriously at the causes of, and potential solutions for, over-population.

The aging demographic

Increases in individual longevity in the last century present us with another problem; looking after our increasingly aged populations. In 1900, the life expectancy of an average late-Victorian male was 49 years. Now, in the UK, we can expect a male to live until he is 81 years old. In Russia, a male may expect to reach 70 years old.

The developed world has failed to devise a reliable system of funding their elderly populations. The fiscal upsets of 2008 onwards revealed multiple flaws in both design and distribution of many financial products, including pensions. At a time when government increasingly needs individuals to financially take care of themselves, there has been a catastrophic loss of confidence in financial markets, which has drifted firmly into the conscious psyche of everyone. Confidence in the ability of these markets to handle the self-funded provision of pension funds has declined to the extent that many now see the placing of serious and hard-earned money into a pension fund as a gamble, and ask themselves whether the money will be there when needed. The problem can only get worse. Technology may help to extend longevity in defiance of disease, but the numbers of the elderly grow remorselessly, and care for them must be funded. How?

Pension fraud

Many have lost significant sums of money from their expected pension fund, resulting in a lowered standard of living in retirement. Since the developed world demographics suggest an expanding and fitter elderly population, this band of silver-haired folk will need sufficient money to survive. Where will this money come from? If this does not come from personal savings, then it must come from taxation. We must hope that personal savings ratios improve from their present abysmal levels, since failure to provide for our futures means yet further taxation burdens on the young. This increased savings hope isn't certain. If the individual is expected to either contribute to, or be entirely self-funded for, their retirement, then the very least that those in charge of that money (government) might do is to engineer reliable stability in the pension system. Tinkering with the pension regulations and altering them to effectively rob those who invested, rightly, in their retirement provision is nothing short of a national disgrace. Must we all take a job in the state sector in order to receive a decent pension? It is beginning to look that way.

Born pre-1950

As life expectancy has improved, the concomitant health implications to society of an older population seems to have come as a complete surprise. Extreme age and the numbers who now expect to live well into their 80s, 90s and even beyond brings with it ever-growing costs of care, which the economy has never been structured to fund in any modern sense of the actual realities. There is a growing realisation that the importance of diet, exercise and generally taking care of oneself is not only crucial, but that widespread failure to do so will result in a funding crisis of care at the heart of local government. Devolved authority, as has been suggested in Chapter 5, should be able to address the problems of healthcare both in terms of education and the specific needs of their locale. It may be that a higher density of the elderly in a given area would result in higher taxes in order to properly fund care for them. At least this would be a known and locally-understood factor in local politics. Such appreciation of the facts, coupled with a well-managed approach to care, may well attract the newly-retired generation to take up residence in an area for just such reasons.

What to do?

What can be done to deal with this appalling mess? Candidly, this means some decent and truthful management of the serious problem of inadequate pension funding. Why should we leave the problem to our children? Are we so dishonest that we are unable even to face our lack of willingness to deal with this glaringly obvious problem? The elderly are living longer and this reality will not simply go away. However the pension fraud is analysed, it is obvious that unless there is a completely new approach to thinking about this very serious problem, the current fixes of increased retirement age and additional taxation are fraught with difficulty (as is the new and risky policy of allowing people to cash-in their pensions). We may see some potentially unwelcome assistance from technology in the solution to this problem. When costs of the human genome analysis come down to manageable proportions, we may be better placed to fund specific groups of the elderly based upon much more accurate personal biological data. There will be many ethical questions that must be answered; technology that is able to accurately determine lifespan will affect questions of life insurance and other health indicators sure to excite the human emotions.

What can be done to introduce some honesty into the savings and pensions industry? We have examined this travesty in other chapters. Why continue to subsidise debtors at the expense of savers, who often depend upon their investment income for a decent standard of living? Government can perhaps con this generation, but the young will take note. It will be very difficult to persuade working people to save for their retirement when their parents did so and paid the price for their thrift by being stolen from. Any personal or centrally-funded pension provision will only be worthwhile if future corporate behaviour is honestly reported in annual accounts. This information will ensure that pension fund investments made in industrial companies are able to be made on sound criteria. Some restoration of confidence in corporate affairs might then be possible, but we can expect this to take some years.

Failure to clean up corporate accounting will be a missed opportunity for all of us to invest in our futures if the corporate representatives are allowed to ignore their earlier mistakes. The consequences of these mistakes have been forced upon us by the greed of a few executives who have been granted (or awarded themselves) inappropriately large salaries and bonus incentives that were not linked to performance. These remunerations have rarely been linked to true accountable performance, which should reflect the managerial skill that the executive brings to the company. For many years, I was paid by results. Had I failed to produce those results, my pay cheque would have been almost nil.

How does *anyone* persuade someone else to pay them millions to lose fortunes? Are the truly insane running the asylum?

How can we deal with future population growth?

Let's remind ourselves again of the growth rate of the human species:

1789 – 1 billion
1918 – 2 billion
1961 – 3 billion
2004 – 6 billion
2050 – 9 billion?

We would not wish anything more than a dramatic improvement in developing-world living standards, needs-based as those improvements must be. The challenge is to educate potential and current consumers in the 'needs, wants and desires' business – see Chapter 7. Excessive and wanton consumption by such enormous numbers of people will only exacerbate global waste, and further pointless manufacturing of pointless products. A programme of education designed to ensure awareness of needs and wants early on in a young life might offer the next-generation student the intellectual framework within which to exercise responsible choice. Developed Western societies, with their celebrity sales men and women, are in a fabulous position to be able to help here since they are admired for whatever reason across the globe for their achievements. For example, if a currently high-profile celebrity endorses a product, or a style of living that it is possible for the consumer to emulate, then there are many people who find that desirable, and therefore aspire to do the same. Might there be the opportunity to sell some good habits before the bad are learned?

If responsible acquisition becomes a sincerely-felt individual responsibility, there is every chance that collective changes in consumptive behaviour might be to the lasting benefit of all of us. How can we have some influence here? If enough of us say NO to pointless products, and illustrate our disapproval by simply refusing to buy, the decision to cease production will be swift. It is that simple.

The planet does not need future generations to simply exist and consume what they want to consume and then die. To be human is more than this. The personal recognition of our design capabilities and the recognition that we are a tiny part of a much bigger plan is a start. We can do very little on our own, so we therefore need one another. Can't we do much better at managing our impact on the planet than we are currently doing? Yes, of course we can, and we know this. Prominent educated comment has recently been made which says this:

"There is a possibility that children born today may witness the end of our civilisation, unless we stop talking and start doing what we know to be right, changing, radically, our behaviour".

That comment is very serious; we have to learn to recognise that so many of us living together brings greater responsibilities, which were unknown to previous generations. We should be intelligent enough to appreciate that the opportunity being given to us is unique. This much we owe to our descendants.

Born post-1995

This demographic group deserves protected status. If global birth rates do eventually begin to decline, as they must, the problem of just where the tax income will come from is pressing. Despite determined efforts by extreme groups of people to effect change by violent means (I also implicate politicians who are guilty for failing to understand why this is), there remains a positive and optimistic mood amongst young folk in particular. This augurs well for the future.

In conversation with various nationalities of twenty-somethings in India during the winter of 2013–2014, I came to the conclusion that although my generation is concerned about basic personal freedoms being removed because of technology, the young feel a lot of freedom is actually being bestowed upon them as a result of technology, particularly through social media. This has profound implications for the future of the political collective and the direction the world will take. The young have become used to being able to express an immediate opinion using this social media, and feel that the Facebook[1]-Twitter[2]-Instagram[3]'-type system does have a long-term relevance. When asked what might come next, they have no idea. But they are very aware of the jobs not being available after graduation... they understand the grand con being perpetrated by governments.

Bright young people are asking themselves searching questions of educational relevance; if *not* going to university is a sensible option, they'll take that decision. The fine balance between debt-funded acquisition of higher education and the likely payback in future years is of necessity examined by the young very closely. This is why an accurate and highly important department of national forecasting is so important. Don't persuade a bright youngster onto a false career path – the resulting disillusionment is destructive in the extreme.

Born 1950–1995

The system persists in taxing this grouping as hard as possible, working them as hard as possible and making life as financially demanding as can be. Demands placed on modernity means hard work, hard hours and substantial living costs. There are fewer mothers able, or willing, to care for their children at home. The contribution to the household finances made by two working adults means less attention and time can be afforded by working parents to their children. This is profoundly sad, since it is widely agreed that having a mother at home is of incalculable benefit to small pre-school children, and when they attend kindergarten. This is not to malign working couples, but it is sometimes a choice freely made. To what extent the second salary contributes to 'needs' as opposed to 'wants and desires' (see Chapter 7) is anybody's guess. Going to work to fund a fancy but unnecessary car or holiday might be a distortion of priorities, but it remains, or so one hopes, a matter of choice. To do so at the expense of the wellbeing of young children is more questionable, however. The word 'priorities' comes to mind.

Perhaps a return to some form of 'married tax allowance' is apposite, since this rewards stability and both encourages and recognises the enormous value of a stay-at-home mother. However much money this might be, it would never financially compensate for not 'working' in the traditional sense, but at least there would be an acknowledged value in this vital role.

SUMMARY

There are more of us, appearing at a faster speed than at any other time in history. We need to understand the chronic problems of poorly-managed reactions to burgeoning city growth and we need to plan and forecast with far greater reliability than we have so far. Government forecasts tend not to come with a certificate of reliability. This requirement must be taken far more seriously; the key to a successful future for the majority of the

planet's populace lies in understanding what our real needs are and when and where we are likely to require them. Once more, management, decent honest management, can deal with this – and it should be undertaken at the highest levels of cooperation.

9

THE EXISTENTIALIST PLANET

"Design by wholesale is grander than design by retail".

Unexplored potential

How often have we discussed amongst ourselves and heard the following: "We only use about 10% of our capabilities; if we used the other 90% what could we achieve?" The exact percentage we use is a matter of conjecture, but let's use 10% for a brief analysis. There are 8,766 hours in a year (365.25 x 24). If we take an eight-hour sleep period in each 24-hour cycle, this reduces to 5,844 waking hours in a year. 10% of these hours will give 584.4 hours annually, or around 96 minutes per day usage of the engineered design. This is a pitiful usage rate of the finest engineered product in history. Even so, this statistic is, in the opinion of many observers, wildly optimistic, making the proposition even more ludicrous. The wastage is simply phenomenal, assuming that we can agree that we could actually function to the maximum capability all the time. We appear to both acknowledge and be happy with this underperformance. We seem to spend very little time exploring the potential of the unused time that we often acknowledge is wasted.

The institutionalised human

I would suggest that by the age of 10 we become 'hard-wired' into the domestic environment in which we are raised, hard-wired into our parents attitudes and, above all, hard-wired into the so-called education system into which we are thrust. Chapter 4 covered education questions of this type. All this ensures an extremely limited field of creative thought and latitude, and it can take us many years, if ever, to understand the linear and confining scope of formal education. Further, I suggest that if we are cognisant and able, then by the age of 50–60 years our conditioning can be both questioned and eventually unlearned, or released. Welcome to an idea of 'consciousness'.

Are we admitting to a collective embarrassment at our poor performance? Are we justifying our shortcomings to an in-built design failure? By accepting an under-use of capability without properly knowing the potential of the whole design, we demonstrate an incredible level of both arrogance and stupidity. We cannot know everything, and if we did, would there be anything worth knowing after all? I wonder if at that point we would technically descend into total and complete stupidity, since we would all know 'everything'. There is a strong possibility that we would take for granted all possible knowledge. If we knew our full capabilities, we would have boundaries that we do not have now; nothing would be possible, only probable, then definite and absolutely without risk.

This is an interesting question to which nobody appears to have a clear answer. It might be worth some basic speculation, if only to eliminate various hypothetical options. This speculation might lead us to reasons which explain why we are the way we are. The human species is, as far as we are aware, the only species concerned with reason in addition to simply surviving. This we cover in Chapter 14. Let's take it for granted that the human being is capable of both mental and physical activities. We can only guess at other species' capabilities, which undoubtedly are present, but we simply can't discuss this with them. Physically, we are fully aware of our limitations. We cannot fly unaided, we cannot run particularly quickly, we can move in water unaided, but not especially far. We do therefore seem to accept the limitations of what we can and cannot do in the physical world. What we wish to achieve we invent things to accomplish if necessary, and it seems that we have a pretty fair handle upon our physical-world capabilities. This is not true when we consider our mental capabilities.

Since Gutenberg's invention of the printing press, the authority of passed-down oral tradition has been in steady decline. Written history is usually clear enough in terms of recorded fact, but it is not always capable of illustrating the necessary and timely 'spirit' of those facts. Small wonder that subsequent written tradition – in some cases labelled as history – is often misinterpreted. What we now call 'reading between the lines' is not a problem in oral tradition because appropriate emphasis can be given where necessary, but the printed word often forces us to assume a spirit of authorship. A period of time over

500 years will more than cover the original tracks of any story, so we are often left with just writing or, perhaps more accurately, the printed words.

So where is this mythical 90% of unused mental ability? Who proved that it is, or was, there? Why do we think that it might exist? This is where we need, at the very least, to consider seriously possibilities of external intelligences such as extra-terrestrials and the secret programmes apparently undertaken in North America, unknowingly funded, as we indicate in Chapter 12, by the taxpayer. If we are to believe a small percentage of highly credible witnesses, ex-employees at Groom Lake, Indian Springs and other facilities, we are cooperating with either extra-terrestrial beings or forces of future-human origin, and have been doing so since the late 1940s. These beings appear to have advanced capabilities and an understanding of the physical world that we have yet to grasp. It is all too easy to be cynical and write this off as fantastic: 'they' wouldn't do that to us would they? And so on. Yes, 'they' would, and yes, 'they' may well be doing so. I can only urge the reader to take a detailed look at this information and come to your own conclusions. As an indication of just how limited our own horizons are there can be no better demonstration.

Historical clues

Before 1439, we have to seek out the more permanent options of how our history was recorded. Hieroglyphs in the ancient Egyptian genre demonstrate a desire to record for posterity. More difficult, but possibly just as important, are the colossal monuments in Britain such as Avebury[1], Callanish[2], and Stonehenge[3], which, because they were constructed of stone, have survived for thousands of years. Here is where 90% of the 'unused human capability' mystery might begin to be explained. Why were these dolmens erected, and why in such a specific manner and place? Life in this era really was nasty, brutal and short. Why then devote such effort to apparently ceremonial construction? It seems fairly certain that shelter was not a design criteria. We need to ask, were these monuments actually so non-essential? Why on earth were they built? For example, Callanish is a very imposing construction, and located on the Isle of Lewis in the Outer Hebrides[4] miles from any current population density. In ancient times there is ample evidence that the local population was far more numerous than it is today, which would justify construction in terms of the number of people it was built to serve. Even so, why were these enormous monoliths erected? How were they shaped and assembled? We are entitled to both wonder about this and to ask these questions, since our forebears must have had sincere reasons for going to such lengths of time and effort to construct them.

Consider the largely forgotten world of 'earth energies', respect for the elements and the incredible achievements involved in raising these structures. Contemporary technology cannot lift more than 200 tons. How were blocks in excess of 1000 tons moved in ancient times? No satisfactory answer is forthcoming. What tuning mechanism existed to connect the folk to their environment? We understand now, courtesy of the dowsing fraternity and other 'connected' people, how the earth is crisscrossed with subtle energy lines. This energy is with us all the time, and it would seem that our forebears were far more connected with this energy than are we. Did they actually use much more of their brain capability than we are used to doing today? Were they really tuned-in to earth energies in a way that we are only now beginning to comprehend? It may be that early man was far more in empathy with the planet than we know, and knew the importance of a truly close understanding with his environs. Are we somehow able to recall a lost capability, which we intuitively feel is there, but have forgotten how to access? This may explain our phenomenal stupidity when we look at how we have abused Planet Earth. Simply put, did we begin to remove our communication cord with the planet when we began to cover our feet?

Metaphorically, has everything that we clothe ourselves with, including our attitudes to our environment and towards the other species with whom we share the planet, removed our natural cooperation with what surrounds us? We have become greedy, domineering and numerous. We believe in our apparent ability to control everything else. We have become arrogant and over-confident towards everything. We have become used to using available natural resources to the point of outright plunder. We have set about dominating the planet, and anything that obstructed our way towards complete domination has been obliterated.

The natural cycle

Much is written about climate change but, again, there are enormous amounts of sometimes conflicting data available offering information on what exactly might be going on with the world's climate. There are some incontrovertible truths, whether or not you are of the opinion that we face an imminent Ice Age, or that we are destined to perish in heat of our own creation. The polar ice cap is said to be melting at an unprecedented rate, but is it? Hasn't it melted before? Many are of the opinion that it has, and that we happen to be seeing part of a natural cycle which the planet has experienced before. This time, however, we happen to be here to witness it and be a part of the changing circumstances. Regardless of the natural historical perspective, and whether or not we do contribute anything to the current changes, we still owe it to the entire global community of all species to behave rather better than we have hitherto, and to make the place vastly more comfortable for both humans and the other inhabitants. Our position in terms of consumption is critical. It is crucial that we are completely aware of the environmental consequences of what we do.

Ecological insensitivity

Is global ecological degradation the necessary impetus for the evolution of our sensitivities? When we realise that we are only one of many species on our planet, which is full of great diversity, we should have more respect for the impact of the evolutionary part we play. Most informed commentators have arrived at a similar conclusion that we are doing our habitat few favours. New scientific thinking has pretty well concluded that everything is connected, and seems to confirm that for every action there is very definitely a reaction. Whilst this general conclusion has seemingly yet to reach a wide enough audience, even the most reclusive media-resistant individual will know that unless we change our behaviour, the portents, particularly for successive generations, are far from good.

It is now common knowledge that we should be responsible for the successful maintenance of our environment. If we genuinely care about our habitat, we have to begin to consider alternatives to our current profligacy and our attitudes to the space we occupy. We can be certain of one thing – demand for change, not political platitudes, must come from each one of us. We have a window of opportunity before our potential to damage the planet becomes irreversible. We need to stop the senseless wasteful behaviour that has become habitual, and stop assuming that we can behave as we like without negative consequences.

Why are we living with wastage and pollution?

Each individual bears responsibility for the welfare of Planet Earth. We are exhorted to constantly remember:

Don't waste food, use leftovers.

Don't leave the water running when you clean your teeth.

To turn off the lights when we leave a room.

Turn off gadgets, rather than leave them on standby power.

Only use ours car when we have to, otherwise walk.

On an individual basis one could add to this list *ad infinitum*. When we receive unsolicited junk mail our reaction is "here's more wood wasted" or "how many trees did this lot take to produce?" There is a danger that the individual contribution we can all make may stop at a little more recycling and a little reduction in car use – all of which are valuable and make huge collective sense, but these efforts are simply not enough to make the big enough difference in our behaviour that the planet so obviously needs. Letting other people make the effort isn't going to help at all – this involves all of us doing more. How? You might like to conduct a survey of your own – how much uninvited waste does your household take in, then put out again? For example, ten years ago my monthly bank statement consisted of one A5-sized piece of paper, containing all the information I needed. Now, they send me four A4-sized pieces of paper which contains the information I need, and much more information which I don't need and for which I didn't ask. This is unnecessary. Waste concerns us all, and we can do far more to stop it.

Sophisticated packaging is an elderly person's nightmare, and in later years I will surely wonder how on earth I can open the packaging to some product that I have purchased. We all have, or should have, dearly-held 'grumpy old men' or 'grumpy old women' views on the sheer pointlessness of much of the packaging waste that is generated around us as a result of buying consumer products. (Meanwhile, you don't have to be grumpy, or old, to realise the patronising stupidity of the famous packet of peanuts bearing the warning "caution, this product may contain nuts". The day that I buy a packet of peanuts expecting to find inside something else other than peanuts will be my last – the world has truly to find another more sensible way of stating the obvious.)

Environmental abuse is a much-covered subject, and huge quantities of data are available to the dedicated researcher. It is extraordinary to see the advice handed down to us through the media in times of hardship. The blindingly obvious advice we are given bears testament to the enormous waste that would appear to be normal in everyday life. What is difficult to believe is how on earth have we embraced waste with quite such enthusiasm? It seems that only when we are hit in our pockets do we finally pay attention and change our behaviour. If that is truly what it takes to gain the collective attention, economic hardship will indeed contain a silver lining.

The challenges for us to deal with are numerous. How do we stop polluting-behaviour whilst maintaining a level of sensible economic activity, sufficient to keep realistic expectations and hopes of the expanding world population alive? As discussed earlier, the more we realise what our true needs are, and try to consume accordingly, the nearer we are to determining what action truly needs to be taken. The dawning realisation that if you do not have the money then you cannot obtain the product is putting a brake on unnecessary consumption. Lack of available credit annihilates false confidence and you have to face financial facts.

No buy, no make

When we don't buy an item, and countless other people don't either, production of that item will cease. Jobs might be lost and a period of manufacturing adjustment will be inevitable, but there is no other sensible choice or option. We might then begin to see a world economy based upon needs production, with potentially exciting consequences for our expanding world population. This may be seen to be a lofty ambition, but we have little choice but to embrace this sort of change before we have change forced upon us. In any climate of economic hardship and restraint there will be an unintended silver lining. Pointless consumption will certainly be on the decline, as unnecessary expenditure subsides. This must be a good thing for the planet. This must be a good thing for landfill sites. This must be a good thing for all of us.

Travel costs and the freedom to move

It is just as important that we pay a real price of travelling to where it is that we wish to go, either by car, aeroplane, train, bus, tram or horse. Every method of transportation has some cost. It is totally indefensible that we can take commercial aeroplane flights for nothing other than government taxes on aviation. This type of flight was available in the old Soviet Union when a flight from Vladivostock to Moscow cost almost nothing. This was more a reflection on old communist inefficiencies, rather than the business plans that now make such journeys possible at modest personal cost.

Are we prepared to accept curbs on our freedom to travel, because of our inability to pay what our journey really costs? Do we know the impact our journey makes on the atmosphere by polluting aviation emissions? Do we care? Everyone who acknowledges that this is a problem has a moral dilemma; voluntary restriction simply will not work fast enough. Travel by car often proves to be an inelastic demand; for example, we may have to use it to go to work and we have to pay what it costs regardless. There are many things we may not want to do without. Is optional leisure travel one of them?

We are reluctantly left with the price mechanism as the practical alternative, which must mean that the cost of travel tickets should reflect the real cost of taking us where it is that we want to go. It is right to expect that a fair profit margin be included in that ticket to the provider of the travel. Nobody wishes to restrict freedom to travel, but the fact remains that an unpleasant result awaits us should we fail to address this very real problem, which is one of too many people travelling at a cost that encourages more atmospheric degradation. We need to charge realistic consumer prices. We will then discover the true level of realistic demand.

We become part of what we are around

We do become part of what we are around, and these surroundings are a reflection of our cumulative everyday behaviour. We ought to remember that we are part of what we live on too, and that is Planet Earth. We have lost our innate ability to be a working part of the natural world that surrounds us, simply because we think we have found our way of doing things to be the 'right way' of doing things, and because all too often it has just always been done that way or it is simply easier.

Some form of return to intellectual realism might well be apposite; we really don't have to know everything. This may sound heretical, but we are none of us inferior because we don't know everything. Planet Earth has, after all, been here for a long time. We ought not to presume on her hospitality. We need to remember, constantly, that we are a part of the whole, not above the whole. We are all interconnected and we bear a collective responsibility for everything within and around us. Some humility may not be amiss. If enough people question and eliminate poor habits in their lives, we will be on the path of change. The skill for us all is knowing where to look for behaviour that damages the planet and, having identified the problem, act to prevent further abuse.

When we vote by our actions to stop nonsensical consumption, the production of pointless products will cease. This will force manufacturers to be much more in tune with what it is that we really need to purchase. Waste levels will drop dramatically.

Enough talk; positive action now

In order to comment with any degree of confidence about the 'carbon issue', which I have largely put to one side here, please see Peter Taylor's[5] book *Chill.* This seminal work appears to prove that the current economic thrust towards carbon reduction is both pointless and scientifically unsubstantiated. This doesn't mean that we can relax our vigilant attitude toward climate change, but it does explain the facts, and we have clearly been misled from the word 'go'. He confirms my point that elimination of waste is the top target. Furthermore, he seems eminently qualified to comment. Polly Higgins[6], a lawyer who has launched the 'Ecocide' initiative, proposes a law for life and for peace, which places people and the planet first. This law would create an overriding duty of care, and make ecocide an international crime. This has highlighted environmental misuse in a manner calculated to attract a thoughtful and sympathetic audience. To present environmental degradation, ecocide, as a crime against humanity is masterful.

SUMMARY

Our world is our only home. It is time we consciously acknowledged this. What wealth there is should be available to succeeding generations, not simply stolen now to mortgage the future. To use a boxing ring metaphor, the bell has been rung for the end of the round and we continue to fight; we haven't heard the bell. Our behaviour has become so materialistic that we have utterly lost the ability to demonstrate the necessary gratitude for simply being here. We have distorted costs, generated waste and shown powerful disregard for our collective history. We individually take so much for granted that this effectively removes us from the planet as surely as the soles of our shoes do the same thing. We are divorced from the whole and individualise so totally that we are no longer able to appreciate simplicity, to see the beauty in nature or in each other for what it is – the most amazing show on earth. Surely an element of refocus, a pause, an acknowledgement that we have gone too far, might be apposite? The planet can support the volume of population we envisage by 2050, if we care to manage the

prospect in a common sense manner.

Whatever our view on climate change, the evidence suggests that we do need to alter our consumptive behaviour, pay realistic costs of consumption and perhaps accept that not every person alive has the ability or the wish to join in the madness of hyped materialism. If the mad dash to 'become' could transform into the slow realisation of how to 'be', we may have the time to fully appreciate the wonderment of where we are, of who we are and how we relate to where we live – once more, we are part of the whole and we may not step outside the natural world however hard we try. Once we understand this, we know that the boundaries of all we are really are far bigger than we ever imagined and we begin to understand from within ourselves our true place in creation, our immensity and the value of our contribution to the whole. We have overstepped the mark; we are pushing our luck and we must stop doing so. If we can return to simple appreciation, simple gratitude and some mental relaxation, and take a fresh look at all we do and why we do it, we cooperate with our natural world. This is not an option – it is vitally necessary. Failure to change is not an option.

10

SUGGESTIONS FOR WORLD GOVERNANCE

"Politics, Science and Economics do not need conscious voters and consumers. Their independence of publicity, their sense of autonomy and responsibility, their search for meaning changes values – the inner values gain, the outer ones lose. This is bad for political seduction and consumerism".

Two important questions

For the world to function properly, a total rethink of how we organise ourselves internationally and locally is vital. Simply put, we have to provide honest answers to the following two questions:

1. Where is the population?
2. Where is the economy?

Without tiresome statistical analysis by each country, it is perhaps digestible for our purposes to group world populations into three main groupings:

1: Developed economies.
2: Developing economies.
3: The African economy.

1. Developed economies

A: World population percentage estimate 2008 – 20%
B: World gross domestic product (GDP) percentage 2008 – 55%

2. Developing economies

A: World population percentage estimate 2008 – 66%
B: World gross domestic product (GDP) percentage 2008 – 42%

3. The African economy
A: World population percentage estimate 2008 – 14%
B: World gross domestic product (GDP) percentage 2008 – 3%

What is interesting here is the alteration in the statistics since 1988. The developed economies are down 8%, while developing economies are up 8% and Africa remains mired where it was. It is obvious where the biggest problem of wealth creation and distribution lies. Irrespective of the natural resources available to African nations, their peoples make little or no progress. It is a 21st century global challenge to both Africans and the international community that Africans make the best use of their natural assets to the benefit of their impoverished populations. It is wrong that they have made no progress whatsoever in the last two decades. The immediate answer appears to be to sell everything to the Chinese, which will end in tears.

The imbalance between developed and developing economies is marked, but so is the trend *towards* the developing economies. Will this continue in the coming decades, or is the dearth of credit and finance in the consuming Western developed markets likely to strangle growth at developing level? Does this mean that an almost 0.5% annual swing away from developed to developing nations over the last 20 years is likely to continue, or at the very least, stabilise? It is unlikely, given the severe and deep shock to both currency and commodity markets that began in 2008. The era of 'take for granted' growth is over and some reassessment of the world economy is both necessary and overdue. A wider recognition of the need to recalibrate the world economy may be accepted by a wider geopolitical audience. These numbers may be telling us that this may be the situation for some time to come. Indeed, if these current figures can be sustained for the next few years, it will be an achievement for the developing countries to hold their recently gained positions of growth. In my view, if by 2018 the situation is as per the 2008 figures, this will be a big plus to those vulnerable economies who need a continuation of Western consumptive exports. Any slide backwards in GDP toward the developed economies will be disastrous for the developing countries. So much for the status quo. Bearing in mind the simplified numbers given above, what might be done to eliminate the more nonsensical results of global mismanagement, and ensure a more equitable life for all global inhabitants?

A radical reinterpretation of our normal methods of statistical analysis must be applied. In order that world population basic needs requirements are to be met, we know that nothing short of a complete reworking of asset distribution is required. What follows are some very simple ideas, a broad framework that is designed to stimulate organisational thought in alternative directions to those on offer today, which don't work very well. Radical reform in our attitudes to global governance is needed. So why not think the hitherto unthinkable? This is not in any way a plea for a 'One World Government' or 'New World Order', which would be born out of the moneyed and powerful, determined to preserve the status quo and their personal vested interests, meaning no real change at all. This would be instead to reinforce a properly functioning United Nations, representing everyone and every nation. Some wider recognition of the need to recalibrate the world economy may be accepted by a global audience to be both necessary and overdue.

We might call this body 'The United Free World Trade Association' (UFWTA), lest we forget the importance of free trade to all nations. We would be entitled to ask for certain criteria to be met. Some suggestions are provided below. In order for the concept and encouragement of personal freedom to be established, enhanced and maintained, we must insist that free trade be meaningful and enforceable by international law. At the same time, we have to acknowledge that those nation states not yet within the orbit of democratic government organisation must be encouraged to develop their commercial infrastructures. We can hope that democracy might follow. After all, it is a proven fact that communism and socialism do not provide adequate incentives at either the personal or national level, but isolating those states would be pointless. We do not need a two-tier world.

United Free World Trade Association

Below is a population and GDP breakdown table, based upon one world representative per 35 million of population, and the same based upon gross domestic product:

POPULATION				*GDP*		
DEVELOPED	20%	=	39	55%	=	106
DEVELOPING	66%	=	127	42%	=	81
AFRICA	14%	=	27	3%	=	6
TOTAL	**100%**	**=**	**193**	**100%**	**=**	**193**

The enormous imbalances between population and income distribution in gross domestic income terminology are easily seen from the breakdown provided above. A world population estimate of 9 billion estimated for 2050, when divided by 35 million, will give around 257 'heads' for representation purposes. Therefore, we have contingency room for an expanded population number between now and 2050. The number 193 above represents a 2012 population estimate of 7 billion, divided by 35 million. These representative numbers are large but not unwieldy enough to obtain balanced decisions. There is, however, a serious problem. The wealthy countries will look at this table and say, yes, we will hold the majority based upon GDP, and so we should. The developing nations will say, what will change? Africa will nod sagaciously, as Africa must.

There are, at the time of writing, some 196 nations, some with UN recognition, some not. However, the population numbers reveal two facts: the developing and African nations represent 80% of the people numbers, and only 45% of GDP numbers. They are then quite right to observe that if that is the case, and they have the majority of the serious problems of basic human needs, what can and will change if the globe is governed solely in the moneyed interest? Therefore, the permutations that the above tables seem to offer are invalid in each direction. This is the challenge; how can we calculate a workable mixture based on these incontrovertible facts?

It is possible to envisage two forums, one based upon nationhood (Nation Forum) and one upon GDP mix (Economic Forum). This means that every nation would at least have one seat at a meeting of every state, all 196 of them. At the very least, those nations that do not enjoy any influence whatsoever will get to be seated in a forum where their futures are discussed. They might even offer some positive suggestions to ensure a functional and non-'talking shop' atmosphere. The Economic Forum is the challenge; how can we effect a sound and meaningful representative body where developed and developing interests are properly served? There is no proposal here for two separate systems, one economic and another based upon population numbers. A Nation Forum would give countries a chance to discuss their concerns. Any decisions must of necessity go to the Economic Forum, where proportionate interests would be best served. GDP representation of the developed economies need yield only nine representatives to developing nations and Africa, and then we are almost in equilibrium:

DEVELOPED ECONOMIES:	97 representatives	50%
DEVELOPING ECONOMIES:	88 representatives	46%
AFRICAN ECONOMY:	8 representatives	4%

How can we justify this transference of nine representatives without discrediting the whole idea? We are unable still to see a working and equitable mix emerging, but we are getting closer. Without endless and unproductive number engineering here, the point is that there must be a method of arriving at a formula agreeable to the nations of the world which will offer a more workable solution to the same problems of human need that continually go unanswered. Why should there be hungry people in the world? Why should children die of malnutrition when others die of calorific over-consumption or morbid obesity through overeating? Some form of genuine performance-based organisation, with globally-acknowledged power to actually deliver basic needs solutions to problems of food, water and shelter distribution, is long overdue. Some suggestions follow.

Restoration of national viability

At the outset, the implementation of genuine free trade is a prerequisite of the comity of nations. The principle is not enshrined in the Universal Declaration of December 1948. This is an omission. All registered nations should have the right to hold a United Free World Trade Association (UFWTA) licence. The suggested criteria are presented below. Without such a licence, any nation should be subject to a UFWTA-agreed export tariff surcharge, significant to the imposition of what are today known as trade sanctions. This may focus organisational minds.

Any nation wishing to participate in the global economy may hold such a UFWTA licence on six counts:

1: That it maintains a democratic system of government, and has done for a period of ten years. Such democracy must be so defined by UFWTA articles. Any removal of democratic rights from citizens ensures suspension of free trade export privileges for a minimum period of five years. Any military coup would have disastrous consequences for a nation, and would focus minds on maintaining the quality of a democracy.

2: That any non-democratic but non-military system of government allows and permits genuine free trade, allows freedom of travel and communications. This will allow communist states to develop trade and industry, permit the increase in personal living standards and leave open the possibility of future democratic demands. To ignore or isolate communist states, especially China, would be counterproductive since the alternative may be the encouragement of repressive measures as a reaction to international loss of recognition. It would also ignore a lesson of history.

3:. Any new democratic nation created should serve a probationary period of five years, during which time it is permitted to enjoy the same privileges as registered nations. This period of probation is designed to demonstrate commitment to the free trade comity of nations, and to nascent democracy. (This may also prevent 'fake democracy' being claimed by opportunists).

4: The notified register of nations stands at 196, as at 2014. Each nation should be entitled to a seat at the UFWTA.

5: Any nation outside the UFWTA will be subject to export trade penalties – and may not freely trade with UFWTA states.

6: Licensed nations must subscribe to a 'preventative anti-war mechanism'. Failure to do so will result in the loss of the UFWTA licence.

Summary

Our challenge remains: we have increasing populations in cities the size of functioning nations. This calls for proper, real, non-corrupt and meaningful answers to the problems raised by the sheer volume of humanity. It is blindingly obvious that real power must devolve to what is termed 'locality', whatever the size that locale might be. In some cases, this is colossal. We cannot ignore inefficiencies; ultimately people will revolt against the waste of tax revenues because their lives are made more difficult than common sense tells them is right and proper.

11

WHAT NOW AND WHAT FUTURE?

"Science can describe everything, except the one thing that really matters".

War – why we fight and sit together afterwards

Mankind is, as usual, at war somewhere or other. Usually, war involves men dressing up in coloured clothes and killing each other with machines. A wise observation says that testosterone should come with a health warning – it brings life to the womb and destroys it on the battlefield. War stands between civilised behaviour and barbarism; we need to question this habitually ridiculous state of affairs. We will resolve very few of the distribution problems faced by the hungry in the developing world unless we deal with the stupidity and pointlessness of war. We have considered the worldwide and historical consequences of war. We have also discussed the nuclear situation, but is there any point in banning, or trying to ban, nuclear war or nuclear weapons? As observed in Chapter 2, we can't un-invent these weapons. The only obvious solution is the abolition of war itself. Isn't the very idea of having to think about 'abolition' utterly absurd? After all, war is simply part of our collective failure to communicate, a final breakdown in the diplomatic process. We are conditioned to accept the inevitability of war if we don't get our own way as a nation. We are used to the availability of the war option.

War is ingrained in our psyche. Inescapably, the warring factions always finish by sitting around a table together. From start to finish, millions will die; women, children and the elderly are particularly vulnerable. Yet victor and vanquished always sit together afterwards, as any examination of history will demonstrate.

War abolition

Could war actually be abolished, forbidden, eliminated? Under the current political structure of nations, this is impossible or at best unlikely. Some nations already have the means of war, while others have an alliance to obtain the means of war. Others still are simply damaged by the fallout of their neighbours. Either way we are back to strong and weak national political realities. People seem to care not so much for their own survival, but they care enormously to be able to eliminate their enemies. We all know that the international ability to destroy ourselves could find its way into the wrong hands; that way lies World War Three. So why do we run this risk?

The simple fact is that it is impossibly difficult to continually focus peoples' conscious attention on this, the most serious of the problems facing us today.

War is a ridiculous and expensive waste of humanity. The United Nations is a conspicuous failure, as was the League of Nations, formed after World War One. War between the 'weaker' nations, or smaller economic nations, remains a traditional affair, and is firmly non-nuclear. War between any of the larger concerns, principally the United States, Europe, Russia, China and India, runs the very real risk of global annihilation. Such a war would confirm our complete stupidity. However since global free trade is so important to everyone, the prospect of this kind of war does, thankfully, seem to be unlikely. But the costs of deterrent provisions are astronomic, with more and more and more updated weapons to be paid for, and more customers to find for the old versions. How stupid can we be?

Preventative anti-war mechanism

Let us assume a scenario involving an inquisitive state of 100 million people, a state which has designs on a contiguous nation of perhaps ten million people. For simplicity, let's assume the larger state to be State A, and the smaller one to be State B. State B speaks the language of State A, and State A uses this as a pretext to 'acquire' State B in the name of greater security and co-nationalism. They may have been separated by historical treaty. Alert readers will spot a comparison with the late 1930s central European situation; this would be apt. Rather than undertake the usual sabre-rattling and general threats that precede an invasion of sovereign territory, a possible method of popular agreement might work as follows:

1: State A declares its formal intention that it wishes to acquire State B and clearly presents its reasons for so doing. This is a clear statement beyond simply 'extending influence'.

2: State A must hold a referendum asking an unambiguous question of every registered voter whether they agree with what is proposed, or not.

3: 75% must vote in the affirmative or negative. Less than this will leave open the possibility of a slight majority either way, enabling future claims of an invalid result. This would be a conclusive result reflecting real opinion.

4: The same subject and question may not be revisited for ten years from the date of any referendum result. This will prevent cynical manipulation of the result.

5: State B must hold a referendum asking a similar unambiguous question of every registered voter whether they agree with what State A proposes.

6: 75% must vote in the affirmative or the negative. This, as with State A, gives a clear mandate or otherwise.

7: The results and the rules of this process would be monitored and supervised by the UFWTA. Any failure to comply would be met with the withdrawal of the National Trading Licence that must be held by all participating democratic nations.

This ultimate sanction, and the imposition of punitive export tariffs on those nations which fail to engage with the rules, would materially affect any country which would seek to acquire territory and influence by force. This means that unilateral declarations of war, or unlawful incursions into another nation's territory without that nation's agreement, would seriously undermine those regimes and nations who decline to join international civilised methods of behaviour. Their wallets would be hit, and hit hard. We saw in Chapter 10 why this would be so. The uninvited Russian incursion into Ukraine in March 2014 is a classic case. In the absence of an internationally agreed framework of sanctions, the Western nations expelled Russia from the G8 and waited for the inevitable 'tit for tat' reaction.

Given that 20% of us hold 55% of the world's finance, shouldn't we be ashamed that so many starve? Shouldn't we be ashamed that so many lack access to clean water? Shouldn't we be ashamed that so many lack basic shelter? Shouldn't we be ashamed that so many die of preventable disease? Shouldn't we be ashamed that we spend millions on instruments of war? If the world's nations were properly represented, a forum would exist to begin the process of admitting the pointlessness of armed conflict. Persuading the military-industrial complex is the hardest proposition; vested interests currently continue to hold sway, while the poor get poorer and the rich get richer. We are once more reminded of the absurd fact that 85 people hold more wealth than the entire bottom half of the global population does.

The outlook

Small wonder that when the economic outlook is poor, we feel that the future looks somewhat bleak. It needn't be so. The phrase 'steady state economics' has been mentioned, and it is apt. If we can play our part in stabilising the planet, rather than rushing madly for 'growth', the benefits are shared amongst a greater number of people, not just the 20% who already have 55% of the money and who seem intent on expanding this share. To have the individual courage to change is a tremendous contribution. Any concerted group effort to carry out change is therefore wonderful. The benefits to everyone and the environment will be widespread. When we are really capable of acknowledging our interconnectedness with everything, and we stop behaving with a blinkered arrogance that the planet is ours to plunder as we like, we might bequeath a balanced environment for future generations. We all deserve a fair share.

Local commerce

At a local level we are witnessing initiatives which anticipate a reduction in the availability of affordable oil supplies. This presupposes a significant change in our ability to buy certain goods, and places responsibility for local needs on local people. 'Transition' towns are a good illustration. Examples of two such towns in England are Penzance in Cornwall and Glastonbury in Somerset, which became keen to engender local awareness of a potential problem of insufficient energy, for such a shortage will bring in its wake demand and supply problems of many kinds.

Increasingly we are being asked once more to 'Dig for Victory.' Digging is fine, if you have somewhere to dig, and are strong enough to dig, and have an inclination to dig. 'Growing your own', using public transport or walking more are all actions that we know reduce waste and unnecessary consumption, but in times of greater need we may require stronger local business and community infrastructure to help everyone, not just the able-bodied. As a result of the possibility that we might need to face a different kind of future, we should support local businesses because changed circumstances could mean we might not be able to travel very far to buy our needs. That's all very well, if these businesses can supply our needs at a price we are willing to pay, and at a time when we need them to be open and accessible. So we need to remind ourselves why we have lost so many local businesses, and why those that remain must be more acutely attuned to the needs of their customers.

Chain stores

It is worth remembering why the supermarkets, and other multiple chain stores, came into existence and why they are so popular. If you live in a community that has lost its pharmacy, grocer, butcher – ask yourself "why did this happen?" The answer isn't simple. As an apprentice territory salesman in the early 1970s, I visited independent chemists selling well-known brands of over-the-counter medicines. Since then, independent local pharmacies have closed down at a steady rate everywhere, and folk have been forced to make longer journeys to have their medicines dispensed. This is a classic illustration of individual businesses failing to supply what their customers wanted to buy, when they wanted to buy it, at a price they were prepared to pay. The chain stores picked up the challenge, and the results are here for us all to see with cloned identical branches of national chain stores offering identical products, present everywhere. We are increasingly limited for real independent choice. If local businesses are to be successful they will have to offer the range of goods required by local people. Are you prepared to pay considerably more to an independent supplier to keep both that business afloat and your supply line local?

If we are serious about supporting local businesses, we have to remember that they cannot buy in the colossal volumes that will enable low prices to be passed on to the customer. We might also acknowledge:

"The bitterness of poor quality remains long after the sweetness of low price is forgotten".

A customer needs to be reminded why a local business is charging slightly higher prices, and why that price is worth paying. Given that most of us seem to agree that the human species must alter its behaviour for the good of all, imagine for a moment the benefits that positive change could bring. What might our grandchildren look forward to? What next? Our ability to adapt in a changing environment enables us to survive. What happens when we get our voice? At present, if you are able to achieve any response to your communication sent to a government department, you may be sure that it has been composed by a secretary or a research assistant. The truth is likely to be that the minister was "too busy to read his/her mail". Nothing less than a full reappraisal of how our ruling classes behave and perform is being asked for. They will not succeed without determined reform and influence to make a difference.

Restore accountability

As highlighted in Chapter 5, we are simply asking for a genuine restoration of governing ability to listen to the electorate and act upon their wishes. We are, in any event, part of a fast-changing global geopolitical reality. The more people who question what they do, and who recognise that some things are not working properly, are beginning, in many cases unwittingly, to support change. The current political theatre is a self-fulfilling self-replicating fact – if enough folk support empowered local community and its aims, and feel in sympathy with it, the more political representatives will need to listen. After all, an unsatisfied group of people in any electorate which is able to bring itself to the attention of the authorities should be listened to and have their views considered. We are simply asking the politicians to *listen*. It is of supreme importance that the majority of people are able to have their confidence in representation restored.

The non-negotiable need for all of us to cooperate effectively in managing our future in a balanced way means that all of us must play our part. There should be no exceptions and no licences purchased by wealthy corporations to enable them to by-pass the rules at the expense of others. Remember, if we don't buy their products, they must close down; it really is that simple. If we don't care for corporations' attitude to taxation or, put basically, their skill at playing by the rules in order to pay next to nothing, just stop buying their goods – or change the rules. Can those huge international changes now underway find their way down to local community level? An uncertain and ever-changing commercial world means that the days of a 'job for life' are long gone. This has compromised our real freedom, for unless we are able to support ourselves and have responsibility for providing our own basic needs then we are doomed. Our fiscal commitments, when allied with a real sense of job insecurity, may have the mental effect of trapping us in our job. If we are simply average, or not particularly outstanding at what we do, we worry about the possibility of redundancy. The ability, or freedom, to tell our boss what to do with his job is fine in times of full employment. Those days seem to have gone forever.

But is this a disaster? How might we be free to choose another lifestyle and maintain our commitments? A paring down of personal finances to the truly necessary is to restore an element of freedom. There is no point in working hard to fund what may no longer be so important to us. Occasionally, we need to review what it is that we work so hard to fund. Debt is modern day slavery, as we have explored, and there is no escape unless you are freed from fiscal obligation to others.

A future ignored

Why do most older people, who have both time and a wealth of experience, appear to ignore the future? Is this because they have more 'past'? Is this because they have learnt to 'be' rather than striving to 'become'? There are a significant number of experienced people who can help us to achieve the changes we all need, people who may be able to persuade the media to broadcast our messages. I am convinced that we have amongst us very many older people who have a tremendous contribution to make, yet many of them are mistakenly convinced that advancing years automatically brings with them a degree of wisdom that entitles them to pass world problems on to the younger members of society, illustrated by phrases such as:

"Seen it all before".

"Never mind, the young will take care of things, it's their turn".

"What goes around comes around".

More is needed than this. I have yet to reach official retirement age, but I find myself getting more rebellious and more insulted by patronising stupidity, and I am less able to be compartmentalised by an uncomprehending box-ticking bureaucracy. The less we agree with the consensus, the harder it becomes to find sufficient like-minded 'rebels'. You need to be awake to perceive how poorly we are being served by power-hungry self-serving people who are determined to retain power once they have it.

A new United Nations

Who has the intellectual audacity and credibility to provide a framework for a reinforced and meaningful United Free World Trade Association, whose remit is above national interest?

Above all, we need to redeploy military expenditure. War has dominated the history of the human race for thousands of years; we owe our grandchildren a better legacy than perpetuating failure to deal with the expensive results, both economically and personally. The whole planetary future depends on genuinely free trade. This is, it has to be admitted, a massive requirement. It does lie at the heart of humankind, who have the right to live in peace. Article 3 of the UN Resolution 217, 1948, confirms this. We must be up to this challenge – it is no longer enough to shrug and say "that's how things are". One cannot pretend to have all the answers, but individuals must be prepared to at least air the questions and ask for the answers, which is better than simply shaking one's head and wandering away muttering at the insanity of it all.

UN Resolution 217A, 10 December 1948

We are therefore reminded of the previous attempt at a Universal declaration of Human Rights, proclaimed by general Assembly Resolution 217A (III) of December 10th, 1948. That this has not succeeded in the last 60 years is indisputable. However, as a hesitant first attempt, there should be, amongst the 30 Articles, enough to encourage future attempts to solve the burning issues of the moment, which in truth seldom seem to vary. The words Freedom, Dignity, Education, Rights, Life and Liberty are writ large. So is the failure to realise them in too many instances. I present the 30 Articles here, since we must begin somewhere. Perhaps we might make something of this skeleton, and flesh it out with more productive action and not merely rhetoric. It really is about time we did...

This Declaration was intended to be well-publicised throughout all member countries, in places of education particularly. The political status of countries was unimportant to the Declaration. The following is directly quoted:

*

PREAMBLE:

Whereas recognition of the inherent dignity and contempt for human rights have resulted in barbarous acts which have outraged the conscience of mankind, and the advent of a world in which human beings shall enjoy freedom of speech and belief and freedom from fear and want has been proclaimed as the highest aspiration of the common people.

Whereas it is essential, if man is not to be compelled to have recourse, as a last resort, to rebellion against tyranny and oppression, that human rights should be protected by the rule of law.

Whereas it is essential to promote the development of friendly relations between nations.

Whereas the peoples of the United Nations have in the charter reaffirmed their faith in fundamental human rights, in the dignity and worth of the human person and in the equal rights of men and women and have determined to promote social progress and better standards of life in larger freedom.

Whereas member states have pledged themselves to achieve, in cooperation with the United Nations, the promotion of universal respect for and observance of human rights and fundamental freedoms.

Whereas a common understanding of these rights and freedoms is of the greatest importance for the full realisation of this pledge.

Now, therefore, The General Assembly proclaims This UNIVERSAL DECLARATION OF HUMAN RIGHTS as a common standard of achievement for all peoples and all nations, to the end that every individual and every organ of society, keeping this Declaration constantly in mind, shall strive by teaching and education to promote respect for these rights and freedoms and by progressive measures, national and international, to secure their universal and effective recognition and observance, both among the peoples of member states themselves and among the territories under their jurisdiction.

ARTICLE 1:
All Human Beings are born free and equal in dignity and rights. They are endowed with reason and conscience and should act towards one another in a spirit of brotherhood.

ARTICLE 2:
Everyone is entitled to all the rights and freedoms set forth in this Declaration, without distinction of any kind, such as race, colour, sex,

language, religion, political or other opinion, national or social origin, property, birth or other status. Furthermore, no distinction shall be made on the basis of the political, jurisdictional or international status of the country or territory to which a person belongs, whether it be independent, trust, non-self-governing or under any other limitation of sovereignty.

ARTICLE 3:
Everyone has the right to life, liberty and security of person.

ARTICLE 4:
No one shall be held in slavery or servitude; slavery and the slave trade shall be prohibited in all their forms.

ARTICLE 5:
No one shall be subjected to torture or to cruel, inhuman or degrading treatment or punishment.

ARTICLE 6:
Everyone has the right to recognition everywhere as a person before the law.

ARTICLE 7:
All are equal before the law and are entitled without any discrimination to equal protection of the law. All are entitled to equal protection against any discrimination in violation of this Declaration and against any incitement to such discrimination.

ARTICLE 8:
Everyone has the right to an effective remedy by the competent national tribunals for acts violating the fundamental rights granted him by the constitution or by law.

ARTICLE 9:
No one shall be subjected to arbitrary arrest, detention or exile.

ARTICLE 10:
Everyone is entitled in full equality to a fair and public hearing by an independent and impartial tribunal, in the determination of his rights and obligations and of any criminal charge against him.

ARTICLE 11:
1. Everyone charged with a penal offence has the right to be presumed innocent until public trial at which he has had all the guarantees necessary for his defence.

2. No one shall be held guilty of any penal offence on account of any act or omission which did not constitute a penal offence, under national or international law, at the time when it was committed. Nor shall a heavier penalty be imposed than the one that was applicable at the time the penal offence was committed.

ARTICLE 12:
No one shall be subjected to arbitrary interference with his privacy, family, home or correspondence, nor to attacks upon his honour and reputation. Everyone has the right to the protection of the law against such interference or attacks.

ARTICLE 13:
1. Everyone has the right to freedom of movement and residence within the borders of each state.

2. Everyone has the right to leave any country, including his own, and to return to his country.

ARTICLE 14:
1. Everyone has the right to seek and to enjoy in other countries asylum from persecution.

2. This right may not be invoked in the case of prosecutions genuinely

arising from non-political crimes or from acts contrary to the purposes and principles of the United Nations.

ARTICLE 15:

1. Everyone has the right to a nationality.

2. No one shall be arbitrarily deprived of his nationality nor denied the right to change his nationality.

ARTICLE 16:

1. Men and Women of full age, without any limitation due to race, nationality or religion, have the right to marry and to found a family. They are entitled to equal rights as to marriage, during marriage and at its dissolution.

2. Marriage shall be entered into only with the free and full consent of the intending spouses.

3. The family is the natural and fundamental group unit of society and is entitled to protection by society and the state.

ARTICLE 17:

1. Everyone has the right to own property alone as well as in association with others.

2. No one shall be arbitrarily deprived of his property.

ARTICLE 18:

Everyone has the right to freedom of thought, conscience and religion; this right includes freedom to change his religion or belief, and freedom, either alone or in community with others and in public or private, to manifest his religion or belief in teaching, practice, worship and observance.

ARTICLE 19:

Everyone has the right to freedom of opinion and expression; this right includes freedom to hold opinions without interference and to seek, receive and impart information and ideas through any media and regardless of frontiers.

ARTICLE 20:

1. Everyone has the right to freedom of peaceful assembly and association.

2. No one may be compelled to belong to an association.

ARTICLE 21:

1. Everyone has the right to take part in the government of his country, directly or through freely chosen representatives.

2. Everyone has the right of equal access to public service in his country.

3. The will of the people shall be the basis of the authority of government; this will shall be expressed in periodic and genuine elections which shall be by universal and equal suffrage and shall be held by secret vote or by equivalent free voting procedures.

ARTICLE 22:

Everyone, as a member of society, has the right to social security and is entitled to realisation, through national effort and international cooperation and in accordance with the organisation and resources of each state, of the economic, social and cultural rights indispensable for his dignity and the free development of his personality.

ARTICLE 23:

1. Everyone has the right to work, to free choice of employment, to just and favourable conditions of work and to protection against unemployment.

2. Everyone, without any discrimination, has the right to equal pay for equal work.

3. Everyone who works has the right to just and favourable remuneration ensuring for himself and his family an existence worthy of human dignity, and supplemented, if necessary, by other means of social protection.

4. Everyone has the right to form and to join trade unions for the protection of his interests.

ARTICLE 24:
Everyone has the right to rest and leisure, including reasonable limitation of working hours and periodic holidays with pay.

ARTICLE 25:
1. Everyone has the right to a standard of living adequate for the health and wellbeing of himself and of his family, including food, clothing, housing and medical care and necessary social services, and the right to security in the event of unemployment, sickness, disability, widowhood, old age or other lack of livelihood in circumstances beyond his control.

2. Motherhood and childhood are entitled to special care and assistance. All children, whether born in or out of wedlock, shall enjoy the same social protection.

ARTICLE 26:
1. Everyone has the right to education. Education shall be free, at least in the elementary and fundamental stages. Elementary education shall be compulsory. Technical and professional education shall be made generally available and higher education shall be equally accessible to all on the basis of merit.

2. Education shall be directed to the full development of the human personality and to the strengthening of respect for human rights and fundamental freedoms. It shall promote understanding, tolerance and friendship among all nations, racial or religious groups, and shall further the activities of the United Nations for the maintenance of peace.

3. Parents have a prior right to choose the kind of education that shall be given to their children.

ARTICLE 27:

1. Everyone has the right freely to participate in the cultural life of the community, to enjoy the arts and to share in scientific advancement and its benefits.

2. Everyone has the right to the protection of the moral and material interests resulting from any scientific, literary or artistic production of which he is the author.

ARTICLE 28:

Everyone is entitled to a social and international order in which the rights and freedoms set forth in this Declaration can be fully realised.

ARTICLE 29:

1. Everyone has duties to the community in which alone the free and full development of his personality is possible.

2. In the exercise of his rights and freedoms, everyone shall be subject only to such limitations as are determined by law solely for the purpose of securing due recognition and respect for the rights and freedoms of others and of meeting the just requirements of morality, public order and the general welfare in a democratic society.

3. These rights and freedoms may in no case be exercised contrary to the purposes and principles of the United Nations.

ARTICLE 30:

Nothing in this Declaration may be interpreted as implying for any state, group or person any right to engage in any activity or to perform any act aimed at the destruction of any of the rights and freedoms set forth herein.

*

Everything on the above list of articles in the UN Resolution points to Freedom, Rights, Liberty, and Respect.

Other very important considerations are mentioned on this list such as 'enjoyment', 'public order', 'welfare', 'education' and 'adequate standard of living' (all things that so many of us take for granted).

It should be noted that Article 21 states quite clearly:

"Everyone has the right to take part in the government of his/her country, directly or through freely chosen representatives".

It has been said that democracy is the "least poor method of government", and perhaps that is so. In which case, let's make the best of the best option that we have.

Isn't it time for all of us to value and uphold our democratic rights ?

SUMMARY

As the global population grows, so does our pressing need to resolve our problems of inequality and unfair distribution of needs-based assets. If we are to avoid the constant repetition of endlessly failing attempts to solve age-old problems, we stand to face never-ending and increasing pressure from those unfortunate enough to live in failed states. This is why a genuine United Free World Trade Association is crucial, or at the very least such an organisation that can give some hope to those nations outside the real world power bloc as it exists today. The tragedy of thousands of people fleeing their homelands in order to try and find a peaceful existence in stable countries for their families is testament to chronic mismanagement and a failure to understand different mentalities. Trade is the passport to economic progress and prosperity; without it there is no hope and no political stability, which in turn impacts world peace. Some effort to spread wealth more evenly without patronising subsidy is essential if we are to escape the dreadful prospect of yet more violence and the inevitable slide back to the Dark Ages.

The United Nations as it stands today appears to be toothless and at best inconsistent. We can reorganise in a fresh way should we care to recognise the malaise in an honest and frank manner.

12

THE GRANDEST LIE?

"Man needs to choose, not just accept his destiny".

Extra-terrestrial contact

It is apparent to anyone capable of analytical thought that our wisdom quotient as a species is abysmal. We are often unable to reconcile the law of unintended consequences with our technological output. This is nothing new, but as we make further progress technologically, we have reportedly become more interesting to those civilisations said to exist outside our planet. There is a widespread, and informed, view that extra-terrestrial (ET) races exist and that contact with them has been regular and ongoing.

When we unearth the facts (no pun intended) and if needs be redirect the military complex dollars to more constructive and positive use, we might be ready to join an intergalactic community. This is a regular and consistent theme amongst researchers. This chapter, which begins this book's deliberate and, some would argue, necessary diversion from the previous 'real-world' subjects so far covered, is emphatically not simply an examination of ET or Unidentified Flying Object (UFO) phenomena, but has been included to make the point that it is an important subject if indeed we are not alone. I will leave the results of research and deduction to you, the reader. My intention is to reveal where this potential might take our civilisation, and the consequences of ignoring the possibility of there being ET civilisations. In order to do this, we have to make 'Truth' a uniting and common currency. It is as well to recall the words of twice-President of the USA Ronald Reagan[1], who observed that we would bury our differences quickly if faced with an off-planet threat. It is a pity that such an event has to be a prerequisite for cooperative civilised behaviour in the here and now.

What if..?

What has the interested observer of such phenomena to make of the seemingly never-ending confusion of often conflicting presentations, articles, books, films, claimed witness testimony and endless conversations? Until evidence is converted to proof, how are we to determine the motives and sincerity of those who offer themselves as agents of clarification? Almost every researcher at some point draws negative criticism; one person's snake oil salesman is somebody else's harbinger of the New Dawn. It is very possible to take seriously an individual who seems by all reasonable personal observation to be telling the truth, yet that person may later be exposed as a fraud and a liar.

The 'truthseeking' community therefore has the problem of adding increasing numbers of enquiring minds at sufficient speed in order to effect timely change of attitudes. For example, if 9/11 was the false-flag event that many claim, it is of scant interest to those now living if this is not established for another century. It is of scant interest to the relatives of those who perished. As for ETs, I ask that you thoroughly investigate the subject, since if it is true that governments are cooperating with off-world intelligences then it has enormous implications for almost everything we do and how we do it. (Concluding comments on 9/11 may be found in Chapter 13. *If* that is the greatest cover-up in history, what else is possible?)

Rules of engagement

One of the challenges of the Internet age is the personal ability to sift through what is true and what is not. You can use only your intuition. Try to separate from your disbelieving and battered mindset – it has been called 'mind chatter' – and both look and listen to this material with as open a mind as you can muster. Once an individual researcher or whistleblower comes to your attention, you now are able to easily enquire further into who and what they are, who else is impressed with what they have to say, who confirms their story and why, and who has had parallel experiences and when. Literature is also available in some quantity.

The same rules of engagement always apply: check your source with great diligence. The conspiracy theory community work steadily, as they are similarly disappointed with the status quo and simply want, in most cases, to reveal the truth. There may well be an international cover-up on the ET subject, for what might seem good reasons to those in charge. We might ourselves know that they are good reasons if we were ever allowed to be a party to the facts, the details of which we have been denied.

So... if we are not alone?

For many decades, the world community has witnessed countless thousands of aerial sightings of UFOs, reported countless off-planet 'abductions' of humans, of which more later, and seen extraordinary mutilations of animals, the demonstrated surgical dexterity of which seems impossible to explain. We do not possess the technology to undertake this surgery in the field or, if we do, it is a clandestine capability restricted to 'black operations'. These statements may be bold, but what is undeniable is that the UFO phenomenon has been subject to a well-documented cover-up at the highest levels of government. What is crucial to proper analysis is the differentiation within the UFO subculture between the sensationalist and dodgy video salesmen, and the serious researchers and campaigns for the disclosure of government-held facts.

It is also reported that the USA and other governments are in strategic and material cooperation with ET representatives from whom they have obtained technology, the details of which have not been disclosed or shared. If this is so, why have we been left out of the communication 'loop' with these races? For those who scoff at the very idea of high-level government involvement, the UK Ministry of Defence (MOD) ran a desk devoted to this subject in order to accumulate data. It was manned by Nick Pope[2], author of various books on the subject. Although Pope has been accused of being a cover story in himself, authorities surely must monitor anything that could be potential ET phenomena. That, it might be argued, is a sign that the subject is indeed taken seriously.

Can we cope with the truth?

We sometimes hear that evidence of ETs is withheld because "we couldn't cope with it" – '*it*' being the fact that we are not alone, and never have been. If this is so fanciful, why not open the files to wider scrutiny? That 'they' may be visiting us is nothing fresh either. There is a vast amount of documented evidence in ancient structures which demonstrates that visitations may have been going on for millennia. Cursory examination of the construction of the major Egyptian pyramids, and many other similar structures in South America, demonstrate a technical ability to move granite blocks heavier than we are able to move today. These structures were built with a precision that clearly illustrates advanced capabilities, so why should ET involvement always be ruled out as "laughable nonsense"?

However, reports suggest ETs appear to have renewed interest in us now, because our technological advances seem to be beginning to make us an interesting prospect, and therefore we may have something to offer off-planet civilisations. If we are prepared to acknowledge that a greater non-earthly community exists, ancient versions of Homo Sapiens probably didn't have much to contribute to such a galactic community. Our slow development into a technically capable society seems to have begun with the nuclear detonations over Japan in 1945. It is widely believed that this is the point when we came to extra-terrestrial attention, so they came to look again at what we were up to. They found Homo Americus and Homo Sovieticus. This mattered to them because by demonstrating a capacity to destroy the planet, our activity might eventually have profound consequences for the elliptical progress of those planets that surround us.

The USA's developing Strategic Defence Initiative (SDI) is a classic example of offensive space weaponry that could be deployed, whilst being dressed up publicly as merely a preventative system. Quite what we would contribute to an intergalactic community at present is a good question.

Humankind back to the sandpit?

If ET intelligences are present today, though, an announcement of this fact might well present problems. Dogmatic religion, for instance, would have to answer many questions, which it almost certainly could not do. Perhaps the simple truth is that humankind *isn't* prepared for this contact. This truth has, however, reportedly been manifest on our behalf and without consultation – how does one prepare the world, though, without 'letting the cat out of the bag'? Many feel that we *are* ready for interaction with off-planet intelligence, and that we actually need it. This attitude can be readily forgiven, as we seem to be making such a mess of things that any positive contribution ought to be gratefully received. But maybe we do not seem to be playing our own planetary game well enough to satisfy the rules of engagement that intergalactic relationships appear to observe. Given mass contact, there is every chance that we would shoot first and ask questions afterwards. Such a misguided action is more likely, however, if the rules of engagement haven't been discussed in advance. It is true that most of us are probably not prepared for this type of eventuality.

Put crudely, perhaps we are not advanced enough to be allowed to join in with the big boys and girls. We still kill each other, we let some starve whilst others get morbidly obese, we plunder our planetary resources with no regard for the future and we unthinkingly rely on technology for our future, without intelligent philosophical questioning. We haven't worked out the simplest ideas of cooperation between ourselves. Until we achieve cohesion here on Earth, our invitation to join in the bigger picture will probably remain unissued. We have to learn to give up fighting. We cannot legislate for this alone; we must educate for it. We don't yet deserve an invite to a more sophisticated party. This means we will have to sort ourselves out, properly and without ambiguity. This has to start with our own person, driven from within. We are unlikely to accept a lecture from others on this subject; it happens when we finally realise for ourselves that the bigger picture is being falsely reported, and it begins to really matter to us. Until we do, we remain vulnerable to speculative explanation as to what is really going on when we discuss ET invaders or visitors, depending upon our viewpoint.

As I mentioned at the beginning of the Introduction, I became aware of something 'going on' in 2006. What is was then was unclear, and many other people were similarly unaware, yet the top of the information egg was being removed, slowly but very surely. A process, at least, has been started.

Our restlessness with our current situation leaves us wide open to any form of apparent redemption; this could take the form of the arrival of the Strong Man, as already mentioned, or simply our willingness to put inordinate volumes of faith in any sudden mass-ET contact. Those who do not shoot at them might hail them as redeemers instead: "They must be good and beneficial; it's all positive, they are fine with us". This is how we might explain and justify our utter lack of control in managing the presence of off-planet races, because this will be the reality. If we can't sort ourselves out, 'they' might. But there is widespread agreement that 'they' will never do this, or that if they did it would be a disaster. If you believe that outsiders will "sort us out", you have lost all belief in our ability to manage our future and the future of our children. Worse, you've lost the belief in yourself. Why voluntarily give the future away to unknown and unelected entities without debate? Make no mistake, these presences, if they are here, are uninvited by almost all of us. What agreements or treaties may have been arrived at on our behalf is anybody's guess.

Abductions

Whether it is happening in a realm of mind or in physical reality, if you have experienced an 'abduction' type of ET contact, did you ask for this? I thought not. If this had happened in your everyday life, the perpetrator would be in a court of law, swiftly. Since you have no control over this, you might reluctantly come to comply with a situation you would never normally tolerate, otherwise you are unable to begin to justify why you are putting up with this violation. You are being taken advantage of, full stop. If this is happening, then why? One possible explanation for this interference is genetic manipulation; there seems to be no other credible explanation. This ties in with Dan Barusch's[3] testimony. If you were a three foot-tall 'grey' ET you'd probably be looking for a few better body parts too, especially if you regret your collective mistakes made long ago to abandon one path of anthropomorphic development in favour of another that turned out to be a huge mistake. Where could you go to obtain fresh parts? This could explain the genetic requirement. It also repositions Planet Earth as a genetic warehouse, to which we do not have a set of keys.

Correcting future mistakes?

Interestingly, one theory is that the greys are not extra-terrestrial at all, but human visitors from another time. If these little fellows are us from our future, might we be looking at the physical consequences of no exercise, looking at screens or holo-displays all the time and being fully technology-driven? It might explain the reported frail bodies (you don't need much of a body to do little physical effort), big head (bigger brain with telepathic capabilities and other enhanced mental functions), small mouth (no need to eat much either since you have a small body), big eyes (receive all external stimuli and work as a camera/thought transference system), small legs and arms (again, little physical effort required) and no ears (nobody talks, all communication is telepathic). This reflects our increasing tendencies to lack of exercise, more time in front of screens of one type or another, and our willingness to adopt more technology into all aspects of our lives. Can we take a long view and place ourselves thousands of years into the future and look at what we might become?

Is this what we are seeing with the greys? Did we morph into chronic frailty? It is not an impossible leap of imagination to connect these observations with what appears to be happening to the human race today. Life expectancy is growing, yet simultaneously we suffer more and more chronic disease and frailty. Employing some subtle logic to these factors could well tie the present to the future. Will we regret the direction we took from a distance of anything from 10,000 to 60,000 years ahead?

Are many of our ET contacts therefore of human origin? There are humanoid similarities, so it should be considered. I do not propose to regurgitate the wealth of data on this phenomenon, which is widely available. Writers and researchers on the abduction phenomenon have shrewdly asked that if this *isn't* happening in physicality, and yet folk all over the world report similar experiences but who don't know of each other's existence, then what is going on? If this is some mass-collective mind experience it still explains little. Abduction has been examined in great detail by, for example, the late Dr John Mack[4] and Dr Kenneth Ring[5]. Either way, we have a problem.

Fact or fiction?

'Facts' are definitive truths, based upon proof, but they are somehow incomplete except in relation to a purpose, a whole. The "don't take my word for it, check the facts for yourself" exclamation from some researchers is an admission that what has been said is incredible. But isn't the listener, or the reader, entitled to rather better? What is the listener/reader paying for, if not an enhanced opinion? Speculation simply requests that additional questions be asked. If such speculation provokes greater interest, which then adds some positive material to the debate, all well and good. What needs to occur is a direct contribution to the truth, otherwise the merry-go-round continues; but it is not always merry. This leads us elsewhere. In short, we require credibility.

You may be reluctant to investigate further, or don't have the required amount of time (substantial), so I offer some bare bones of testimony that you might find illuminating. Further comment is made in Chapter 13. Again, the testimony of Dan Barusch is riveting and seems to me to be a sensible exploratory avenue. His story ties in with the evidence of Charles J. Hall[6] in his quadrilogy series *Millennial Hospitality*. Barusch maintains that grey 'ET' visitors are indeed ourselves from our future thousands of years ahead, and who have the capacity to travel in time. Hall offers complimentary evidence and personal experiences of on-the-ground contact with a 'tall white' race. He also offers convincing scientific conclusions in his fourth book in the series. He maintains that Einstein[7] didn't quite get all the numbers required. I thoroughly recommend reading these books for an intimate experience of what purports to be ET practicalities when visiting Planet Earth.

If we fail to reorganise...

As mentioned above, if we fail to get a grip it has been suggested that there is the prospect of uninvited assistance coming to our aid. We are unlikely to be overtly invaded in the traditional sci-fi manner, as we have observed, as this seems not to be the style of ET or future-us interests. It has been suggested that their techniques would be those of persuasion and deception; they would present themselves as agents of change. This makes sense, since an old-fashioned conquest by violent means would further depreciate planetary assets and be counter-productive. For external agencies, it may be easier by far to integrate and ingratiate. As we have seen, the abduction scenario appears to indicate that their species is biologically deficient and that they seek our genetic material. If so, we are being utilised, pure and simple. There can be no other logical explanation; this is manipulative behaviour without cooperation. As a balance, some abductees do claim that they have very positive experiences, with unfolding relationships between the ETs and their human subjects, so there may be some ambiguity here, but the tendency does seem to be towards these scenarios being uninvited.

The available reports also tell us that the abductors are not suited to our environment. This might be so for some races, but not necessarily for all races, since it is commonly held that there are several differing ET species.

If – and this is a big 'if' – we subscribe to the view that innovations such as free energy systems have been reportedly 'buried' for many years, the deep space programme of the USA and technology-sharing cooperation with ET intelligences or future-humans will eventually need to be both exposed and the reasons for their long suppression explained – but we need to accelerate the process of social preparation and education on such issues so that our civilisation doesn't fall apart when it happens. If such claims are true, aside from the scandal of all the undeclared financial costs of all this secrecy and hidden technology, presumably held back for military advantage as well as social concerns, it also remains the grossest insult to us all that a tiny few maintain the handle on information that means we do not in fact need to plunder the planet of natural resources. There must be collaboration occurring with the financial wielders of power as well as the political. As we have noted, 85 people possess more money than 3.5 billion of us. Derived technology from 'other' sources would almost certainly render fossil fuel extraction unnecessary and obsolete, and ruin many long established income streams – which may be part of the problem.

Obsessive and pointless secrecy is becoming more and more difficult to maintain, as those who reportedly worked in black operations in the USA are willing to testify. Detailed examination of this on the Internet will yield what would appear to be positive, trustworthy and intellectually provocative information that cannot and should not be ignored, although, as ever, a degree of deliberate misinformation out there also has to be taken into account. This calls for a degree of personal sophistication in order to filter the huge amounts of misleading propaganda from the truth. A significant proportion of this period up to 2047 will reflect our willingness to absorb the importance of the decision that we must take as a species – do we properly acknowledge the critical condition in which we find ourselves, and take the sensible decisions we can take to ensure our future? Or, do we accept the blandishments of the New World Order as offered by leading political figures for the last few decades? If we accept this, we lose our freedoms. We also lose our influence to help direct what comes next. The New World Order *will* succeed if we do nothing. Then it will be far too late to do anything about it.

SUMMARY

To the uninitiated but mildly curious reader, much of this chapter will seem fantastic. It has often been remarked that the truth can be stranger than fiction. Nothing is easier for those in elected authority than to utterly deny these "fantastic stories" as science fiction, fables, prurient, ridiculous, along with many other pejorative adjectives. As I have suggested, try for a moment to step outside any preconceived negative ideas you may have on the question of ET intelligence – for what if even a fraction of this is true? To lend credibility to this subject, there are highly qualified people involved in ET research whom it may be fairly said are not 'bonkers'. As we have observed, something is going on. This alone is worthy of sophisticated and informed research. Above all, the mixture of questions we are required to answer in this area is broad and all-encompassing. Not only are we asked questions of science, we are asked questions of philosophy too. The investigators and truthseekers ask us to question the very foundations of society, the reported extent of scientific discovery and the veracity of

information we receive. The global consequences of any admission that we are not after all dependent on fossil fuels would be enough to ignite an enormous debate on just what else has been withheld from the world community. One may be forgiven for assuming that this alone would unite world opinion in firmly rejecting any 'New World Order' and foment an insistence on clear, truthful and real investigation on what else has surely been hidden in the vested interest.

What would follow an official acknowledgment of other intelligences being amongst us would itself be a huge challenge; the initial chaos of the necessary change would be horrendous. So much better then, if we grasp the opportunity to carefully prepare the ground, disclose the truth and be proactive in changing our social organisation for ourselves, in good time and in our own time.

13

BEYOND CONSPIRACY THEORY

"To see what is right and not to do it is want of courage".

Inferential scrutability

'Conspiracy theory' is an inevitable, and perhaps necessary, thought process in a world of sometimes obvious deception, but it can also be in danger of being exposed as self-serving by negative and hysterical self-promotion. Laudable though many efforts are to expose the truth, the overall approach is all too often scattered and uncoordinated. It is useful to remind ourselves of David Chalmers' description of the 'Knowability Thesis':

"For any truth S, it is possible that someone knows S".

This is different from the 'Scrutability Thesis':

"Every truth is scrutable, or derivable from a limited class of basic truths".

Whilst I am determined not to be overly analytical, the above definitions are classic conspiracy theory indicators. They assist us in channelling or processing what we told by the theorists. As Chalmers indicates, 'inferential scrutability' isn't especially troubled by questions of analysis or *a priori* truth – fertile ground indeed for below-par explanations of events that seem to us to be suspect. Note the "limited class of basic truths". This can offer much upon which to build.

The poor and declining reputations of our political representatives lends us more and more to seeking alternative offerings of the 'Truth', but too many of us seem no more inclined to do the research on conspiracy theories than we are willing to do research on regular media offerings. As already noted, we are often exhorted by speakers, authors and filmmakers to "not take my word for it – do the research yourself". This presents a paradox: on one level we should indeed probably all make the effort to find out more, yet at the same time quite why we should repeat verbatim the work and offerings of those to whom we often pay to hear an enhanced, more factually-informed view of what interests us is also a reasonable question. Either way, the reality is that, on inspection, conspiracy theories do sometimes start to seem more factual than the 'official' versions of events, when what is presented by authorities as "The Truth" seems even more fantastic by comparison. The mainstream media lie too often, so we give up. We no longer trust what we are offered by way of 'news', nor do we trust the organisations that provide it. As we have observed, a free press is a mirage.

Conspiracy theorists, or truthseekers, depending upon your viewpoint, must, however, retain a credible and reliable relationship with the absolute truth, which I argue must always be based in scientific fact, or at least take a fully logical, rational approach. If something is untrue, it is not factual, and this usually becomes obvious over time. Issuing ever-more seemingly incredible variations on what are essentially forecasts is unhelpful.

What is the interested observer to make of the never-ending confusion and conflicting opinion around conspiracies? Until evidence is converted to proof, how are we to determine the motives and sincerity of those who offer themselves as agents of clarification? If one person's snake oil salesman is indeed another person's bringer of the New Dawn, how can we learn to tell the difference? The truthseeker community therefore has the problem of amalgamating sufficient interested opinion on a timely basis – introduction to the more incredible aspects of their views at an early stage of personal interest can confirm to newcomers that they have found a crowd of nutcases. But the more people who demonstrate credible concern with the mainstream reportage of an event – in other words, a report that seems to be both unlikely and untrue to them – the more likely the case may be made for a serious forensic investigation to be mounted on a timely basis.

The crop circle phenomenon is a classic example of what became a debunked and seemingly widely discredited phenomenon – discredited due to outright lies and misrepresentations by unscrupulous press agencies. This physical manifestation of patterns in the crops is no modern occurrence; its origins go back hundreds of years. Whatever personal take one may have on this extraordinary manifestation of calling cards left overnight (usually, although daytime events also occur) in the agricultural fields of England and elsewhere, a more balanced explanation is called for. The negative publicity and downright lies peddled in the national media in the early 1990s put paid to continuing and important ongoing proper research into just what was happening in the fields. Twenty-five years later, any mention of crop circles will bring forth a comment such as "they're all hoaxed, of course" from people who have never been within a mile of any of these formations, of which there have been *thousands*. This means that any progress in terms of continuing investigation remains very difficult, and misguided opinion holds sway. This is too often the way that many alternative theories are dealt with by the mainstream.

It remains true that institutional lying must be successfully eliminated, or we will continue to hear conspiracy theories which highlight and indeed encourage our distrust of elected government, and which continue to undermine trust in that most delicate area of philosophical discussion; politics. This is the art of social organisation, and it's serious. It is of scant benefit to anyone to attend yet another conference denouncing the Bilderberg Group[2], Majestic-12[3], The Nazis[4], The Masons[5], and any other organisation that by intense research might be said to have a 'darker agenda', working under the New World Order[6] umbrella. This much we know already. But if truthseekers' further claims are not supported by factual proof, those claims remain speculation. More than this is now required.

Clearly, we need fresh collective deep thinking and reasoning when we consider our current situation, which both environmentally and economically remain under pressure. Whether we like it or not, we are looking at nothing less than an entire re-examination of what we do and how we do it, what is important to us and why; and a questioning of moral values away from nihilism and individualism and towards genuine community. This means total reform of the way the franchise works. This is essential, or we face an Orwellian future not of our choosing, but one which we unconsciously invite. Inaction means connivance with others unknown to us, taking us in directions we neither voted for nor approved of.

To this end, conspiracy theorists, with their presentations that bring awareness of New World Order threats and the like, are actually highlighting nothing other than what senior politicians of the Western alliance have been seen to be in the mainstream media for ages. We should not be surprised at this; we have been clearly told for years what the agenda is. So we need to consider this truth, and what we can do with it. Factual investigations are the most important area of truth research for deeper insights, and this is where we need to be extremely vigilant. How can we be sure that what we discover is factual? The Internet is an ever-expanding potential minefield of data, much of which may be successfully discounted. My late wife found that website articles accompanied by loud music often present the poorest quality of content. This may or may not be valid, but it is necessary to discover filters that are applicable to what it is you wish to uncover. The ability, or lack of it, to spell is surely another indicator of reliability.

YouTube power

YouTube will yield enormous volumes of lectures, videos, seminars and radio recordings, which examine any subject in which you care to show interest. Whistleblowing reporters are particularly interesting; look at Project Camelot[7], for example. Kerry Cassidy[8] and Bill Ryan[9] have unearthed an incredibly interesting group of people prepared to blow the whistle on the most extraordinary government and extra-governmental organisations. I have mentioned several names in other chapters. If one tenth of what they claim is true, it seems we have no idea that we have been born. We have no knowledge of what has been technically achieved in our unknowing absence – or rather, what has gone on underneath our feet, literally in some cases. We have no idea of the enormity of the military-industrial complex, its siphoning-off of colossal numbers of tax dollars without accountability or the incredible power it exercises way beyond presidential seniority. Dr Steven Greer[10], of the Disclosure Project[11] movement in the USA has assembled an impressive array of US military personnel who are prepared to testify before Congress under oath in order to relate their experiences of apparent extra-terrestrial contacts. You simply couldn't make some of this up. I defy any imagination to dream up the methodology of the American deep space programme, the back-engineering projects of extra-terrestrial equipment and the cooperation between the human race and others perhaps from our future.

Until recent claims were made public via the Internet through the likes of Greer's work, we had no idea that government collusion with ET beings was anything more than a fantastic assault on our individual credibility. Similarly, did we have any idea that travel faster than the speed of light was possible – at 670 million miles per hour? This is the briefest of descriptions as to the type of material that is available for you to consider. The majority of people have simply no idea that this material is there, while those that do cannot really know how credible or otherwise these contributions are without careful discernment. What is certain is that at least some of the whistleblowers do seem to be very credible indeed, and are unafraid to provide details of their provenance and experience. Many have held high-ranking positions in both regular military intelligence and in the military-industrial complex, sometimes via black operations. It isn't overly difficult these days to establish personal credentials, and we have to do this with these messengers. Liars and frauds need to be exposed quickly.

Many are willing to accept an alternative view, simply because it makes sense to them and a weight of evidence is there to be found. This explains why there is often a stark and instinctive rejection of the 'official' line. Intelligent people become fed up with being constantly being fed lies. This highlights the educational challenge once more; the onus is on us to filter what we are told, and we must educate ourselves to do it. But it is unquestionably the case that there are common threads that unite the most extraordinary experiences of some individuals. The idea that truth can be stranger than fiction applies to inter-governmental cover-ups to a staggering degree.

What is indisputable is this; that if just 10% of conspiracy claims are true, the foundations of an admittedly poor democratic system are founded upon sand at best. The entire planetary population has, by various degrees, been systematically conned, deceived, lied to, stolen from, murdered, starved, infected and generally abused beyond satire.

9/11

Of all claimed state conspiracies, the events of 9/11[12], as inadequately reported by the authorities, certainly do not appear, on closer inspection, to be the result solely of overseas terrorist activity. Many suspect that either 'inside' aid was given, or the events were wholly planned, with the aim of giving a mandate for the New World Order-sponsored wars and restrictions on freedom that have followed. This is one area of research that I do urge anyone to spend time on, if only to satisfy yourself that such a claim does have a foundation in reality. It must be the greatest false-flag event in history, and therefore one of the greatest crimes of the 21st century. This is nothing short of a total disgrace, and an insult to humankind all over the globe. None of which you will ever be told of, officially. The official line will remain accepted by the majority, with appalling results for the possibility of a peaceful future. When qualified airline pilots, architects and structural engineers question the veracity of the official report into the events of 9/11, we are fully entitled to ask serious questions and to expect an honest answer. These people, after all, have the credentials which qualify them to comment on this event, and they have personal reputations to maintain.

If the events of 9/11 – which is the biggest atrocity to occur in recent years yet to be satisfactorily explained – were to be investigated as the crime it undoubtedly was, regardless of who was responsible, it should not be inordinately difficult to investigate this event forensically according to the usual rules of crime scene investigation. Instead, no such proper investigation has ever been conducted, with full responsibility simply being given to Middle Eastern terrorists from the start.

We outlined some of the many problems with 9/11 on page 67, but a final point of evidence should also be considered. For those who believe the official report to be a truthful explanation of the facts, then exactly how is it that World Trade Centre Building 7 later collapsed in apparent sympathy with the twin towers which fell some hours earlier – despite never having been hit by an aeroplane and with just a few fires? This is a fair question to ask; it's simple enough and requires a truthful answer. The official explanation of unusual structural behaviour due to supposedly concentrated heat is woefully inadequate on inspection. Many believe the building was brought down deliberately to cover evidence of 'authorised' involvement in the events of the day. Just what is required to unlock the recorded evidence in a court of law to establish the real facts?

Before the truthseeking community, and those who present what we understand to be a 'conspiracy theory', can go too much further in other areas, in general there has to be a greater connection with the facts. In short, there needs to be a far greater 'hit rate' with the conversion of theory into fact. 9/11 is a classic example of a high-likelihood theory where many seemingly indisputable facts *are* being gathered to provide a strong case against the official version. If, as many authoritative and qualified observers claim, there has been a monumental cover-up, we have to find a way of either proving once and for all that this was potentially the worst criminal event of this century, or the authorities charged with disseminating the government version of the 'facts' must answer the legitimate concerns of qualified observers. Other conspiracy subjects must follow suit with comparative fact-gathering diligence if they are to find similar legitimacy.

Frankly put, we currently have no better opportunity of highlighting deceit and mismanagement at the highest levels, if it exists. 9/11 was no individual assassination; this has involved thousands of deaths, in a busy metropolitan district of a major US city. In order for alternative viewpoints – call them theories if you will – to be laid to rest with due reference to the known facts, this simply has to be faced. At stake lies the ethical behaviour of the Western world's only superpower. If the US (or, perhaps more specifically, traitorous forces within it) is indisputably found to have acted against its citizens in this manner, God help us all. The consequences are too awful to contemplate. Other ideologies will have every right to vigorously pursue their own 'truth' doctrines in the face of blatant hypocrisy, and say "we told you so". The 'infidel' will have been found guilty at the top of its voice, and in doing so alienate the entire population of the planet. The USA will lose what credibility it has left and become a pariah state by its own definition.

Truth on trial

9/11 is the opportunity for all sides to finally nail the truth and to display the facts. Truth is beyond conspiracy theory; it is the next step. The question of what we do with the truth will then exercise independent minds. If guilty verdicts for Western culprits were to be realised after due process, what to do with the miscreants, never mind the terrible fallout of confidence in the legislature which would surely occur? How we manage such a truth would be a task of such magnitude that one wonders how it could ever be done without hysterical, emotional and, in many eyes, entirely justified retribution. That challenge faces the civilised world, and those areas of extremist opinion would enjoy the torment that the USA, and any other collaborative agencies, would face. But that is no reason to leave this crime to history; we need to know what happened, if only to stop an even greater miscarriage of human management in the future.

SUMMARY

As we have observed, it is important to be extremely careful in sourcing opinion on such seemingly fantastic scenarios. Again, we must be mindful of the truth constantly; if it seems fantastic it may just possibly be fantastic – but surely not all of the claims can be a pack of lies told by those out to deceive the gullible. The ability to 'sift' information remains vital. Should a line of research promise a deep and interesting journey, be ready to spend considerable time and effort pursuing just that. It is difficult to avoid the conclusion that the more deeply hidden the facts, the more liberty and prosperity we all stand to lose as a result. An open mind is a pre-requisite; an open and free society is a global necessity.

14

COHERENCE, CONSCIOUSNESS AND SPIRITUALITY

"In the absence of an acceptance of Coherence, we carry on using the kind of rationality which will create conflict because it will concentrate power and wealth and it will continue to devastate the environment".

The human condition

We are all unique, as is our view of the universe and everything contained therein. Our view of an all-encompassing God, or not, is unique to each and every one of us. In our quest for survival we have unique thoughts, individual to us alone, but we share thought patterns, sometimes logical and sometimes non-sequential. We also share the ability to suffer the anguish that accompanies the human condition, which is often because of loneliness, isolation, fear of loss and the sheer burden of life without a known connection to any source.

We sometimes struggle for deep meaningful answers to these questions, at some point during our earthly lives. When we examine some of our emotional senses, we may have come to very basic conclusions that life is to be aware, to feel, to care, to love... it also means having a very definite respect and understanding for our position on the planet, ourselves and all living creatures. We should be aware that in order to *be* rather than to become, we can avoid the regression that appears to be taking place amongst the human race. So many people drown in a sea of debt that they effectively join the animals once more in looking for their next meal as their prime objective on a daily basis. In other words, more people than ever are in 'survival' mode. We hear words such as 'coherence', 'consciousness' and 'spirituality', used often as a type of common currency amongst aware and open-minded people, for example at conferences where such folk gather.

What, though, do we really mean by these words, and how can we relate to them in our everyday lives? I offer some simple explanations here, since these words often mentally frighten people. They can sometimes convey a pseudo-academic language that seems to stray into the scientific realm – therefore 'they can't apply to me'. Once more, plain language is helpful.

Coherence

Coherence seems to be the ultimate reality, the oil which enables the parts to function as one immense connected unit. The function of one part is dependent on the next part, so everything is a part of the whole. In the known universe everything appears to be tuned together, thereby producing a system of true coherency, which means everything working together systematically. Co-creating a healthy world with the certain knowledge that we are interdependent will give us the courage to discover the necessary skills of love and cooperation in order to create a different future. This has been called 'The Intelligent Aether' by Jim Lyons. Jim was a chief engineer on future technology programmes and spent time examining the idea that the cosmos is *not* held together by gravity. 99.999%, he maintains, is the fourth state of matter, or plasma. This self-organising field creates cosmic structure and also organises the information (mind, or 'Bosonic') world energy field, or the torsion field. This is something that has been observed in some crop circles.

This is a simple but smart description, and calls into question the word 'nothing'. There is no such thing as empty space. There is a simple way of considering 'The Whole', since this resembles a complete jigsaw in its entirety. Every single piece fits beautifully, and there are no exceptions. Not one of us can defy the system; when we understand this we may be able to better see where it is that we fit into all this, for fit into it we do. This engineering is so precise that there is an intense and harmonious beauty to the construct, in much the same way that when you look in the mirror, the image cannot be improved. So it is with natural engineering... it is the ultimate machine, superbly oiled and constructed to last all lifetimes.

Consciousness

Consciousness may be described as being awake. Quite literally, if you are not unconscious, then you must be awake. This is, for many people, rather different to being aware of one's consciousness. So to be 'aware', or truly 'awake', rather than going through habitual motion, to be confident in your quiet knowledge and to take your place in the natural order, is to possess attributes of consciousness. We might describe some of these attributes as clear vision, or the ability to see all sides of the equation; joy, or the ability to enjoy the moment and go with the flow; time to ponder and reflect and to acknowledge our dependency on one another and the need to be honest. This knowledge may make one's daily passage through life simpler and easier. This has been described as a step towards enlightenment, because it is. It has been said that we should make our experience on earth all the more precious – we have as yet no absolute evidence that consciousness is accomplishing a similar task elsewhere in the universe, although the claims of ET visitations (Chapter 12) may yet throw a new light on this. The premise of interconnectedness is that we have potential access to an unlimited field of information. This is by virtue of our membership in an unbounded domain of consciousness.

We considered in Chapter 9 the 'hard-wired' concept, the 50-year period to unlearn much of what we have become, because we are around it all the time. Institutionalism, our recognition and emergence from it, is a conscious decision.

Spirituality

Spirituality is the 'intention' which, when coupled with the realisation that some action must be taken, gives us a direction in which to go. The same traditions and skills that nourished our ancestors, who had a more direct relationship with the natural world, are experiencing a renaissance. We are starting to ransack our past to discover a rich pattern of existence, as the monuments our forebears left us seem to testify. Many of us spend so little time outside that we no longer have much natural connection/communication with our habitat. When we rediscover deeply hidden lines of communication with ourselves and our planet (which come from within) such as the ability to dowse earth energies, this is testament to the power of spiritual communication. This we may choose to call a skill, but it is in fact an innate ability. This is bringing us back into a more harmonious and coherent relationship with the planet, and is as direct a contact with Mother Earth as one could wish for.

The anthropomorphic God

At some point long ago in the pre-Christian era, animism (the belief that all matter in some way possesses a spiritual dimension) was a functioning and respected belief system. To the casual modern eye, this might seem oddly naive and even immature. At what point did an anthropomorphic deity assume divine status at the blatant expense of everything else? Our collective arrogance at our practical domination of the natural world somehow qualified us to nominate a God looking much like us. When asked to visualise God, the instant mental image for many is of an elderly, wise-looking gent with long hair and a beard, sitting in judgement on a throne with a benevolent smile on his face. Our religious histories specify the prophets as humans; they sit 'at the right hand of God the Father' or sit under trees waiting for enlightenment, and they are most definitely presumed to be of human origin. So God, since he is 'the Father', became human in our own image. The ancient written word confirms the anthropomorphic concept of divine authority, be it Jesus Christ, Mohammed or Buddha. But God does not have to be portrayed in our image; God is omnipotent.

When people are insecure and adrift, the Church is no longer the first authority to whom they turn. The old saying "religion is what people do with their solitude" is no longer wholly valid. In times of uncertainty one may listen to anything that answers the cry for help. In our increasingly desperate quest to acquire meaning to our lives, some of us have a tendency to cherry-pick spiritual meanings from other cultures, particularly those of the East.

It is interesting to note that Eastern religions do not descend into the patronising dogma of Western religions, and therefore appear to have retained larger numbers of adherents. Human control over other species appears to have led us to conclude that God had better be in our image. The following excerpt from *The Upanishads*[1], the sacred Hindu texts, clearly demonstrates an Eastern viewpoint, establishing the idea that, indeed, we're all in this together and that the concept of God is altogether far more encompassing and non anthropomorphic:

"We try to direct our thoughts to the Infinite Light which is God, Truth, Love, and is beyond our understanding. We try to realise that it is everywhere, both outside us, and within us; that we as human beings are carriers of the Divine light here on Earth, that it dwells in our hearts, that our bodies are the Temple of the Living Spirit, and we should let this Spirit shine through our eyes, speak through our words, be felt through our deeds. Then we send a thought of peace and love to all those around us, to our family, our friends, those who we love, those whom we do not love, to all living beings on the earth and beyond".

From the unreal to the Real,
From darkness to Light,
From death to Immortality,
Peace.

The Shaman Chant 1, iii, verse 28, *The Brihadaranyaka Upanishad*

Some people may be highly spiritual folk who feel that they are simply detached from society, and that what is right and even 'proper' for them is simply not part of society's equation. As they see it modern society does not represent them adequately. What can we offer people who feel disconnected from the existing system? Those of us who realise that change is necessary will call for deep and lifestyle-altering change, for everyone. How we plan and implement these changes will depend on how far and how fast each of us is prepared to go. The greater the degree of personal responsibility we take, the easier the overall task becomes. Be kind to other people, because in some sense they *are* you.

SUMMARY

An awareness and an admission that there are other ways to deal with each other than simply waging war can be developed into understanding. We need to be open to the possibilities of discussing our way through our

difficulties rather than aggressively muscling our requirements to the head of the personal or the international queue. Before we reach that happy state of affairs, we could usefully consider a more open, and in some ways more relaxed point of mental view: the realisation that we hold so many answers within us, and that continual materialism is not and never will give the answers to what we think are our problems. It is natural that we should seek a higher understanding of our position in life, and it is natural that the acquisition of that understanding will take time. Until we realise this for ourselves – and this can never be taught – we will search for answers and dig deeply into any culture or belief mechanism in order to satisfy our curiosities. This explains our keen interest in Eastern philosophies; we are always seeking solutions to what we believe to be our spiritual undernourishment caused by materialism.

It could be said that a personal acknowledgement of these three 'States of Grace' indicate a powerful awareness that there is more to life than we have been educated to understand. They take us further in our realisation that to 'be' is vital, that the moment is true realisation, that the now is particularly special, and that we are uniquely special in our ability to be able to really enjoy that fabulous position. We waste inordinate amounts of time trying hard to ignore this incontrovertible fact. We waste huge amounts of time protecting tomorrow and worrying about, and feeling guilty about, our pasts. This is corrosive and pointless. There may be different roads, but the destination remains the same for all of us. Nobody is immune from error.

Were we to really understand this, we would realise with stunning clarity that much as we are all born, we are destined to move on eventually and surrender the physical. We ought to take steps to think about what it is we have in common – which is everything. In much the same way, some thought devoted to what comes next is not wasted thought, but is an acknowledgement that in some way we may yet understand that there is more to life. It may even make our lives less of a trial than we are determined to make them through our own mismanagement. Another step towards what we are pleased to call 'enlightenment'? We are endowed with three priceless attributes; the ability to achieve a high degree of consciousness; the ability to become internally truly free; and the extraordinarily deep ability to love.

EPILOGUE:

UNREALISED HEAVEN

"Drop the idea of becoming someone, because you are already a masterpiece. You cannot be improved. You only have to realise this to know it".

At some point in our lives, the jigsaw of life heads for completion and those things that confused us become much clearer. The fabulous simplicity in everything, where once it seemed so complicated, enables us to view life with an objectivity we may not have possessed even a few years ago. As one seven billionth of the global population, we are nothing. Yet when we look in the mirror, we are everything. We are therefore nothing and everything, a realisation that is so simple and yet so complex that what results is the most elegant simplicity of all. This realisation can help us to accept that we will never, can never, know everything. This doesn't matter; it doesn't make us inferior. Rather it releases us to understand how we relate to our surroundings, and all we encounter is our part in the grand theatre. We are all actors in this play. We all matter and we all need one another. Any 'sunrise' is a new dawn. So it is with finally growing up. It's personal and at the same time collective. Once we identify and deal with our ego, we are 'there'. We all need to grow up at some point. We all need to wake up at some point. That is true freedom.

We sometimes stand in our own way, seemingly determined to interfere with common sense and equally determined to ignore basic principles of cooperation with one another, our environment and even our real and true selves. Why must we endure catastrophe to achieve change? We don't need to and we shouldn't. We should simply grow up. Once we grasp the fact and understand that we are the unrealised heaven, we will have achieved a level of sufficient understanding to make some realistic progress as a functioning society. Everybody deserves to be a part of what is heaven, since that is what we were designed to be.

NOTES

ACKNOWLEDGEMENTS

1. **Jim Lyons** – Visiting professor, dowser, linguist and aeronautical engineer, scientific adviser to the Centre for Crop Circle Studies.
www.dowsingresearch.org.uk
2. **Hamish Miller** – Blacksmith, dowser and author. Born 1927, died 2010. *www.penwithpress.co.uk*
3. **Andy Thomas** – Author, mysteries researcher, lecturer, co-organiser of the Glastonbury Symposium. *www.truthagenda.org*
4. **Iain McGilchrist** – Neuropsychiatrist, fellow of All Souls College and author of *The Master and his Emissary: The Divided Brain and The Making of the Western World*, published in 2009.
5. **Thomas Hobbes** – Philosopher and author of *Leviathan*. Born 1588, died 1689.

INTRODUCTION

1. **Glastonbury Symposium** – Annual conference devoted to 'truth, mysteries and new frontiers'. *www.glastonburysymposium.co.uk*
2. **David Chalmers** – Philosopher and author of *Constructing the World*
www.consc.net

CHAPTER 1

1. **Frances Fukuyama** – Author of *The End of History and The Last Man*, published 1992. Co-signatory of the 'Project For The New American Century'. Born 1952.

2. **Robert Kagan** – Author of *The Return of History and The End of Dreams*, published 2008. Born 1958.
3. **Jalaluddin Rumi** – Persian poet and theologian. Born 1207, died 1273.
4. **George Walker Bush** – 43rd President of the United States of America 2001–2009. Born 1946.
5. **Scott McClellan** – White House Press Secretary, author of *What Happened?*, published 2008, a summary of US government reaction to the events surrounding September 11th, 2001.

CHAPTER 2

1. **Isaiah Berlin** – Philosopher and historian. Born 1909, died 1997.
2. **Johannes Gutenberg** – Printer and publisher, inventor of the printing press 1439. Born 1395, died 1468.
3. **William Caxton** – Printer and book retailer, introduced the printing press to England. Born 1415, died 1492.
4. **Voltaire** – French philosopher, historian and author of 99 books. Real name Francois Arouet. Born 1694, died 1778.
5. **Denis Diderot** – French philosopher, writer and art critic. Born 1713, died 1784.
6. **Jean le Rond d'Alembert** – French philosopher and mathematician. Born 1717, died 1783.
7. **William Pitt the Younger** – Twice Prime Minister of England 1783–1801 and 1804–1806.
8. **King George III** – King of England 1760–1820. Born 1738, died 1820.
9. **Napoleon Bonaparte** – Artillery officer, came to power in France 1799, declared Emperor Napoleon I 1804–1814. Born 1769, died 1821.
10. **Edmund Burke** – Whig Member of Parliament for Bristol 1774–1780. Born 1729, died 1797.
11. **'Peterloo' Massacre** – 1819: Dragoons slay 20 members of the public at a reform rally at St Peter's Field, Manchester, UK. 700 casualties overall.
12. **Wellington, Duke of** – Victor of the battle of Waterloo, twice Prime

Minister 1828–1830 and 1834. Born 1769, died 1852.
13. **Charles James Fox** – First Foreign Secretary, three times Secretary of State 1782, 1783 and 1806. Born 1749, died 1806.
14. **Dunwich** – Famous 'Rotten Borough' that returned two members of Parliament despite being mostly submerged off the south coast of England. Abolished by First Reform Act and absorbed into East Suffolk.
15. **Lord John Russell** – Four times Prime Minister of Great Britain, 1852, 1846–1852, 1865–1866 and 1865–1866. Born 1792, died 1878.
16. **Bertrand Russell** – Philosopher and mathematician, Author of *A History of Western Philosophy*, published 1945. Born 1872, died 1970.
17. **Queen Victoria** – Queen of England 1837–1901. Empress of India 1876–1901. Born 1819, died 1901.
18. **Lord Melbourne** – Prime Minister of Great Britain 1835–1841. Queen Victoria's mentor in the early years of her reign. Born 1799, died 1848.
19. **William Ewart Gladstone** – Four times Liberal Prime Minister of Great Britain, 1868–1874, 1880–1885, 1886 and 1892–1894. Born 1809, died 1898.
20. **Benjamin Disraeli** – Twice Prime Minister of Great Britain, 1868 and 1874–1880. Created Earl of Beaconsfield 1876. Born 1804, died 1881.
21. **3rd Viscount Palmerston** – Twice Prime Minister of England 1855–1858 and 1859–1865. Foreign Secretary 1852–1856. Born 1784, died 1864.
22. **Robert Owen** – Welsh industrialist mill owner, philanthropist and originator of the Trade Union Movement. Coined the phrase 'socialism'. Born 1771, died 1858.
23. **Sir Robert Peel** – Twice Prime Minister of Great Britain 1834–1835 and 1841–1846. Born 1788, died 1850.
24. **Lord George Bentinck** – Leader of the Tory party in the House of Commons 1846–1850. Horse racing stable owner. Born 1802, died 1848.
25. **Joseph Paxton** – Creator of the Crystal Palace for the 'Great Exhibition' of 1851. Member of Parliament and architect. Born 1803, died 1865.
26. **Viscount John Morley** – Cabinet Minister under Gladstone, Gladstone's official biographer. Born 1838, died 1923.
27. **Richard Ashetton Cross** – Home Secretary in Disraeli administration 1874–1880. Lancashire solicitor, created 1st Viscount Cross in 1886.

Born 1823, died 1914.

28. **Versailles Treaty** – Signed 1919 in Paris, France, and concluded The Great War of 1914–1918.

29. **Hernán Cortéz** – Spanish Conquistador of South American Aztecs. Born 1485, died 1547.

30. **King Edward VII** – King of Great Britain 1901–1910. Born 1841, died 1910.

31. **King George V** – King of Great Britain 1910–1936. Born 1865, died 1936.

32. **Fidel Castro** – Communist leader of Cuba 1959. Born 1926.

33. **Adolf Hitler** – Leader of German National Socialist Movement (Nazis) 1933–1945. Author of *Mein Kampf*. Born 1889, died 1945.

34. **Joseph Stalin** – Politburo President of the Union of Soviet Socialist Republics (USSR) 1929–1953. Born 1878, died 1953.

35. **General Erich Ludendorff** – Military leader of German armies 1914–1918. Born 1865, died 1937.

36. **Benito Mussolini** – Italian Fascist leader 1922–1943. Born 1883, died 1945.

37. ***Mein Kampf* by Adolf Hitler** – Volume 1 published in 1925. Volume 2 published in 1926. Translates into English as 'My Struggle'. Sets out Hitler's thinking for Germany's post-Versailles Treaty future.

38. **Clement Attlee** – Lawyer and Labour Party Prime Minister 1945–1951. Wartime cabinet minister under Churchill, responsible for Home Affairs. Born 1883, died 1967.

39. **Winston Churchill** – Twice Prime Minister 1940–1945 and 1951–1955. Born 1874, died 1965.

40. **General de Gaulle** – Prime Minister of France 1958–1959, President of France 1959–1969. Leader of wartime Free French government in exile in the UK 1940–1944. Born 1890 – died 1970.

41. **Richard Mulhouse Nixon** – President of the USA 1969–1973. Author of *The Real War* published in 1980. Born 1913, died 1994.

42. **John Fitzgerald Kennedy** – President of the USA 1961–1963. Assassinated in Dallas, Texas, by gunshot. Born 1917, died 1963.

43. **Organisation of European Economic Cooperation** – Created 1948.

44. **Charlemagne** – Ruler of Europe 768–814. Crowned Emperor of the Romans by Pope Leo in 800. Born c742, died 814.
45. **John Lennon and Paul McCartney** – Songwriters, members of the 1960s group The Beatles. Lennon born 1940, murdered by gunshot 1980. McCartney born 1942.
46. **Leonard Cohen** – Canadian poet, musician, author and songwriter. Born 1934. *www.leonardcohen.com*
47. **Bob Dylan** – Singer, songwriter. Real name Robert Zimmerman. Born 1941. *www.bobdylan.com*
48. **The Wright Brothers** – Credited with the first manned flight in 1903. Lasted 12 seconds and flew 120 feet.
49. **Hamas** – Democratically elected Palestinian government in 2006.

CHAPTER 3

1. **Islamic State** – Extremist Islamic revolutionary group.
2. **Boko Haram** – Islamist group. Translates into English as 'Western education is forbidden'.
3. ***Charlie Hebdo*** – A satirical magazine published in Paris, France.
4. **Barack Obama** – Democratic President of the USA 2009. Born 1961.
5. **Saddam Hussein** – Sunni B'ath party leader of Iraq 1979–2003. Born 1937, executed 2006.
6. **Lord Balfour** – Tory Prime Minister of Great Britain 1902–1905. Author of the 'Balfour Declaration'. Born 1848, died 1930.
7. **David Ben-Gurion** – Twice Prime Minister of Israel 1948–1953 and 1955–1963. Born 1886, died 1973.
8. **Al-Qaeda** – Translates into English as 'The Base'. Idea formed by Al Qtub, an Egyptian, in 1955. Said to have been officially formed by Azzam and Osama bin Laden in 1988/89.
9. **Menachem Begin** – Twice Prime Minister of Israel 1980–1981 and 1981–1983. Commander of 'The Irgun' (see 10 below) 1942. Born 1913, died 1992.

10. **'Irgun'** – Organisation devoted to ridding Israel of the English, and establishing the Jewish State of Israel. Created in 1931, disbanded in 1948.
11. **Martin McGuinness** – Member of the IRA (see 12 below), Deputy First Minister of Northern Ireland Assembly 2007, member Sinn Fein. Member of UK Parliament 1997–2013. Born 1950.
12. **Irish Republican Army** (IRA) – Devoted to reuniting divided Ireland through terrorism. Established 1922, disbanded 1969. Not to be confused with breakaway groups such as the 'Provisional IRA'.
13. **The RAND Corporation** - Or 'Research ANd Development', a thinktank research company. *www.rand.org*

CHAPTER 4

1. **Paul Stiles** – Author of *Is the American Dream Killing You?,* published in 2005.
2. **St Andrews University** – Based in Fife, Scotland.
3. **Scientific and Medical Network** – An interdisciplinary networking forum and educational charity exploring science, medicine, philosophy and spirituality. *www.scimednet.org*

CHAPTER 5

1. **3rd Marquess of Salisbury** – Also Lord Salisbury/Viscount Cranborne. Tory Prime Minister of Great Britain 1881–1885, 1886–1892 and 1895–1902. Foreign Minister under Disraeli 1874–1880. Born 1830, died 1903.
2. **Herbert Henry Asquith** – Liberal Prime Minister of Great Britain 1908–1916. Earl of Oxford and Asquith 1925. Born 1852, died 1928.
3. **David Lloyd George** – Liberal Prime Minister of Great Britain 1916–1922. Present in cabinet through the Great War. Born 1863, died 1945.
4. **Tony Blair** – Labour Prime Minister of Great Britain 1997–2007. Born 1953.

5. **Charles Ponzi** – Italian national credited with the invention of 'pyramid selling'. Born 1882, died 1949.

CHAPTER 6

1. **YouTube** – Video-sharing forum company established 2005, acquired by Google in 2006.
2. **Google** – Internet search engine company formed in 1998 by Sergey Brin and Larry Page.
3. **George Orwell** – Writer, real name Eric Blair, author of *Nineteen Eighty-Four, Animal Farm* and *The Road to Wigan Pier* amongst others. Born 1903, died 1950.
4. **The Open University** – Designed for distance learning, inaugurated in 1969.

CHAPTER 7

1. **Colonel Muammar Al Gaddafi** – Libyan dictator 1969–2011. Born 1942, died 2011.
2. **The Taliban** – Literally, 'Students'. Nationalist and fundamentalist Islamist organisations in Afghanistan and Pakistan.
3. ***Hidden Persuaders*** – Written by Vance Packard, published 1957. Born 1914, died 1996.
4. **Stephen Hawking** – Theoretical physicist and cosmologist. Author of *A Brief History of Time*, published 1998. Born 1942.
5. **Robert Mugabe** – Zanu PF Head of State of Zimbabwe, formerly Southern Rhodesia. Democratically elected Prime Minister 1980, assumed Head of State title in 1987. Born 1924.
6. **David Ricardo** – Author of *Principles of Political Economy and Taxation*. MP 1819. Born 1772, died 1823.

7. **Fred Harrison** – Author, and director of The Land Trust.

CHAPTER 8

1. **Facebook** – Social media website.
2. **Twitter** – Social media SMS system. Messages are restricted to a maximum of 140 characters.
3. **Instagram** – Photograph-sharing web platform.

CHAPTER 9

1. **Avebury** – Prehistoric stone circle complex in Great Britain near Marlborough, Wiltshire. Silbury Hill is adjacent.
2. **Callanish** – Standing stone monument near Stornoway on the Island of Lewis, Outer Hebrides, Scotland.
3. **Stonehenge** – Iconic monument of standing dolmens near Amesbury in Wiltshire, England. Believed to date from around 2500 BC.
4. **Outer Hebrides** – Chain of islands off north west Scotland. From Barra in the South to Lewis in the North is approximately 130 miles. 15 inhabited islands. Population is approximately 25,000.
5. **Peter Taylor** – Climatologist and author of *Chill*, published 2009, an exposure of the myths surrounding climate change. Born 1948.
6. **Polly Higgins** – Lawyer and proponent of an international law of 'ecocide'. *www.eradicatingecocide.com*

CHAPTER 12

1. **Ronald Reagan** – Actor and President of the USA 1981–1989.

Governor of California State 1967–1975. Born 1911, died 2004.
2. **Nick Pope** – Ministry of Defence employee 1991–1994, tasked with running the MOD's UFO 'desk'. Left MOD 2006. Author of several books on the paranormal. Born 1965.
3. **Dan Barusch** – High Security Clearance operative located in Indian Springs. Intimate contact claimed with ET beings of humanoid origin.
4. **Dr John E. Mack** – Psychiatrist and author with special interest in 'abduction' experiencers. Professor Harvard Medical School. Born 1929, died 2004.
5. **Dr Kenneth Ring, PhD** – Author of *The Omega Project*, published in 1990. Professor Emeritus of Psychology, University of Connecticut. Also researches 'near-death' experiences. Born 1936.
6. **Charles James Hall** – Author of the *Millennial Hospitality* quadrilogy. Weather observer at Nellis Air Force Base, Nevada, USA. Contact claimed with 'tall white' extra-terrestrials. *www.millenialhospitality.com*
7. **Albert Einstein** – Scientist. German citizen, emigrated to USA 1933. Became US citizen in 1940. Published 'Theory of Relativity' 1916. Born 1879, died 1955.

CHAPTER 13

1. **Crop circles** – Swirled patterns occurring in agricultural fields. Records go back to the 1600s, with photos available from 1932. At first largely circles and rings, their development into extraordinary glyphs in recent decades has attracted great fascination and controversy. Current reports can be found at: *www.cropcircleconnector.com*
2. **The Bilderberg Group** – A committee of the powerful and moneyed interests. Meets under Chatham House Rules – which means complete secrecy. Said to have been formed in 1954.
3. **Majestic-12, or MJ-12** – A top level military/scientific committee of twelve, said to have been formed in 1947 after the Roswell UFO crash.
4. **The Nazis** – National socialist movement begun in post-war Germany,

elected by 'democratic vote' in 1933, led by Adolf Hitler. Formed from the German Workers' Party,

5. **The Masons (or Freemasons)** – Organisation originally of stone masons that has grown into a flourishing networking group of the influential.

6. **The New World Order** – Ongoing global power project admitted to by various politicians, including both US Presidents Bush and Clinton, and British Prime Ministers Tony Blair and Gordon Brown.

7. **Project Camelot** – Available on YouTube and dedicated to publicising 'whistleblowers', especially dealing with hidden technologies, black military budgets and paranormal-themed unpublicised material. *www.projectcamelotportal.com*

8. **Kerry Cassidy** – Co-presenter of Project Camelot.

9. **Bill Ryan** – Co-presenter of Project Camelot until 2010. Now runs Project Avalon. *www.projectavalon.net*

10. **Dr Steven Greer** – Chairman of The Disclosure Project.

11. **The Disclosure Project** – *www.projectdisclosure.com*

12. **9/11** – The destruction of the World Trade Centre twin towers and WTC building 7 in New York, the attack on the Pentagon in Washington DC, and the crashing of Flight 93 on September 11th, 2001.

CHAPTER 14

---

1. ***The Upanishads*** – Sacred Vedic texts in Sanskrit. Highest form of sacred thought: 'the closer one's soul is with everything' or 'sitting close to'.

INDEX

Photography by James Burns

The beautiful cover photograph for this book, *A Future World Vision*, was taken by James Burns, from his growing portfolio of impressive images entitled *London from the Rooftops* ...

On his website, James writes: "*London from the Rooftops* is my mission and my ode to the city that I love and the city that made me who I am. My teenage years were marked by a curiosity and fascination with my surroundings... My journeys led through the back streets, to the housing estates, the top floors of tower blocks, and eventually to the rooftops. Something compelled me to explore London's remote aerial limits so I could build in my head my very own version of what the black cabbies call 'The Knowledge'.

The journey started in some form in the late 1990s, but it really began to take shape in 2003 when I realised how the camera was the easiest way for me to express and document this growing connection that I felt with London.

By 2004 The Princes Trust had recognised my passion, helped me to find my first local authority clients and to get set up in business as a professional photographer. Two years of intense photographic activity followed and, by 2006, *London from the Rooftops* had really begun to take shape... Not content with just shooting from social housing high rises, I set about gaining permission to shoot from central London's office blocks. Years of building contacts and relationships passed whilst all the time I was strengthening my portfolio in the knowledge that one day it would be my defining body of work.

The mission goes on; London never stops and neither will my enthusiasm for its wonderful energy, diversity, architecture and culture."

Find out more about James Burns and his work at:

http://londonfromtherooftops.com

Books by Andy Thomas

The foreword to *A Future World Vision* was written by Andy Thomas, author of many books including these, both available as signed copies from *www.vitalsignspublishing.co.uk*...

The Truth Agenda: *Making Sense of Unexplained Mysteries, Global Cover-Ups and Visions for a New Era* [404 pages, VSP]

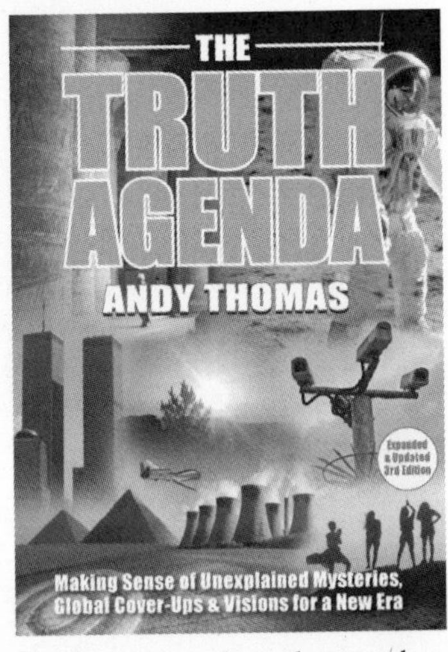

The Truth Agenda explores some of the most famous unexplained mysteries and global cover-ups of recent history. What is the truth about UFOs, pyramids, psychic phenomena, consciousness research, visions of the future and ancient prophecies, and what is their connection to famous conspiracy theories concerning the Moon landings, 9/11, the New World Order and claims that the world is covertly run by a powerful ruling elite..?

Leading mysteries researcher Andy Thomas pulls the many threads together in a refreshingly accessible overview, addressing the issues in a credible analysis which suggests that the world we live in may be very different to the picture presented by the establishment, but that we can all help to create a far more positive future. *"An essential guide"* – KINDRED SPIRIT

Conspiracies: *The Facts – The Theories – The Evidence* [292 pages, Watkins Publishing]

JFK, Watergate, the Gunpowder Plot, Princess Diana, Dr David Kelly, 9/11, the Moon landings, chemtrails, HAARP, false-flag attacks, ETs, the New World Order and far beyond... Since the political intrigues of the Roman Empire, nearly every significant event of the last 2,000 years has sparked off a conspiracy theory. Andy Thomas sifts the evidence of more than 30 major examples and dramatically highlights the core issues in a balanced and meticulously-researched overview. *"Highly recommended"* – PHENOMENA

THE AUTHOR

Richard Smith

Two generations of both domestic and international involvement commercially in ophthalmic optics (*www.eyemasters.co.uk*) has taken Richard to 25% of UN-recognised countries. Living overseas in his formative years has given him a deeper than usual fascination with global geopolitics, which, coupled with his role in manufacturing optics, offered many varied insights into different overseas mentalities. Richard was a founder member of Hamish Miller's Parallel Community project, formed in 2006. He now lives in East Sussex with his partner Annie and runs a spectacle dispensing business from home.

Richard was once a council member of the now defunct Centre for Crop Circle Studies (CCCS) in the 1990s, having been introduced to this phenomenon near his home in 1988. Richard says: "I understand the importance of the bigger picture, and consciously try to avoid pure focus on my speciality. Excessive reductionism is persuading us into technological solutions that lack concomitant wisdom". This is just one of the themes that have fuelled this, his first book, *A Future World Vision*.